EVERY DAY LASTS A . ...

Richard S. Hollander was devastated when his parents were killed in an automobile accident in 1986. While rummaging through their attic, he discovered letters from a family he never knew – his father's mother, three sisters, and their husbands and children. The letters, neatly stacked in a briefcase, were written from Cracow, Poland, between November 1939 and December 1941, vividly depicting day-to-day life during the Holocaust. At the same time, Richard's father, Joseph Hollander, who had entered the U.S. illegally in 1939, was fighting the government to avoid deportation to Poland and certain death. Hollander was astounded to learn that his father saved the lives of many Polish Jews, but – despites heroic efforts – could not save his family. Now in paperback, the book features a new preface by Richard S. Hollander and a speech written by Joseph that was not included in the critically acclaimed hardback edition.

Richard S. Hollander's grandmother, aunts, their spouses, and their children wrote the poignant and powerful letters from Cracow, Poland (1939–1941) that comprise the bulk of this book. Mr. Hollander is the author of *Video Democracy*, a look at the impact of interactive technology on American politics. He has been a reporter with two daily newspapers and with WBAL-TV in Baltimore, Maryland. Presently, Mr. Hollander is president of Millbrook Communications in Baltimore, an advertising and marketing firm representing professional sports teams and Maryland Public Television.

Christopher R. Browning is the Frank Porter Graham Professor of History at the University of North Carolina, Chapel Hill. He is the author of seven books on Nazi Germany and the Holocaust, including *The Origins of the Final Solution* and *Ordinary Men*, both winners of the National Jewish Book Award in the Holocaust category.

Nechama Tec is Professor Emerita of Sociology at the University of Connecticut, Stamford, and author of seven books. Her *Resilience and Courage, Women, Men, and the Holocaust* won the National Jewish Book Award. Others won numerous prizes and were nominated for the Pulitzer Prize and the National Book Award.

EVERY DAY LASTS A YEAR

A Jewish Family's Correspondence from Poland

Introduced and Edited by
Christopher R. Browning
University of North Carolina, Chapel Hill

Richard S. Hollander

Nechama Tec
University of Connecticut, Stamford

Annotated by
Craig Hollander
Christopher R. Browning

CAMBRIDGE
UNIVERSITY PRESS

CAMBRIDGE
UNIVERSITY PRESS

32 Avenue of the Americas, New York, NY 10013-2473, USA

Cambridge University Press is part of the University of Cambridge.

It furthers the University's mission by disseminating knowledge in the pursuit of education, learning, and research at the highest international levels of excellence.

www.cambridge.org
Information on this title: www.cambridge.org/9781107668768

First published 2007
Reprinted 2007
First paperback edition 2014

A catalog record for this publication is available from the British Library.

Library of Congress Cataloging in Publication Data
Every day lasts a year: a Jewish family's correspondence from Poland /
Richard S. Hollander, Christopher R. Browning, Nechama Tec.
    p. cm.
Includes bibliographical references and index.
ISBN 978-0-521-88274-3 (hardback)
1. Hollander, Joseph Arthur. 2. Jews – United States – Correspondence. 3. Jews, Polish – United States – Correspondence. 4. Refugees, Jewish – United States – Correspondence.
5. Holocaust, Jewish (1939–1945) – Poland – Influence. 6. Jews – Poland – Correspondence.
I. Hollander, Richard S. II. Browning, Christopher R. III. Tec, Nechama. IV. Title.
E184.37.H65A4 2007
940.53'18 – dc22   2007017924

ISBN   978-0-521-88274-3 Hardback
ISBN   978-1-107-66876-8 Paperback

To Joseph Hollander – who left us their story and forged his own.

Contents

Introduction and Acknowledgments

The historian trying to write about the life and death of Polish Jewry during the Holocaust faces a major dilemma. Most of the surviving contemporary documents are those written by the Nazi perpetrators, not the victims. Not only were some 90 percent of Polish Jews murdered, most of the records of the Jewish communities as well as the personal papers, letters, and diaries of individual Polish Jews were destroyed as well. The constant uprooting of the Jewish population as well as the looting and confiscation of Jewish property that both preceded and followed their destruction were not conducive to the preservation of such precious documents. The Ringelblum Archives for Warsaw and a substantial amount of material from Lodz are the exception. There are no comparable collections of surviving Jewish documentation from other cities in Poland.

The postwar memoirs and testimonies of the survivors are, of course, one essential source for historians trying to compensate for the loss of so much contemporary documentation, but postwar memories – filtered through catastrophe and survival – cannot fully recapture the perspective and state of consciousness of an earlier period when not only was the Holocaust not yet known but for most was totally inconceivable. The rare surviving diaries and letters written after the German occupation but before the mass murder – particularly from cities other than Warsaw and Lodz – are therefore an invaluable historical resource to recreate the world of Polish Jewry on the edge of destruction. They allow us entry into the lives and consciousness of those who sensed the terrible danger but did not yet know the outcome, of those who struggled with unprecedented problems but who also had to continue dealing with the joys and tensions of everyday family life, of those who hovered between hope and despair.

This extensive collection of letters written to Joseph Hollander in New York by his family in Cracow between 1939 and 1941 is especially rare and valuable in two regards. First, the collection is a near complete run of letters – only a few that were apparently lost in the post seem to be missing – extending over more than two years. The letters allow us to chart change over time. Second, they preserve for us nine different voices – six women and three men – spanning three generations. We can see the same events and experiences from different perspectives and vantage points.

The publication of this extensive collection of letters posed serious challenges. The vast majority of the letters were handwritten, not typed. Most were written in Polish, reflecting the relatively assimilated, urban, upper-middle-class standing of the family. However, the two oldest correspondents (Joseph's mother and his brother-in-law, Salo) who were in school before World War , when Cracow was still part of the Habsburg Empire, wrote in German. So did another brother-in-law, Munio, who was educated in Vienna. Professor Barbara Bernhardt both transcribed and translated the bulk of the Polish-language letters and some of the German letters. Joseph's mother employed an old nineteenth-century style of German handwriting that is mystifying to the nonspecialist. Jeannette Norfleet provided the necessary expertise to decipher, transcribe, and translate the mother's contributions to the correspondence. Some additional letters in Polish that came to light near the end of the project were translated by Joanna Asia Mieczkowska and Nechama Tec. This project could not have been even conceived much less brought to completion without the essential help in transcription and translation of these individuals.

The Hollander family's involvement was key. Craig Hollander's initial analysis of these letters in an award-winning undergraduate essay at Columbia University helped set this project in motion, and Ellen Hollander provided valuable advice and support.

As is often the case in publishing a book, the title is one of the last matters to be settled. The letters offered a wealth of possibilities. "Every day lasts a year" was written by Berta Hollander on May 26, 1941, as she waited anxiously to receive her son Joseph's next letter.

My son, Craig, did the initial scholarly research on the letters from Cracow as part of an undergraduate thesis in the history department at Columbia University. Craig's insight and analysis were invaluable. Craig received his doctorate in history from Johns Hopkins University in 2013.

People Frequently Mentioned in the Correspondence

Joseph (Józiu) Hollander (born 1905): the recipient of the family letters from Cracow

Lusia (Felicia) Hollander: Joseph's first wife

Berta (Beila) Hollander (born 1866): Joseph's mother

Mania Nachtigall (born 1890): Joseph's sister, wife of Salo (Gabryel) Nachtigall

Klara Wimisner (born 1893): Joseph's sister, wife of Dawid Wimisner, mother of teenage daughters Lusia and Genka

Dola Stark (born 1901): Joseph's sister, wife first of Henek Stark, then of Munio Blaustein

Lusia (Dola) Wimisner (born 1924): Joseph's niece, Klara and Dawid's younger daughter

Genka (Genia, Eugenia) Wimisner (born 1921): Joseph's niece, Klara and Dawid's older daughter

Dawid Wimisner (born 1890): Joseph's brother-in-law, husband of Klara

Salo (Gabryel) Nachtigall (born 1878): Joseph's brother-in-law, husband of Mania

Munio Blaustein (Bransdorfer): Joseph's brother-in-law, second husband of Dola

Jan Schreiber: Joseph's wife's brother, living in New York City

Regine Hütschnecker: Munio Blaustein's sister, living in Switzerland

Feliks Palaszek: Joseph's former business associate

Henek Stark: Joseph's brother-in-law, Dola's first husband, died in Soviet-occupied Galicia

Arnold Spitzman: fourteen-year-old refugee boy Joseph and Felicia take under their care in Italy and travel with to the United States

Adele: Joseph's wife's relative, living in Vienna

Leo, Paula: Joseph's cousins, living in New York City

EVERY DAY LASTS A YEAR

1. **Dola Stark.** Joseph's youngest sister contemplated divorcing her husband Henek, who abandoned her and fled to Soviet-occupied Eastern Galicia. After Henek's death, Dola anxiously sought Joseph's approval of her sudden marriage to her newfound love, Munio Blaustein.

2. Klara Wimisner. Joseph's second eldest sister wrote Joseph that "we live like on a volcano" but also expressed her faith in God. Occasionally she despaired, as when she wrote, "The more I get to know people the more I treasure dogs."

3. Eugenia "Genka" Wimisner. Klara and David's firstborn was the moodier sibling. "I do not feel alive," she wrote. "What I see is quite black."

4. **Lusia Wimisner.** Genka's cheery younger sister, who excelled as a seamstress and discovered her "true talent" as a teacher in the Cracow ghetto. The opposite of her older sister in temperament, she wrote, "I see everything in bright colors. I have enough joy of life for this whole highly respected family of ours."

5. Dawid Wimisner. Klara's husband and Joseph's brother-in-law. He wrote infrequently to Joseph. The family made numerous references to his energy but also to his irascibility. He occasionally tried Joseph's patience with his complaints.

6. Salo Nachtigall. Mania's husband and Joseph's brother-in-law. Salo belatedly considered the option of leaving Poland. "Many people register themselves for emigration overseas," he wrote. "In order not to blame ourselves later we are thinking about doing the same."

7. **Amalia "Mania" Nachtigall.** The eldest of the three Hollander sisters. Her son, Ignacy, died before the war. Reacting to the swirl of events, she wrote: "Sometimes, I feel like somebody asked me to sing after my tongue was removed."

8. **Vita Hollander.** Joseph's wife and author Richard Hollander's mother was born in the United States. Vita and Joseph were married in 1945, hours before he was shipped overseas to fight the Nazis. Joseph's letters to her from the European front speak of his search for his family.

9. Joseph Arthur Hollander. This photo is Joseph as a young man in Cracow. He was the youngest of the four Hollander children. After he arrived in the United States in December 1939, the U.S. government made every effort to have him deported back to Europe.

10. Joseph Arthur Hollander. He enlisted in the U.S. Army and returned to Europe as a soldier. He wrote Vita of his powerful reactions to defeating Germany.

11. **Joseph and Vita Hollander.** Pictured at a cousin's wedding. They had a storybook marriage and died together in a car accident in 1986.

12. **Saul and Berta Hollander.** Parents of Joseph, Mania, Klara, and Dola. Saul died of natural causes before the war. Berta was the family matriarch, who is credited with the extraordinary family cohesion in the midst of the most dire circumstances.

13. Refugees Dr. Joseph A. Hollander, 12-year-old Arnold Spitzman, Mrs. Felicia Hollander, and Marek Morsel (from left) arrive in New York City, December 6, 1939. Photographer unknown, courtesy of Nick Spitzman.

Preface

Richard S. Hollander

We are perpetually children. No matter our age, they are the adults and we are their children. There seems to be an emotional barrier to envisioning our parents *before* our own birth – and certainly before our parents met each other and married.

My father, Joseph Hollander, and I had a close, loving, and mutually respectful relationship, but we never ventured into his sealed past of Holocaust, immigration, and the family left behind to die in concentration camps. As stated in the chapter "Joseph," the creation of a wall was simple to understand: neither my father nor I wanted to inflict emotional pain on the other. It was better to live in the present and the future than the past.

I didn't volunteer to explore my father's past; it was thrust on me. In a dark attic, I literally stumbled on the briefcase containing the letters and numerous personal documents that comprise this book. Yet far from embracing what I now consider a gift, I left the letters untouched in the tan leather Air India briefcase. The compulsion to have the letters translated and ultimately published was only marginally related to my relationship with my father. As far as I knew, we had nothing in our relationship to repair – it was an absolute joy and privilege to be his son. In fact, if memory serves me correctly, the very last thing I said to him as he stood on the front lawn of his Westchester house on that bright afternoon in October 1986, waving "goodbye" to me; my wife, Ellen; and our three children, was "I love you." One cannot improve on that.

What compelled me to move forward on this project was to further Holocaust studies and to give breath, substance, and meaning to my father's family. I don't know why he never pursued the same task – maybe leaving the letters and attendant documents behind was intentional.

Every Day Lasts a Year was a work in progress from its inception. Dr. Christopher R. Browning, one of the nation's foremost Holocaust scholars, instantly recognized the value of the letters as primary source material. Here was this treasure of material from the victims of Nazi atrocities. As a rule, losers don't write history. And the fact that the central characters were women – my father's mother and three sisters – made the letters historically significant from the perspective of gender.

Since Cambridge is an academic press, it seemed clear from the beginning that the focus of the book would be the letters. Chris wisely said he would place the letters in historic context, and recruited Dr. Nechama Tec to look at the sociology of the family dynamic. Even my son Craig, then in college, would contribute to the project, annotating and researching. Finally, I would write a brief biography of Joseph. In this manner, *Every Day Lasts a Year* would be a Holocaust history book giving insight into one Jewish family living in Cracow, Poland. Joseph was less of a participant in the story than he was a recipient of mail.

The traditional path is that a thesis evolves into a book. With *Every Day Lasts a Year*, the path was reversed. The book became the catalyst to uncover powerful themes in my father's life.

As I began to research my brief biographical sketch of Joseph, his hidden world opened up for me. What I was too timid to ask him in life became a living, vivid, and compelling story after his death. Delving into the research, I was worried that the Joseph Hollander that would emerge wouldn't measure up to my extraordinary ethical, moral, caring, and loving father. What son or daughter would want to shatter an idealized image?

To my relief and joy, the Joseph Hollander that rose from the archives and research was even more heroic, courageous, and brilliant than the image I carried with me. All the great qualities he possessed as my father were there in abundance in the crucible of the Holocaust.

I call this book a work in progress because thematically it is far broader in scope than a translation of letters, however important the letters may be. Without losing its initial focus of the letters from Poland, for me, *Every Day Lasts a Year* evolved into an intensely personal and emotional investigation into my father's world, and what started as a brief biographical sketch was transformed into a wealth of universal, compelling themes.

One cannot read the story of Joseph's escape from Nazi-occupied Poland, serendipitous arrival in the United States, and immediate detention by authorities without cringing in embarrassment for our government. What compassionate and just government would expend an astonishing amount of time and energy to deport to their inevitable deaths a couple and a 12-year-old child?

There is the story of Joseph the son who worked frantically and desperately behind the scenes to rescue his family. When one places Joseph's tireless and imaginative rescue efforts in the context of his deportation peril, the story becomes heroic. Yes, a Hollywood ending would have been better, but that does not detract from Joseph's obsession to free those he loved.

What of Joseph the GI who was sent into the caldron of a fallen Germany to seek news of survival and dreading the inevitable? Even with the perspective of decades, I cannot begin to fathom the emotional tsunami that must have engulfed my father sifting through the wreckage of Germany, European Jewry, and his family.

Finally, who was this beautiful woman that Joseph the future husband met on a train who would later rescue him? They had almost nothing in common. My mother Vita was a shy artist who knew little of the world beyond Brooklyn and whose foreign-language skills never extended beyond high school Latin. He was a multi-lingual, highly resourceful lawyer/businessman who had traveled extensively and had been previously married.

So, pick your story. Select a theme. I would never have known Joseph Hollander prior to my birth if it were not for the opportunity to contribute to this history book, but through research I was blessed to be able to reconstruct his life *before* I was born. I saw a real person, and his image was untarnished.

The publication of *Every Day Lasts a Year* set in motion a number of events that have and continue to affect the father–son relationship.

In January 2008, two months after this book's publication, I was standing in a living room in an exquisite home in the Hancock Park section of Los Angeles about to give a book talk. My cell phone rang. It was my son, Craig: "Dad, you're not going to believe this. I just heard from Arnold Spitzman's son."

This book tells the story of how my father rescued the 12-year-old Arnold from a sickbed in Italy and brought him to the United States. As with my father and his then-wife Lucia, the U.S. government attempted to deport Arnold and refuse him sanctuary for the duration of the war. My father boldly asserted at their immigration hearing that he would be responsible for Arnold and that the young refugee would not be a ward of the state.

While researching the biographical chapter on my father, I attempted to locate Arnold. I knew he lived most of his adult life in Brazil, but despite several phone calls to Brazil and other efforts, I was unsuccessful. But shortly after the book was published a young man named Nicholas Spitzman was sitting on a Miami beach reading it. He couldn't believe his father's story was in print or, to be accurate, on the Internet.

Nick correctly assumed that Craig had a Facebook page. He wrote to Craig: "I have randomly found your father's book on the internet and have been googling around to try and find a way to get in touch. To make a long story short, I am the son of Arnold Spitzman."

Every book talk or interview invariably returned to the question of Arnold. What happened to the boy rescued and brought to the United States? Now I would finally be able to answer that question. More importantly, Arnold was, to the best of my knowledge, the only surviving person who could give me insight and facts related to the escape from Europe and the immigration prosecution.

Shortly thereafter, I met Nick in Chicago. Sixty-eight years had elapsed since Arnold traveled on the *Vulcania* from Naples to New York, and Arnold lived a full and highly productive life. While still a teenager, Arnold married an American, Esther Schweitzer. They had two daughters. He served in the army, but did not see combat. As a civilian, Arnold worked in the minerals and jewelry business. In the mid-1950s, Arnold moved to a small city in the interior of Brazil. Later, he relocated with his wife and daughters to Rio de Janeiro, where he became the manager of a jewelry store near the Copacabana Palace Hotel. In the early 1970s, Arnold and Esther divorced and she moved back to the United States with their daughters. Then at age 46, Arnold married a Brazilian, 22-year-old Iris. Nick was born in 1984.

As a reaction to rampant violent crime in Rio (Iris was robbed at gunpoint several times, the jewelry store was robbed, their apartment was robbed), the Spitzman family decided in 1995 to leave Brazil for the United States. After 37 years in Brazil, Arnold and Iris settled in the Florida panhandle beach resort of Destin. The reason why I couldn't find Arnold in Brazil is because he was no longer there.

In March 2008, I traveled with my wife, Ellen, to meet Arnold and Iris in their Destin home. My expectations were unrealistically high. I arrived with a briefcase filled with documents to show Arnold and refresh his memory. There were copies of newspaper clippings, the letter to Eleanor Roosevelt where he is mentioned, transcripts of his testimony at immigration hearings, letters from Poland, and more.

It was gratifying just to meet Arnold. Not only was he a living link to my father's youth, but even in his 80s he was energetic, vibrant, and thoroughly engaged in the moment. Arnold, who was still working every day, was obviously someone who appreciated and relished the gift of the years he gained by escaping from Europe.

We talked and talked. He carefully reviewed the documents. Arnold apologized for not being able to add to the narrative of the escape and immigration trials. I was disappointed that Arnold could not share stories about my father and, in fact, his first wife.

"You have to understand," Arnold explained. "I was a child and your father was the adult. Whatever he told me to do, I did."

Arnold paused for emphasis.

"I will say this. If it were not for your father's kindness, courage, and compassion, I would not have survived. I would never have left Europe and, if I got to the United States, I would have been sent back."

The next day Ellen and I left Destin to return to Baltimore. I was not sure what, if anything, I learned from Arnold. What I took away from our meeting was of far greater significance than an anecdote from 1939 or 1940.

"What a privilege it is," I said to Ellen, getting into the rental car to drive to the airport, "to hear another person describe my father as a hero. Everyone should have that moment to hear someone say his or her parent is a hero."

After the publication of *Every Day Lasts a Year*, the Chicago Shake-speare Theater commissioned the playwright Karen Hartman to write a drama based on my father's life. At the time I'm writing this preface, the script is completed and the play is in its development stage. Essentially, the play is the story of a son fulfilling a father's legacy: after his father's death and the discovery of family letters and other documents, Joseph is not emotionally ready to share his story. In the first lines of his incomplete autobiography, however, it becomes clear that he wanted to explain his story to future generations.

As in reality, the script details how the burden of telling Joseph's story falls on me, his son. Well before anyone conceived of a play, I was acutely aware that I was the keeper of my father's legacy – an emotionally wrench-ing and weighty task. From the instant I saw the briefcase in the attic after my parents were killed and looked at the letters so neatly organized and stacked in chronological order, I knew this was the path my father wanted me to travel. In introspective moments, I realize that there is virtually no higher task or calling than to complete a mission that one's parent was unable to achieve in life. And, if reaching that objective creates a legacy for one's parent, it is both humbling and gratifying.

Karen Hartman echoes my sentiments: "The story of Joseph Hollan-der is to me a story of legacy. In creating the semi-documentary play, I focused on Rich's discovery of the letters and the sudden death of his par-ents, his choice to put them away, and his own children's eventual need to know what was written in the letters. This moving collection poses a universal question: how does the pain of past generations become a gift for the present?"

I have no idea whether the play will be a commercial success, but that is beside the point: I am finally ready to share my father with everyone who reads this book or sees the play on stage. The story I hid from myself and all others for many years has emerged, and I am happy his story belongs to all of us.

PART ONE

JOSEPH'S STORY

Joseph

Richard S. Hollander

His voice was not audible, but he spoke loudly.

He was an ocean away, yet he was a visible pillar of strength.

He was tormented by failure, but succeeded more than he imagined.

He had every reason to abandon hope, yet he created a new world for himself.

Joseph Arthur Hollander is the central character in this book. He left Europe in 1939 and arrived, quite unexpectedly, at Ellis Island on December 6, 1939. As an undocumented refugee, Joseph threw himself at the mercy of the American legal system. By the time he returned to Europe in March 1945, he proudly wore American military fatigues and a U.S. Army dog tag. Then, on July 17, 1945, the enlistee walked into Hitler's office, took an axe, and chopped a block of coffee-colored marble from the Führer's desk. From Berlin, Joseph insightfully wrote to his American bride in English, a language that he had already mastered: "I broke up a piece of Hitler's marble desk on which he signed so many treaties and agreements he never kept and so many murder decrees he fulfilled to the last word" (letter to Vita, July 17, 1945, Berlin).

Mostly, this is the story of my father, a man who was a victim of the Holocaust although he never saw a ghetto, experienced the dehumanizing conduct of Nazi overseers, nor witnessed the indescribable atrocities.

Joseph owed his survival to an improbable sequence of events and a fierce will to survive. He battled against the U.S. government for the opportunity to seek refuge in the country and then battled for the same government in its relentless march to Berlin. To the end, Joseph remained a man of uncompromising integrity, complete humility, and unparalleled determination.

Joseph speaks to us largely through his family, whose members were trapped in a cauldron of hate in Cracow, Poland. The family wrote many scores of letters to Joseph, which are a compendium of prayerful expectations and crushed dreams as well as a valuable historical reference. Unfortunately, we can only guess what Joseph wrote to his family, given that he did not retain copies of his own correspondence (perhaps due to the state of technology at that time). Clearly, the family regarded Joseph as a lifeline. Revealed in nearly every letter is an almost childlike faith in Joseph's ability to provide deliverance. There is no way to calculate the burden of being the only thread of hope of an entire family and its only survivor.

The story of the letters from Cracow begins almost forty-seven years after Joseph's escape from Nazi-occupied Poland. At dusk on October 22, 1986, my parents, Joseph and Vita Hollander, were driving north on a commercial street in suburban Westchester County, New York, returning from a visit to Vita's mother. Vita, who was seventy years of age, was at the wheel. For unexplained reasons, their vehicle suddenly veered off the road and smashed into the wall of a freestanding store on the east side of Central Avenue. The force of the crash jarred the engine block loose and sent it hurtling into the dashboard of the passenger compartment. My parents, who were profoundly in love after forty-one years of marriage, died almost instantly, and within seconds of each other, from massive internal injuries. Their vehicle had crashed into a storefront. I learned of their deaths several hours later in a terse telephone call from a Westchester County police officer who said, "Mr. Hollander, I have some bad news for you. Your parents were killed a few hours ago in a car accident."

Months later, as my parents' only child, I faced the dreaded task that inevitably falls to the offspring of deceased parents: I had to dispose of the contents of the house in which I grew up and that my folks had occupied since 1959. It was as if the house had been left in suspended animation. They were coming home. Food was in the refrigerator; the toothbrushes were neatly placed in their holders; the thermostat was set at a comfortable level.

On the third floor of my parents' split-level home was a crawl-space attic, which was used primarily to store suitcases. This would be the easy part; I had no particular attachment to luggage. As I climbed into the attic, I noticed a plain tan briefcase off to the side, with an Air India baggage tag. When I lifted it, I immediately knew it was not empty. Upon opening the briefcase, I saw stacks of letters, all neatly arranged and held together by rubber bands, in just the precise and organized way my father always kept anything that was important. Every letter was addressed to my father. My eyes were quickly drawn to the stamps on the upper right corner of each letter and to the large, hand-stamped Nazi imprints on the backs. Swastika after swastika after swastika jumped out at me. With a slight tremble in my hands, I pulled out one letter, then another. Most were handwritten, but some were typed. Although unable to read the words, I could immediately tell they were in Polish and German.

Although I had never been told of their existence, I instantly knew what they were and from whom they had come. These were letters from my father's immediate family in Poland – the people he never mentioned, the relatives I never knew, and a world from which he endeavored to shield his family, friends, and, undoubtedly, himself. In addition, my father left a treasure of other documents and photographs, including passports, receipts, household inventories, telephone records, business cards, drivers' licenses, personal phone books, and records of monetary disbursements. On the surface, these were documents that typically clutter desks and files and are eventually thrown out. Yet these records were not discarded.

I understood why my father kept the letters and other documents; they were all that remained of the beloved family he left in Poland. I also realized why he entombed the letters in the briefcase. For him, the reminders of vanished family, friendships, culture, and way-of-life were profoundly painful.

Still consumed with grief from the sudden loss of my devoted parents, overwrought with the painful and draining task of packing up the house in which I had spent so many happy years, and trying to cope with a life seemingly in disarray, I could not adequately focus on the briefcase at that time. So, just like my father decades before, I closed the briefcase, literally and figuratively, and brought it to my house, where it rested for more than a dozen years.

Over time, perhaps imperceptibly at first, I came to believe that my father saved the letters for another reason. If he had truly wanted to erase all of the pain inflicted by the Holocaust, he could have discarded the briefcase. He didn't. He couldn't. That the letters were chronologically organized and neatly secured convinced me that they were left for a purpose. I became convinced that it was my father's unspoken hope that one day I would give a voice to his entire family. This is their story.

Repeatedly, I have repressed anger at myself for not pressing my father to share his journey.

Because of Joseph's shroud of silence about his experience, much of this narrative has been stitched together through shreds of information, travel to Poland, legal documents from the National Archives that are about sixty-five years old, and clues contained in the letters.

Although Joseph never gave an oral history and was incapable of speaking about his ordeal, we fortunately have a remnant of narrative. In 1985, he began writing an autobiography. Sadly, it was never finished. His account was clearly motivated by the births of his three grandchildren. Joseph wrote: "Since the birth of Hillary, our first grandchild, I was toying with the idea of writing my short autobiography – to tell something about my family, myself, the place where I was born, studied and worked. Now, since we are blessed with two more grandchildren Craig and Brett, the undertaking of mine now has a more valid reason." He continued: "I assume as they grow older, they will wonder why they have never known any member of their grandfather's family. It will be difficult for them to comprehend the tragedy of the Holocaust and the loss of all my relatives and finally the miracle of my survival."

*　　*　　*

One wonders why Joseph decided to leave his hometown of Cracow, Poland, in 1939. Far from being the prototypical refugee, Joseph had every reason to stay. At thirty-four years of age, he had a law degree from the venerable Jagiellonian University. Joseph was also director of the prosperous Polish Travel Bureau, Poltour, at 36 Szpitlana Street, off Cracow's main square. And, according to a letter he wrote to a Cracow lawyer in 1947, the family owned real estate in the city. With his prosperity, Joseph could afford a car and custom-made suits even during the worldwide depression of the 1930s. His red hair, green eyes, and quick wit may have helped him win the affection of Felicia "Lusia" Schreiber, who, at five foot eight and 125 pounds, was a statuesque blonde and a champion swimmer. Felicia, eight years Joseph's junior, was repeatedly described by his family as beautiful, with tendencies toward vanity and arrogance.

After Joseph's marriage to Felicia in Cracow on June 28, 1934, the couple moved into a luxurious high-rise apartment with a balcony overlooking the old city. The lobby of their apartment building was appointed with marble and had an elevator to reach the upper floors. From furniture receipts found with the trove of letters, it is clear that by 1939 Felicia was spending a substantial amount for decorating.

As the only surviving male in his immediate family (his father, Saul, died on May 4, 1933, of natural causes), Joseph wore a mantle of familial leadership. Given his social stature, profitable business, and family responsibilities, abandoning everything for the most uncertain of futures seems an unlikely choice. Never known to act on impulse or out of emotion, only Joseph's near-certain knowledge of dire consequences would have compelled him to leave his loved ones, business, culture, and country for the inevitable struggles of a refugee.

Joseph's decision to leave the familiar for the unknown may have been prompted by what he observed during a three-nation trip to Western Europe in April 1939. The journey probably provided Joseph with an ominous glimpse of the future of European Jewry. Indeed, by the spring of 1939, there was nothing subtle about anti-Semitism in Germany; it was ugly and ubiquitous.

The trip apparently was not long in the planning. Joseph received his British entry visa in Warsaw on April 3, 1939; a French visa in Cracow on April 6; and a German visa on April 19, only days before he left Poland. Although we do not know the purpose of Joseph's European trip, one possible explanation for his visit to London was his transfer of more than $4,000 from his British bank account to Felicia's cousin, Emile Deligtisch, who lived in New York. Undoubtedly, while in Germany in April 1939, Joseph witnessed the rapidly deteriorating condition of German Jews, and he must have sensed the metastasis of the anti-Semitic German cancer.

In his autobiography, Joseph chronicles the inexorable spread of the virus of hate outward from Germany. Citing the "total upheaval in

Europe" in the 1930s such as Hitler's seizing of complete power in Germany, the Italian invasion of Ethiopia, and the Spanish Civil War, Joseph wrote:

> unfortunately, we [Polish Jews] didn't realize the enormity of the situation and life and business continued as before. The news of the persecution of Jews in Germany had a bad effect in Poland where a majority of the population was basically Anti-Semitic. Attacks on Jews in many cities, especially the smaller ones, on trains and even in public places were common occurrences. The local authorities, the police, and the federal government did not do anything to stop this. The excesses had the main purpose of robbing Jewish homes and plundering their stores and factories. The situation started to convince some Jews, especially the wealthy ones, that leaving Poland was a necessity. But still it was more talk than action.

On July 7, 1939, less than two months before the Nazi invasion, Joseph appeared at the consulate in the Polish city of Katowice and obtained a one-year visa to Great Britain for a "business visit." Ever prudent, Joseph outwardly maintained a business-as-usual image. In August 1939, for example, he purchased a considerable amount of furnishings for his new apartment, leaving a substantial deposit. One wonders whether the purchase of furniture was an act of intentional deception.

The vexing question is why Joseph's immediate family – his mother, three sisters, their spouses, and children – did not flee with him. Although we do not know the answer, the letters indicate that Joseph had warned family and friends of his fears and reveal the family's remorse at failing to follow Joseph's advice to leave Poland. Nevertheless, it is easy to understand their decision; human imagination could not conceive of the Final Solution. Instead, the family's frame of reference was probably World War I, a time of deprivation and dislocation but certainly not a time of premeditated extinction of European Jewry. Joseph's belief that, in the summer of 1939, he should have insisted that his family flee from Poland, and his knowledge that if he had persisted they might have survived, surely tortured him all of his days. A man who had an unsurpassed gift of logic and persuasion failed when it counted most.

One of the great ironies of Joseph's life is that in the immediate prewar period, he had already embarked on a long and complicated process of saving the lives of many endangered Polish Jews – in all likelihood, almost all strangers. At the same time, he was as yet incapable of leaving Poland with his wife, Felicia, and their respective extended families. The image is haunting. Here was an exceedingly resourceful man working feverishly, at considerable risk, to save Polish Jews and, at the same time, unable to get his own family to heed the obvious warning signs.

In his autobiography, Joseph spoke of his highly successful travel agency in Cracow. With the encroaching shadow of Nazism looming over Poland, the tourism travel business stopped. In a matter-of-fact tone, Joseph writes:

> In 1937–38, Hitler expelled Polish Jews, who came to Germany after the First World War and forced them to go back to Poland. They all had Polish passports with expired validity and the Polish government refused to recognize them as Polish citizens. In order to leave Poland and go to another country a valid passport and visa was a necessity. Hundreds of them came to me for help. Having connections – rather costly – in the Interior Ministry in Warsaw, I traveled a couple of times a month to Warsaw where their passports were revalidated.

Here Joseph is describing his own experience of a crisis that was set in motion when the Polish government set a deadline of October 1938 to revalidate old Polish passports. After that date, Poles living abroad without revalidated passports would no longer be considered Polish citizens, and Polish consulates in Germany often refused to revalidate the passports of Polish Jews living there. Faced with the prospect that Polish Jews in Germany would soon become stateless and hence unable to emigrate from that country, the Nazi regime rounded up thousands of Polish Jews and tried to deport them to Poland. In turn, the Polish government sealed its border, and many of these unfortunate refugees were trapped in no-man's land, left to live in tent cities between the two countries. Clearly, if it were not for Joseph's ability to find greedy and corrupt bureaucrats in the Polish Interior Ministry who, for a price, would revalidate the passports of at least some of these expelled Polish Jews, many more would have met that fate.

> The next problem was to what country a visa could be secured. All Europe was out. Countries like Panama, Bolivia, Cuba, Nicaragua etc... were giving – I should say selling – permits to enter. On this

basis, people could leave Poland. I was swamped with work, which I hated, but I knew I was helping them.

Later in life, Joseph wrote that he met many of the people he had saved who managed to leave the Central and South American nations for new lives in the United States, Canada, and Australia. Without any trace of self-aggrandizement for truly heroic work, Joseph merely reported that the Polish Jews he saved "expressed their gratitude for my help."

One would think that by mid-1939 Joseph had undoubtedly seen more than enough to convince even the most hardcore Pollyanna that there were no happy endings on the horizon. He had helped Polish Jews living in Germany to have their passports revalidated and obtain exit visas to countries in the Western Hemisphere. He witnessed the vicious brutality against innocent Polish Jews, and he had traveled into the heart of the Nazi universe. He had seen Hitler move on Austria and Czechoslovakia. With decades of hindsight, Joseph wrote:

> With all this happening, the Jews in Poland didn't realize the gravity of the situation and continued hoping it would stop. How blind we all were. The easy life blinded us. With all this happening, people started to realize that a danger of war, a German attack on Poland, can be expected. Some, however, believed if it came to war, England and France, having a treaty with Poland, will come to the rescue.

As dynamic and determined as he was, Joseph apparently postponed his personal escape plan. There were still people to help. His autobiography gives some insight into his emotional state.

> I just lived from day to day being very busy to help other people leave the country. Anyhow, being of military age, I couldn't leave according to a new regulation. Towards the end of August 1939, news reached us that Germany was massing an army on the western border of Poland. This created a panic and thousands of people started to move to the eastern part of Poland. And again, I was swamped with work, as the trains were overcrowded. I chartered . . . two sleeping cars, which were attached to a regular overnight train from Krakow to Lwow. This I succeeded to arrange for four days.

One has to marvel at Joseph's lack of editorializing. There is not a hint of self-congratulations for making arrangements for a last-minute evacuation. The rail exodus from Cracow to Lvov on the chartered sleeping cars probably took place in the last days of August 1939.

Three fates awaited the refugees who managed to get to Lvov. A minority crossed over into Romania and then to other sanctuaries. A second group remained in Lvov, only to be overtaken and murdered by the Nazis in 1941. A third group survived by virtue of being deported to Siberia or Kazahkstan by the Stalinist regime prior to June 1941.

Unfortunately, Joseph's autobiography ends abruptly with the brief description of chartering the sleeping cars from Cracow to Lvov. It was written in 1985–6; he was killed in October 1986. The unresolved question is whether he ran out of time to complete the story or was, instead, emotionally incapable of writing the remaining chapters. Fortunately, for those trying to reconstruct Joseph's escape, Polish authorities required passes for international travel. There is documentation of a request for permission to stay in a hotel in the Polish city of Lvov. Located east of Cracow near what was then the Polish southeastern border with Romania, Lvov was the ideal jumping-off point for a quick crossing. Joseph's planning was meticulous. Given the chaos of war, anything short of perfect planning invited disaster. On August 10, 1939, he booked an open-ended stay at a spa in the resort village of Zaleszczyki, which became the exit point for thousands of Poles, including government officials, fleeing the advancing Nazi armies. Then, on September 6, 1939, at the Romanian consulate in Lvov, Joseph obtained a forty-eight-hour, one-time transit visa into Romania.

Ever mindful that government documents are ultimately just paper, Joseph also took several large, loose jewels with him in the event he needed to entice border guards. It is not known how many of the gems found their way into the palms of corrupt immigration officials.

Joseph's passport reflects that on September 18, 1939, seventeen days after the Wehrmacht smashed into Poland and just one day after Soviet forces invaded Poland from the east to secure Stalin's territorial reward for his Non-Aggression Pact with Hitler, Joseph crossed into Romania at the Crisana Bridge. Within weeks of the invasion, Warsaw fell to the Nazis, effectively sealing the fate of three million Polish Jews who were left behind. Joseph's family was among them.

With Joseph at the Crisana Bridge were his wife, Felicia; a fourteen-year-old boy, Arnold Spitzman; the boy's aunt and uncle, Henrik and

Felicia Spitzman; and the boy's seven-year-old sister, Anita. At the outset, Joseph did not have a close friendship with the Spitzman family, but he would later do everything humanly possible to save the boy, who landed in his care. We know little about Arnold. His father, Maximilian Spitzman, was a Polish military pilot who was killed in the early days of the war. Arnold's mother, who owned a store in Lvov, remained behind, attempting to liquidate the family's assets before departing. Like many other Jews, she eagerly sent her children ahead, planning to join them at a later time.

The group found its way to the Romanian Black Sea port of Constanza, where they stayed for eight days. Then they sailed through the Dardanelles into the Aegean and around Greece to Yugoslavia. They received a Yugoslavian transit visa and were able to board yet another ship for the brief crossing to the Italian east coast.

Fascist Italy, which permitted the transit but not the residence of foreign Jews, was far from a permanent safe haven for Joseph. His ultimate destination was Portugal, a neutral country. While in Bologna, Italy, however, Arnold came down with typhus and was hospitalized for a month. For unknown reasons, Arnold's uncle, aunt, and sister decided to leave Italy without him and head for Paris, with the expectation that they would reunite with Joseph, Felicia, and Arnold in Lisbon. To assume that the plans of desperate refugees will work out is to assume sand can be held in one's fingers. Little did Joseph know at the separation from Arnold's aunt and uncle that young Arnold would soon become his responsibility.

At the Portuguese Consulate in Rome on October 13, 1939, Joseph, Felicia, and Arnold received visas for entry into Portugal. As a condition of receiving the visas, however, they had to pledge in writing that they would not return to Italy. Although none of the three realized it at the time, the "never to return" pledge would become a significant issue in a matter of weeks.

Following Arnold's recovery, the three boarded the Italian liner *Vulcania* in Naples on November 26, 1939, and sailed for Lisbon. But when the vessel arrived in Portugal, the three were not allowed to disembark, despite having the proper documentation. In Portuguese, the passport reads: "Prevented from disembarking in Lisbon from the ship *Saturnia [Vulcania]*, on the current date [November 29, 1939] by Port Authority Police."

According to legal documents, at that point Joseph tried but failed to obtain visas to other European countries. Consequently, the three remained on the *Vulcania* as it sailed to Ponta Delgada in the Azores, a Portuguese territory. As on the mainland, Portuguese authorities again refused to accept their country's own visas, issued by the Portuguese consulate. Despite his advance planning, Joseph did not know that Portuguese port authorities required a special stamp from the country's secret police, along with the visa. (Ironically, by June 1940, the Hebrew Immigrant Aid Society had reached an agreement with the Portuguese government to allow Jews who reached Portugal to stay temporarily while making arrangements to proceed to another country.)

By the time the *Vulcania* pulled anchor in the Azores, Joseph, Felicia, and Arnold were people without a home or even a destination. The next stop for the *Vulcania* happened to be New York, although from the trio's perspective, it could have been any port on the globe. As the three crossed the Atlantic, they had no idea that they were heading for Ellis Island. Although Joseph could not know it at the time, he would next cross the Atlantic as a United States citizen and a member of its army, about to liberate Europe from the Nazi nightmare he had once fled on the *Vulcania*.

Captained by Nestore Martinoli, the *Vulcania* cruised into New York harbor on December 6, 1939, carrying the three undocumented aliens among its passengers. We can only speculate as to the thoughts and emotions of the three stateless persons as the vessel slipped by the Statue of Liberty shortly before eight that evening. Did they realize that landing in the United States without proper documents, and with just $28 in cash, would leave them open for immediate deportation? Did they dare to envision that Poland and the loved ones left behind would be reduced to memory? On that dark December evening, did the chill of fear match the chill of the weather?

According to Dr. Marian Smith, a government historian, the illegal aliens were effectively shipwrecked on American shores. What they would soon learn is that the stirring words of Emma Lazarus, which graced the country's preeminent symbol of liberty, had tragically little to do with their reality. Forget the heartfelt appeal to the "tired and poor yearning to breathe free." Save for a tiny crack at the hinge, the government seemed determined to shut the Golden Door.

There were thousands of immigrants whose cases were adjudicated by low-level bureaucrats, totally removed from the highest levels of the national government. Fortunately for the trio, this case seemed to constitute an exception to business as usual for the Immigration and Naturalization Service (INS). Joseph clearly played a key role in mobilizing an interest in the aliens' cause. Soon after their arrival, information about the group's legal predicament reached the offices of the secretary of state, secretary of labor, the INS commissioner, a U.S. senator, two members of the House of Representatives, a federal judge, and the White House itself.

Upon arrival at Ellis Island, the three aliens were initially detained on the *Vulcania*, with the expectation that they would be on board at noon on December 11, 1939, when the Italian liner set sail from New York on its eastbound voyage. Their only immediate contact with the outside world was Jan Schreiber, Felicia's brother, who lived in Manhattan. We do not know much about Schreiber, except that he appears to have been a recent immigrant to the United States. He hired Jacob Lesser, Esquire, to represent his sister, brother-in-law, and Arnold in the brewing legal morass.

With Lesser's help, U.S. District Court Judge Alfred C. Coxe granted a writ of habeas corpus on December 8, 1939, and set a hearing for December 12, 1939. Immigration authorities had agreed to permit the three to leave the ship for the purpose of attending the hearing on December 12. That hearing was crucial, because it was held one day *after* the *Vulcania* sailed back to Italy.

On the scheduled date, the three appeared in federal court before Judge William Bondy, who agreed to a stipulation (docketed January 24, 1940) to withdraw the writ, pending a hearing before a Board of Special Inquiry for the INS, which was then under the Labor Department. After the court hearing on December 12, 1939, Joseph, Felicia, and Arnold were held without bail on Ellis Island.

Once a welcoming way station for immigrants, Ellis Island became the group's prison. According to Dr. Marian Smith of the INS, Joseph was likely housed in a male dormitory while his wife became an occupant of the women's section. They could spend time in a common room reading, writing, or playing board games. Although the guards were nonthreatening and did not treat those held on Ellis Island as common criminals, Dr. Smith said the guards were there to supervise the immigrants.

Always resourceful and ever determined, Joseph pursued a desperate fight to remain in the United States. He used his time on Ellis Island to marshal every resource at his disposal to plead his case. Records maintained at the National Archives in Washington contain court orders, memoranda, phone records, letters, and other references to the case, which serve as a testament to Joseph's efforts.

Nevertheless, over the course of the next year, the U.S. government expended countless hours and taxpayer dollars in an effort to send the three back to the flames of Europe. Indeed, judging by the voluminous legal record, the federal government employed considerable bureaucratic vigor in its effort to expel three harmless individuals who were merely trying to save their own lives.

Less than a week after the aliens arrived at Ellis Island, what might be described as a ritualized ballet between the federal immigration bureaucracy and the trio's allies began to take form. One could easily read the many pages of legal papers and conclude that the U.S. government was inexorably anti-Semitic or, at best, grossly callous. After all, the aliens lost at every step of the Immigration and Naturalization administrative hearing process and all through the federal judicial system. Yet history is painted in shades of gray. What may appear to be a stubborn and intransigent governmental position, hell-bent on deportation, had on the edges some flexibility.

The INS and the federal prosecutors seemed determined to uphold the immigration law; those who arrived on American shores without proper documents had to leave. Under the law in effect at the time, the government sought to deport Joseph, Felicia, and Arnold to Naples, Italy, because Italy was the trio's most immediate port of embarkation. However, because the aliens had signed agreements stating they would not return to Italy, that country was not a viable option. Rather, the three would have to be returned directly to Poland and, most assuredly, death. As the *New York Times* wrote on February 17, 1940, "if they are sent back to Naples they would undoubtedly be returned to Poland."

Of course, the federal bureaucracy did not exist in a vacuum. From the labor secretary on down, the INS was mindful of the media and public opinion. For those trying to change harsh and restrictive U.S. immigration law, Joseph and his companions may have been the perfect test case, because there was no evidence that they had tried to enter the country fraudulently. Rather, the three were literally deposited at the nation's doorstep. And although the INS wanted to avoid any ruling that would leave cracks in precedent, the highest level of INS was, indeed, sensitive to political pressure.

Only two days after the *Vulcania* arrived in New York, Robert T. Crane, executive director of the Social Science Research Council in New York, sent a telegram to the State Department asserting that the case of "Josef Arthur Hollander and companions" has "international significance." He expressed "the hope" that they "will not be deported." Secretary of State Cordell Hull received the Crane telegram and forwarded it to Labor Secretary Frances Perkins, then in charge of the INS.

On December 12, 1939, Byron H. Uhl, the INS district director in New York, wrote a letter to his boss, INS Commissioner James L. Houghteling, briefing him on the case. Uhl stated that the trio's lawyer was going to the local Portuguese consulate to see whether the three would be allowed to be deported to Portugal. "And," Uhl continued, "if unsuccessful as to that, [Lesser] would take steps to have the aliens depart for some South American country."

Four days later, Assistant Labor Secretary C. V. McLaughlin wrote: "It is recommended that permission be granted these aliens to transship to some South American country or to Portugal and in the event they are refused admission to the country to which they proceed, that the responsible [steamship] line . . . return [them] to the country from whence they came." Deputy INS Commissioner Edward J. Shaughnessy wrote to Secretary of State Cordell Hull on December 20, outlining a deal by which the three could remain in the United States long enough to make arrangements to go to another country. From the perspective of the INS, it was the ideal compromise. The government could avoid offering sanctuary to the trio and, at the same time, demonstrate compassion by giving them time to find another sanctuary.

One letter in Joseph's immigration file is particularly noteworthy. The address on the envelope had no street name or number, but the post office had no trouble delivering it on December 22, 1939, just two days after it was typed on Ellis Island. It was addressed to "Mrs. Franklin D. Roosevelt, The White House, Washington, D. C." From the halting language, it is clear that the text was not written by a lawyer or by a native speaker of English. Nor is it known if Joseph, who spoke little or no English at that time, dictated it to someone on Ellis Island with whom he could communicate. In any event, it contained Joseph's less than subtle message; he beseeched the First Lady to intercede and save him, his wife, and Arnold from deportation.

Addressed "My Dear Madam," the first sentence stated: "Please pardon me, my troubling you, by asking you for help, but your well known noble-mindedness and our tragic situation will excuse us. We are Jews, Polish subjects, who were obliged to leave Poland. After three months of wanderings through Rumania, Yugoslavia and Italy we got Portuguese visas in Rome and left for Lisboa with the ship *Vulcania*." He also explained that their visas were not honored by the Portuguese port police and that they had signed an agreement not to return to Italy.

Joseph indicated that they were to have an immigration hearing in January and, of course, that they lacked U.S. visas. He asserted: "We don't know how will be the verdict of the court . . . that is why we are begging you – Dear Madam – for help. When our destination did lead us here, we beg don't send us back to Germany, because that means death for us." Joseph added that they merely sought a temporary stay in the United States while making arrangements for transfer to a third country. He also assured Mrs. Roosevelt that they would not be a public charge. Imploring the First Lady for help, Joseph added: "Dear Madam – save us and don't send us back from this free American country to Germany. We believe in your nobility and are now living with the hope that our apel [sic appeal] will be granted."

Eleanor Roosevelt's mailbox must have been overflowing with equally poignant letters; her reputation for compassion stirred many pens. Yet the National Archives file contains an attachment to the letter from Joseph to Mrs. Roosevelt. It is a typed piece of paper that stated: "In answering them, please say you are doing so at Mrs. Roosevelt's request." Even with the intervening Christmas holiday, Joseph's letter to Mrs. Roosevelt's, along with the attachment, arrived at INS by December 27, 1939.

Almost immediately upon the group's arrival at Ellis Island, Congressman Sol Bloom of New York, chair of the House Foreign Affairs Committee, was also called upon to help. Bloom did, indeed, lobby INS through letters and telephone calls, although he was hardly optimistic.

Unknown to Joseph, the trio also had guardian angels in Providence, Rhode Island, who took up their cause simply because it was just and merciful. Both in deed and in monetary contributions, Archibald and Ida Silverman made it their mission to help Jewish immigrants. Immigrants themselves, the Silvermans often went down to the pier in Rhode Island to assist refugees in their first hours in their new country.

The Silvermans were leading philanthropists and civic leaders in Rhode Island and throughout the international Jewish community. Archibald rose from making costume jewelry in a factory, where he earned less than two dollars a week, to become a bank president and pillar of his community. Ida, who was Rhode Island Mother of the Year in 1954, was the recipient of numerous awards for a lifetime of humane acts, including the establishment of the Jewish Orphanage in Rhode Island. The couple was also on the front lines in the formative years of the State of Israel. Ida, who worked tirelessly to help establish the State of Israel, is buried there. In an editorial eulogizing Archibald, the *Providence Journal* wrote on September 16, 1966: "The city and state will have a difficult time finding someone to fill the void his death has left."

It is not clear how the Silvermans heard about the trio's plight, but when they did, they sought help from an influential friend, U.S. Senator Theodore Francis Green of Rhode Island. A seasoned legislator and scholar of Roman law, Green was dogged in his determination to aid the three aliens who were virtually imprisoned on Ellis Island.

The INS was aware of the political support for the trio. In a handwritten memo to his file on December 21, Shaughnessy, the Deputy INS Commissioner, wrote that Senator Theodore Green of Rhode Island and Congressman Sol Bloom of New York were interested in the case. On January 4, 1940, Shaughnessy wrote a memo to the Board of Inquiry, advising that "when [a] decision has been reached in the case of Mr. and Mrs. Hollander Congressman Bloom's office would like to be advised by telephone." By mid-January 1940, Bloom received a letter from Deputy INS Commissioner I. F. Wixon. The letter referred to phone calls and a letter of December 28, 1939, regarding the congressman's request to release the trio on bond from their Ellis Island confinement. Wixon also responded to Green on January 16, 1940, stating that "there is no authority in law to authorize their release under bond pending their departure from the United States," and that the three were found "inadmissible to the United States either for permanent residence or temporary visit."

Despite the INS's awareness of the political interest in the trio, it persisted in its effort to expel the aliens, who were quickly becoming a political nuisance. On January 10, 1940, Henry Hazard, assistant to the INS commissioner in Washington, wrote to Byron Uhl, the New York district director, asking to be advised of the disposition of the case. Hazard enclosed the letter Joseph had sent to Eleanor Roosevelt and asked that the letter be returned with his report. One can only speculate about Uhl's reaction to Hazard's letter. Yet it must have made Uhl somewhat uneasy that not only his superiors in Washington but also the president's wife were watching events unfold on Ellis Island.

In the meantime, the Board of Special Inquiry convened on Ellis Island on January 26, 1940. Through a translator, Joseph, Felicia, and young Arnold all testified. The three acknowledged that they arrived in the United States without appropriate documents.

The testimony of Felicia and Arnold was quite brief. It was left to Joseph to explain what had transpired. He recounted that the three had never intended to come to the United States. Rather, their intent was to wait out the war in Portugal, with the hope of returning to Poland after the war.

According to the transcript of the proceeding (which is part of the record in a later appeal to the United States Court of Appeals for the Second Circuit), Mr. Galvin, the government inspector representing INS, asked Joseph: "Why did you leave Poland?" Joseph summed up the trio's plight in four words: "To save our lives." To the pointed question as to whether he would "voluntarily" go back to Poland during the war, Joseph replied with one syllable: "No." As shocking as it may seem to contemporary American sensibilities, Inspector Galvin also asked Joseph, "What is your race?" Joseph replied, "Hebrew."

In addition, Inspector Galvin asked Joseph where he wanted to make his future home. Joseph answered: "The only hope I have is that the war will end and that I will be able to return to my home." "Do you mean Poland?," asked the Inspector. "Yes," replied Joseph.

Arnold's illness in Italy and his subsequent separation from his blood relations linked his fate to Joseph's. The link was clearly a moral one for Joseph. Inspector W. J. King asked Joseph: "What obligation have you to support or take care of this boy?" Joseph answered: "Just human interest." Although Joseph stated that he had only met Arnold's parents once in

Cracow, Joseph assured the Board that he would take full responsibility for young Arnold, agreeing to "support him, take care of him, shelter him, and see that he doesn't become a public charge of the government." When Joseph was asked whether he believed Arnold's parents would disapprove of their son living with him, Joseph answered: "No, on the contrary, I think they would be happy about it."

The government's representative also asked Joseph: "Is there any further evidence you wish to present with regard to your application for admission to the U.S.?" Joseph's answer was brief, powerful, and poignant: "I beg for the sake of humanity to grant us a refuge here as we have no other place to go at this time."

Surely, it was clear that the three had ample means of support and would not become a burden to the government. It was also clear that they never intended to come into the country. The dire consequences of deportation, whether to Italy or eventually to Poland, could not have been more apparent. Yet, because the evidence showed that there were "no American stamps or visas contained" in the trio's passports, the government argued that immigration law demanded deportation.

The Board's decision was swift, unanimous, succinct, and crushing. At the conclusion of the hearing, Chairman Galvin announced the ruling: "This Board has voted to deny you admission into the U.S. under Section 13 (a)(l) of the Immigration Act of 1924 as immigrants not in possession of appropriate, unexpired, Consular immigration visas."

In the midst of the group's legal battle to stay in the United States, Congressman Bloom wrote to Joseph on February 3, 1940: "I can assure you, Doctor [of Law], that everything that can be done will be done for you and your dear wife, and, if there was any way by which you could be admitted to the United States, the same would be done, but as you no doubt understand by this time, your entrance into the United States is not according to our law and there is no way that this law could be changed so as to fit your case."

On February 7, 1940, Green acknowledged a letter he had received from Joseph and correspondence from Mrs. Silverman. Green told Joseph he had already written to the INS in Washington and telegraphed the commissioner. The senator concluded: "[I] trust that my communications on your behalf will receive sympathetic consideration." He was wrong.

After their loss before the Board of Inquiry, the aliens noted an appeal to the Board of Review, which was heard on February 7, 1940. The ruling from that hearing is also part of the record in regard to the later appeal to the Second Circuit. In its ruling, the Board of Review traced the trio's arrival at Ellis Island, noting: "They are all citizens of Poland and of the Hebrew race. They do not have passports, visas, or travel documents of any kind." Moreover, the Board determined that the trio "had not complied with the requirements for admission" because they were immigrants without visas. While recognizing that "on humane grounds," the aliens asked not to be deported to Poland, the Board was of the view that they would "be returned to the country whence they came (in this instance Italy)." It concluded that the Board of Special Inquiry "acted properly in regarding [them] as immigrants, in view of their stated intention not to return to their homeland, and in excluding them from admission to the United States."

Although the Board of Review affirmed the decision of the Board of Special Inquiry, it added: "There should be no objection to a temporary stay of their deportation to allow them to arrange for visas to some other country and to transship to such country." As a result, deportation was "held in abeyance" for thirty days to permit the aliens to make such arrangements, "at their own expense."

The trio's legal battle to stay in the United States was hardly over. Although a lawyer by training, Joseph was not familiar with the seemingly Byzantine rules of the American legal system. He could only hope that, on appeal, the courts would overturn the administrative rulings.

On February 13, 1940, Jan Schreiber, "as next friend" of Joseph Hollander, Felicia Schreiber Hollander, and Arnold Spitzman, filed in the U.S. District Court for the Southern District of New York a petition for a writ of habeas corpus against Rudolph Reimer, Commissioner of Immigration at Ellis Island. Schreiber sought to bring the aliens to court to decide "what shall be done concerning the said persons or any of them." In the petition, the group's lawyer pleaded with the court: "That deportation to Poland is fraught with serious and harsh consequences; that Poland is in a chaotic state and a state of great political uncertainty. That deportation to Poland at this time is inhuman and shocking to the senses." The "relators," as they were called, obtained a writ of habeas corpus on February 13, 1940, pending a hearing.

The U.S. government remained steadfast in its determination to close the door to freedom while opening the door to deportation. At a hearing held in federal court on February 16, 1940, before Judge Henry Goddard, the government, represented by U.S. Attorney John T. Cahill and Assistant U.S. Attorney David McKibbin III, vigorously opposed the relators' position. The Justice Department lawyers renewed the arguments that had been successfully advanced at the Ellis Island administrative proceeding: the three did not arrive in a lawful manner and were therefore subject to deportation, regardless of the situation in Europe. The *New York Times* and a Polish language newspaper published in the United States covered the hearing. Pursuant to an order entered on February 17, 1940, without an opinion, Judge Goddard agreed with the government and dismissed the writ of habeas corpus. He also remanded the three to the custody of the commissioner of immigration. However, the judge agreed to stay deportation for ten days, to permit the aliens to note an appeal to the United States Court of Appeals for the Second Circuit.

The trio applied to the United States District Court for an order releasing them on bail, pending resolution of their appeal. Regarding bail, the issue was not that the three *would flee*. The issue was that they would *stay*. Nevertheless, on this issue they prevailed. By another order dated February 17, 1940, Judge Goddard granted the request for bail, with the express consent of the U.S. Attorney, John Cahill. Goddard set bail at $1,000 for Joseph, $1,000 for Felicia, and $500 for Arnold; the total of $2,500 was a rather hefty sum for the time. Nevertheless, after two months and thirteen days at Ellis Island, the three were finally able to leave.

Still, Joseph faced the daunting task of saving himself, Felicia, and Arnold; he attempted to travel down another path. Joseph's Polish passport contains a one-year Mexican visa issued in New York on March 30, 1940. Sanctuary in Mexico looked like the only hope for the group. There are references in letters from Joseph's family in Poland, reflecting that Joseph had informed them that he was likely to go to Mexico.

Later, in a letter of September 13, 1940, to INS's district director at Ellis Island, the aliens' attorney, Jacob Lesser, wrote: "Mr. Hollander, acting for himself, his wife, and the young boy Arnold Spitzman, has been endeavoring to make arrangements to emigrate from this country to some South American country." He added: "Of course, your department recognizes the difficulties attending such effort due to the war conditions, the religious persuasion of my clients, and the general disinclination of most countries at this time to encourage immigration."

In addition, Lesser reported that Joseph had "finally located" Arnold's uncle, Henry K. Spitzman, who, with his wife and Arnold's sister, had made it to Rio de Janeiro, Brazil. They had traveled from Paris to Lisbon to South America. Arnold's uncle was attempting to arrange for the trio's emigration but explained that "under present conditions, it takes a longer time than it otherwise would." Therefore, Lesser sought release of the trio without delay, "upon the giving of such departmental bonds" as INS required. Eventually, Arnold would join his blood relatives in Brazil and live his adult life there.

As Joseph was contending with the federal proceedings, he was constantly aware of the desperate plight of his family, trapped in Poland. The family's letters to Joseph left little doubt that their lives were in extreme jeopardy. On March 16, 1940, Joseph wrote to a lawyer in Poland for help: "I keep receiving letters from my sister and brother-in-law from Krakow, and from the content, I can easily guess that the situation over there is terrible. I have to do absolutely everything in order to help them leave ... I am awaiting your response with impatience since the situation is burning and any delay may be catastrophic." Nor was there anything subtle in a letter to Joseph of April 8, 1940, from his brother-in-law, Salo Nachtigall, who wrote: "We are awaiting news as if for salvation."

In an archaic German script, Joseph's aging mother, Berta, wrote often to her beloved only son. There is but one theme in Berta's letters, as evidenced by a passage from a letter to Joseph on June 2, 1940: "You are my treasure and lucky star. When I get up and go to bed, my thoughts are of you. Why should I not be happy to have such a child, and I am proud of you. I would like to know only that you are happy, what you want is the important thing. You deserve to be happy and content. How happy I am to read your sweet lines. I cannot part from your dear letters. I always carry them with me, and when I am anxious, I reach for your letters." Undoubtedly, Joseph remembered to his dying day the image of his devoted mother sustaining herself with her love of him and the hope that he could miraculously rescue them.

The aliens' appeal was heard in the Second Circuit Court of Appeals on June 20, 1940. In name, the opponent was Rudolph Reimer, the Commissioner of Immigration at Ellis Island. In reality, the power and prestige of the Justice Department was aligned against the group. Lesser, the trio's attorney, implored the court to reverse Judge Goddard's ruling dismissing the writ of habeas corpus and to permit the trio to remain in the United States. He wrote with passion and truth in his brief that "deportation to Poland at this time in effect means the destruction of the relators [i.e., Joseph, Felicia, Arnold] either in body, or in spirit or in both." Stanley Diana, the immigration inspector, challenged Lesser's humanitarian plea. Asserting in the government's brief that "the aliens were afforded a full, complete and fair hearing before the Board of Special Inquiry," Diana urged the Court of Appeals to uphold the Board's ruling.

On July 8, 1940, a three-judge panel of the Second Circuit Court of Appeals, consisting of Judges Thomas Swan, Charles Clark, and Robert Patterson, issued its decision, affirming the lower court. Thereafter, John Cahill, the U.S. Attorney for the Southern District of New York, presented an "Order on Mandate" to the federal trial court. The order, signed by Judge Samuel Mandelbaum on September 9, 1940, directed "the aliens" to surrender for deportation on September 17, 1940, at the federal courthouse. That date was later extended. Although the trio surrendered for deportation on October 11, 1940, deportation did not occur.

Since the *Vulcania* sailed into New York Harbor, the world had changed significantly. Although it would be many months until Pearl Harbor and the entry of the United States into the war, Europe was engulfed in a continental death grip. The law seemed to require the government to return the aliens via the same shipping line that originally brought them to the United States. However, as a practical matter, it had become *totally* impossible for the government to send the trio back to Europe on an Italian line vessel, given Italy's entry into the war in May 1940. Moreover, by late 1940, the INS must have realized that any xenophobic fear of hordes of Jewish refugees landing in the United States was surely ludicrous. Although a few lucky ones might slip through, Europe's exit doors had been sealed shut, as was the collective fate of the continent's Jewish population. Therefore, INS was in a position to discretely allow three wayward and exhausted Jewish immigrants to bide their time in the United States without fear that other Jews would follow.

On September 14, 1940, while the federal prosecutors seemingly remained intent on pursuing the deportation of the aliens, Uhl wrote to the INS commissioner in Washington. Noting the government's inability to send the aliens back "at the present time on account of lack of sailings," Uhl suggested that INS release the aliens under bond, "until such time as their removal could be effected."

In the fall of 1940, INS was moved from the Labor Department to the Justice Department. On September 30, 1940, the Board of Immigration Appeals of the INS considered the trio's "request for release under bond" and granted "parole of [the] aliens for six months," upon posting of a total of $2,500. Signed by the chairman of the Board of Immigration Appeals, the order pointed to the "inability to accomplish deportation" because of the "war conditions" in Europe. The order also noted that the three had been trying to gain entry to Brazil, where "an uncle of [Arnold] has been located." The three were formally released under INS bond on October 11, 1940, in lieu of deportation.

In effect, the three aliens had traded their federal court bail for INS bonds. They could breathe American air, but they were far from free. The aliens still had no legal status. Upon the expiration of the parole, they could still face deportation. In short, their legal odyssey was far from complete.

In the year preceding U.S. entry into the war, Joseph was in that neverland of parole. On the street, he appeared as just another American immigrant. At least initially, however, the INS would not allow him to work, and his tether to freedom was tenuous at best. Nevertheless, he and three others invested a sum of money to establish a travel bureau, the Compass Resettlement Corporation, located on West 42nd Street in New York City. The company's mission was, in part, to extricate Joseph's family.

Knowing that one is the only flicker of hope to so many souls was surely an overwhelming emotional burden for Joseph. Yet, he was relentless in his efforts to save his family. Joseph knew time was his enemy, as every passing month brought new restrictions, indignities, and hardship to the Jews of Poland. At considerable expense, he was able to send sugar, tea, coffee, cooking oil, and even chocolate to his family in Cracow from neutral countries. Clearly, only some of these packages arrived.

In December 1940, Joseph managed to obtain papers for his family from the Nicaraguan Consulate in the United States, which were regarded as nothing short of a miracle by the entire family. Indeed, the news was greeted with unsurpassed jubilation. In the unforgiving bright light of reality, however, what we see are people desperate for a shred of hope. With hindsight, it can be seen that there was very little chance the Nazis would honor the Nicaraguan documents. Nonetheless, the papers seem to have come excruciatingly close to saving Klara, Dawid, and their teenage daughters, Lusia and Genka.

In the meantime, Joseph hired a Washington immigration lawyer, Edward Collins, to pursue his effort to obtain legal entry into the United States. In January 1941, Joseph and Felicia submitted a twenty-page application to INS for a "pre-examination." Once through the pre-examination process in the United States, the immigrants were supposed to go to Canada for a brief period to apply formally for the coveted immigration visas. All legal issues were on the cusp of being resolved. Because the undocumented aliens physically had to leave the United States and reenter legally with a visa, a trip to Toronto was scheduled for March 3, 1941. Everything had been moving perfectly – perhaps too perfectly. As luck would have it, just a few days before Joseph and Felicia were to have their pre-examination on Ellis Island, they were told not to come because of an "investigation."

Although the delay was caused by a Justice Department investigation, the incident that led to it could easily have been penned in Hollywood. The couple's carefully orchestrated plan to reenter the United States legally was derailed by a bizarre extortion plot. Joseph's case would now resonate in the halls of the Department of Justice and even into the office of Secretary of State Cordell Hull.

According to the investigation, in June 1940, Joseph had been contacted at the Compass office by Alexander Gross, a man unknown to Joseph. Gross, who must have heard of Joseph's background in the travel business, asked Joseph if he knew anyone connected with the Honduran government who could help obtain Honduran passports for Richard Abramowicz and his wife, who were friends of Gross trapped in Poland. Gross showed Joseph documents indicating that in Poland Abramowicz was an honorary consular official for the Honduran government. Gross also told Joseph that Abramowicz was willing to spend $2,000 to obtain valid Honduran passports or travel documents for himself and his spouse. Realizing that there was a Polish Jew who needed to be rescued, Joseph agreed to inquire. He went to a colleague, Jacques Sherry, who, in turn, said he knew of a man named Jaffe who claimed to know the consul general of Honduras in New York.

As reflected in a document submitted by Collins to the Department of Justice, captioned "For the privilege of a Pre-Examination," there was an exchange of telegrams between New York and Honduras. Negotiations between Jaffe and Honduras went on for approximately a month, culminating in two official Honduran passports, signed by the Honoduran minister of foreign affairs. The passports were sent to Gross, who then forwarded them to his desperate friends in Warsaw. Amazingly, Abramowicz and his wife arrived in San Francisco on November 13, 1940, Honduran diplomatic passports in hand, and were admitted as citizens of Honduras. The story could have ended on the dock in San Francisco with two Polish Jews grateful for having been saved from extermination.

Several months after Abramowicz's arrival, in the midst of Joseph's own maneuvering for legal residency, the new immigrant found Joseph in New York. One might have expected Abramowicz to shower Joseph – and everyone else along the chain to the Honduran consulate – with a profusion of gratitude. Hardly. Abramowicz demanded that Joseph refund $900 of the original $2,000 that was used to obtain the passports. Joseph explained that he was merely a conduit and did not have the money. In Joseph's sworn affidavit of September 15, 1941, submitted during the investigation, Abramowicz was quoted as saying to Joseph: "If you will not pay, I will go to American authorities and I will make a scandal for you." A "Legal Branch – Hearing" was held on the same date, September 15, 1941, before T. B. Shoemaker and Allan C. Defanny, deputy commissioners of INS's Legal Branch. Collins explained what had transpired, asserting that Abramowicz told "Dr. Hollander [he] would return to him $900 or he [i.e., Abramowicz] would create a scandal."

Knowing that he was guilty only of a humanitarian gesture toward the very person trying to extort money from him, Joseph categorically refused to acquiesce to the demand. True to his threat, it was at that point that Abramowicz requested an investigation of Joseph's role in procuring Honduran passports for Mr. and Mrs. Gross. In a letter of December 30, 1941, from Lemuel Schofield, special assistant to the attorney general,

Collins was notified that "Dr. Hollander's case is receiving consideration and you will be notified when a decision is reached."

Fortunately for Joseph, the INS became suspicious of the man now calling himself "Ricardo" Abramowicz, whose story began to unravel. Abramowicz admitted to INS authorities that he never renounced his Polish citizenship and never swore allegiance to Honduras. Abramowicz also told U.S. officials that he "erroneously believed that the issuance of a Honduran passport conferred upon him Honduran citizenship." The Justice Department concluded that Abramowicz entered the United States under false pretense because his actual nationality was Polish, not Honduran. The conclusion of the INS investigation was "that consideration may be given to the question of the institution of possible deportation proceedings" against Abramowicz. Although Joseph was exonerated, Abramowicz's charges caused a delay of the Hollanders' pre-examination process until May 28, 1942. A precious year had been lost.

If the swirl of events, the seeming uncertainty of the investigation, and the absence after early 1942 of any mail from his family were not sufficient to crush Joseph's spirit, his marriage to Felicia fell apart. Together they had escaped the Nazi inferno and prevailed in a mighty struggle to stay in the United States. But in December 1942, Felicia established residency in Reno, Nevada, and obtained a divorce on January 25, 1943. In short order, Felicia married Julius Deutsch, who was more than twenty years her senior and lived on Fifth Avenue in New York. In April 1944, Felicia went through the immigration process by going to Canada and legally entering the United States.

As for Joseph, he benefited from the enactment in 1942 of an amendment (section 701) to the Nationality Act of 1940. Section 701 allowed members of the U.S. military to apply for citizenship regardless of their legal status. In the words of INS historian Marian Smith, Congress created a shortcut to citizenship. On March 15, 1943, Joseph enlisted in the army, presumably aware that his decision would expedite his goal of remaining in the United States while also providing him with an opportunity to help in the defeat of the evil that had decimated his life and the lives of his family.

A U.S. naturalization examiner wrote to the divisional director with regard to Joseph's petition for naturalization, noting that "the manner of the subject's arrival at a port of entry in [the] United States, together with the means by which he continued to stay" in the country, were presented to the court. In addition, Joseph's attempts to procure Nicaraguan and Honduran passports "in aid of relatives and other individuals in Europe to obtain egress from that continent" were also reviewed.

The federal court granted Joseph's petition for naturalization; he was naturalized in Newark, New Jersey, on November 19, 1943, just shy of four years after the *Vulcania* steamed into New York Harbor.

Repeatedly, Joseph asked the Red Cross for assistance in regard to his family. In May 1943, he was informed by the International Red Cross of his mother's death. On September 24, 1943, Joseph received a note from the Red Cross, indicating that "the names and addresses of your sisters were in doubt." In the spring of 1944, Joseph wrote to the Red Cross, inquiring about his sister, Mania. The Red Cross responded in August 1944, advising that it could not locate her. While searching for bits of information about his family, Joseph was led to Arthur Blaustein in Paris. Initially, he did not realize that Blaustein was the brother of Munio, the man his sister Dola had married during the German occupation. In January 1945, pleading for help, Joseph wrote to Blaustein, stating that he had "tried to get news through different organizations, but everything is in vain."

In the meantime, after Joseph enlisted in the army, he underwent basic training in upstate New York. He was subsequently posted in Ft. Monmouth, New Jersey – an assignment that would again change his life.

A short train trip on February 3, 1944, produced results that lasted more than forty years. On that date, the 7:40 A.M. train from New York's Pennsylvania Station to Red Bank, New Jersey, near Ft. Monmouth, carried Joseph as well as Vita Fischman, a civilian illustrator employed by the army, who was returning to duty following the funeral of her paternal grandmother. By chance, she sat next to a soldier, Joseph Hollander.

Vita and Joseph began a storybook romance that ended in their common moment of death in October 1986. As the couple's correspondence reveals – letters that they both saved – their courtship and marriage were characterized by extraordinary dedication, mutual respect, and an unparalleled love. This yin and yang, left brain–right brain relationship, not only endured but thrived and deepened with time. Many would say that their act of dying together was symbolic of their unending devotion, almost a literary punctuation point for a marriage of two souls inseparable in spirit.

Whereas Joseph had a precise, methodical, and almost mathematical mind, Vita was 180 degrees the opposite. She was a talented cartoonist, portrait painter, and sculptor, able to work in almost any medium. She had been trained in fine arts at Pratt Institute in Brooklyn, New York, and, before the war, was a cartoonist with the Fleischer Studios in New York and Florida, where she worked on the Popeye and Betty Boop cartoons and the feature film, *Gulliver's Travels*. During the war, the army used her talents to draw complex diagrams of electronics equipment.

By Jewish standards, Vita was almost the proverbial Yankee. Her maternal grandparents emigrated to the United States by the mid–nineteenth century, and her parents were born in the United States. With no direct family ties to Eastern Europe, events unfolding in the Jewish community in Poland must have seemed very remote to her.

On a subconscious level, it seems as if Joseph sought someone with no ties to his past, a Jewish community in Cracow nearing extinction. With Vita (whose name means life), did he want to separate himself from the old to fulfill the American promise of a new beginning? Could Vita, with her unbridled optimism and "can-do" values, typical of midcentury Americans, offer him a roadmap to rebuild a shattered life? Could she, with her physical beauty and talent to create, give him hope to transcend the inhumanity of fellow humans, the profound loneliness of being a sole survivor, and the emptiness of his reality?

On February 28, 1945, Joseph and Vita were married in Manhattan by a deputy city clerk. It was one of those classic wartime weddings, with the date effectively dictated by the War Department. The small family reception was followed by a honeymoon that could be counted in minutes rather than days. Their wedding night was spent at a room in the St. Moritz Hotel, overlooking Central Park. On March 1, 1945, one day after the marriage, Joseph's army unit was sent to the European theater to fight the evil that precipitated Joseph's flight from Europe almost six years earlier.

After Joseph returned from the European theater, the couple repeated their marriage vows in a religious ceremony in September 1945. Ever the romantic, the "second" wedding date provided Joseph with an annual opportunity to celebrate a "second" anniversary and to provide a second anniversary gift for his wife.

Joseph had a dual role in Europe. He was part of a victorious military on the march to Berlin. But he was also determined to learn the fate of his three sisters and their families. On March 6, 1945, Vita wrote assuringly to Joseph: "There's one thing you won't have to worry about no matter where you may be – I shall try every possible means of finding out about your family – and if help is needed – it is theirs."

While in Belgium on April 28, 1945, Joseph discovered a letter under his sleeping bag from Arthur Blaustein. He wrote to Vita about the letter, in perfect English: "Mr. Blaustein wants to see me and writes that he has something to tell me about my family. The first thing tomorrow morning (it's midnight now) I will try and get a two-day pass to go to Paris. It is a long trip and I will have to hitch hike. Most probably it will take me around 10 hours each way, but I must go – I wonder whether I'll be able to sleep now. I am too excited."

The Paris trip to visit Blaustein was ultimately disappointing. In a letter to Vita from Germany dated May 7, 1945, Joseph wrote that until July 1943, Blaustein had been in continuous contact with his brother, Munio, and Munio's wife, Dola – Joseph's youngest sister. Blaustein gave Joseph the final three postcards from Munio and Dola. Joseph explained to Vita:

> Every card contained a few words, as a sign they were alive. Those cards were mailed to my other sister in Krakow (because this was the only town in Poland from where letters could have been mailed outside of Germany) and addressed to a certain woman (a gentile) in Paris. Her name and address were used by Mr. Blaustein as his cover address.

Presumably Blaustein, as a Jew, was himself in hiding in Paris and thus could only receive mail through the help of others. Joseph continued:

> To the last card, dated July 3, 1943, my second sister [Klara], the one who lived with her husband and two daughters in Krakow, added the following words (in translation): We are leaving unexpectedly on a transport for exchange. We will send to you our new address after our arrival." This little note was signed by my sister, Klara, and it was in her own handwriting. Two days later on July 7, 1943, Mr. Blaustein sent a card

to my sister Klara's last address in Krakow and it was returned to him with an official remark "returned." Not one word more. It is clear to me that they left Krakow, but neither I know where they have been shipped nor who was shipped. My sister wrote "we." Was it with her husband and children or under "we" did she mean also my oldest sister with her husband. They all had the same documents [to Nicaragua], which I mailed to them in 1940. The only basis these papers could be used by the German authorities was the word "exchange," which my sister repeated in her last note. If she would write "we are leaving with a transport" she would not mention the words "for exchange." I think it was one of those dreadful transports. Can I have any hope to see them yet alive?

The information which I am getting here from the deported Poles (there are over 3 million in Germany) is not good. I was mainly interested to find out whether the Germans have also sent Jews as slave laborers to Germany. Their answer is negative. Only some Jewish women could perhaps hide among the masses of Polish women.... I am using every opportunity to talk to Poles in the camps of displaced persons asking for someone from Krakow in the hope that he may know someone from my family. It's like trying to find a small object in the ocean. Perhaps in a few weeks we will be at our destination. I will be able to contact the Russian administration of displaced persons and with their help find out the truth. I know I am cheating myself, but it is hard to give up the hope and to face the fact that my whole family is lost and no one can be saved.

In the letter, Joseph did say he received "a little consolation" learning from Blaustein that his mother died of natural causes with her family at her side and that she had a proper burial. He expressed the hope that he would be able to visit her grave in Nowy Sacz. The lengthy letter goes on to say that Blaustein thought Munio had friends in the small town where they lived and "through connections he could hide."

On May 2, 1945, upon returning to Belgium "after a long and strenuous trip to Paris," Joseph lamented to Vita that he spent the entire day "in the company of the poor and most unhappy Mr. Blaustein," who had reported "bad news about my own family and a few unfortunate friends." Yet, Joseph never specified the bad news that he learned from Blaustein.

One can tell from reading Joseph's letters to his bride that he continued to harbor hope for the survival of his family. In a letter written to Vita from Berlin on July 18, 1945, Joseph reflected: "If my family would have a chance to write to me, they would use my old address and I would surely receive the mail. The letter which I wrote to Poland to a man . . . in Nowy Sacz where my youngest sister lived for the last few years was returned to me today with a note 'no service.'" He added that telegraph service to Warsaw had just resumed and that a friend learned his mother and sister had survived. In another letter, Joseph said: "The war news changes every hour on the hour." He also wrote: "[A]ny minute [we] expect unconditional surrender."

As late as July 20, 1945, well after Germany's capitulation, Joseph remained hopeful that his family had survived. He wrote to Vita:

> The happenings of the last few years taught me to be always ready to hear about some unexpected news and therefore to keep always calm. It was impossible for me to be undisturbed last night when I received a letter from a person unknown to me with information that she was together with my sister Klara, her husband, their two daughters and a child they adopted in the camp Belsen until May 28, 1944. You remembered the last place I lost trace was Krakow from which they were deported on July 3, 1943. With yesterday's news, I gained almost a whole year. The letter is dated June 26, 1945, and is written in Frankfurt in the Polish language. The woman who writes this letter traveled with my sister and her family from Krakow to Belsen and says on May 28, 1944, two transports each of 150 persons with the best documents have been sent to an unknown destination for exchange against German citizens. My sister and her family was in one of those transports. I am writing to this woman to find out some more details and follow up the trail. You must wonder how she knew my military address. I can't understand it either. She starts the letter: "By pure accident I have seen your letter one hour before I left Liege and I am writing on a train to Paris to find my husband. I know you are from Krakow and I used to work in a bank where you have been a client." She assures me that many people from Poland are alive and scattered throughout the world and pretty soon we'll hear from them. I hope she is right. She doesn't mention anything about my other two sisters and their husbands. As soon as I have more details from her I will notify you.

To be sure, it was an emotional roller-coaster. Over a fragment of a letter, a brief conversation, some official correspondence, Joseph analyzed and agonized, probably knowing in his gut that he was, indeed, cheating himself. On June 12, 1945, Joseph wrote to Vita of his visit to Bergen-Belsen, the notorious concentration camp where he believed Klara and her family had been imprisoned. He noted that, even after liberation by the Allies, "whole families... were scattered through Germany."

> I met two women in the Belsen camp, but they could not give me any information concerning my family. I will spare you and therefore not write about all that I learned and saw. I traveled from one camp to another in this area until after 10 P.M. and drove back through the night. At the last place I was informed that [in] a certain office in Bergen a master list of names of all people deported from Poland to camp Belsen can be found.

He noted that it was almost impossible to get there because all travel had to be connected to a military mission. Driven to find out the truth about his family, Joseph went to Bergen-Belsen a few days later. Although the June 16, 1945, letter is not clear, he noted there was a fourteen-hour delay and that he got back to camp at 4:00 A.M. "How I explained that AWOL I will tell you some day in person."

> I did not find any trace of my family. The camp is filled with people from Poland and at least 6,000 Jewish women (the whole camp is mostly women) some from my hometown. The conditions are still terrible and even though it is two months since the British took over this camp, the people still suffer. I can't say everything in a letter. Just one remark poor people and poor world, where this can happen.
>
> A list of names of all people – even those still alive – is not ready. I was sent from one camp to another in this vicinity and traveled 22 hours around 450 miles. The head-man in Belsen gave me some hope. He is sure that I can find my sister Klara with her family in a camp called Hillersleben... according to his information families with documents of one of the neutral countries were shipped to this place before the Allied armies occupied Belsen. How I will get to this place. As the result of my short visit, I have to write around thirty letters to America and Palestine to relatives of some people from this camp.

Even after the Germans surrendered, Joseph did not know for sure whether his family had perished. He received a letter from the United Nations Relief and Rehabilitation Administration on July 24, 1945, instructing him to work through the military in his efforts to locate surviving members of his family. Joseph's sudden surge of hope each time he saw a faint glow of light undoubtedly mirrored the real but tragically fleeting exhilaration felt by his family when they thought they had received documents giving them sanctuary in Nicaragua.

Those who knew Joseph agree that he was kind and gentle to a fault and never made disparaging comments about anyone. Even when he was justified, he never expressed venom about the Germans. In a letter to Vita on April 28, 1945, written from Belgium, he showed an uncharacteristic anger:

He [a Polish Air Force officer assigned to the RAF] invited me to his table and we had a half hour chat. He flew over Germany many times and told me about the destruction made by our bombing, which I was pleased to hear. At least they have the taste of horror done to other nations. He told me about the millions of Poles, Russians, French, etc. The slave laborers in Germany. This is beyond every description. The tragedy of those people can't be compared with anything similar in the whole history of the human race. How innocent the barbarians look now. The history of the "dark" middle ages can be called a fairy tale in comparison with the "heroism" of the 20th century. They [Germans] have absolutely surpassed the Japanese in the cruelty and inhuman treatment. I don't have a vicious nature and never had, but for them [Germany], to punish them, we have to find something to repay them for what they have done. But I am afraid the penalty which they will pay will be in no comparison with what they have done.

Two letters from Joseph to Vita are enormously revealing of his emotional response to the defeated Germans – a people who brutally murdered his three sisters and their husbands and children; killed his friends and colleagues; destroyed his livelihood, culture, and national identity; and turned European Jewry into ashes.

Upon crossing the Dutch-German border with the conquering U.S. Army on May 6, 1945, Joseph is instantly reminded "of all the cruelty, mischief, evil, unhappiness, destruction and misery brought by them [Germans] on so many millions in the whole world."

It is only very, very little satisfaction for me to see their own towns and villages destroyed and to hear that many of them were killed during

the bitter fighting and bombardments. When we passed the demolished
Dutch towns near the frontier, I felt very sorry for the poor and homeless
people, but the same view on the other side of the border filled me
almost with happiness. I asked myself how is it possible to change so
fundamentally in this same minute? It must have been something deep
in me that could bring such diametric emotions; although everything
happened under the same sky and the same green colored fields on both
sides [of the border].

Among the ruins here and there we could see wonderful tulips or
an isolated lilac tree whose magnificent flowers and smell were such a
contrast to everything around. Sometimes it looked to me like a mirage,
just proof that the world and life could be marvelous. . . .

But for you and everyone with whom you will talk, I would like to
state after traveling for three days on German soil, and deep inside that
country – that they got what they asked for. I saw a few destroyed towns
in England, France, Belgium and Holland and such towns as South-
hampton, Le Harve, Brussels etc. But nothing can be compared with
the thorough job our boys did here [in Germany]. When we read in the
States that so many towns and most of the larger ones in Germany have
been bombed for 30 consecutive days and nights, we really didn't know
what this meant. Towns of 100,000 population and bigger can never be
rebuilt. We drove for hours seeing only ruins of buildings. The destruction is so complete that from the mountains of debris we could never
say whether it was a house, a factory or a church. . . . Sometimes, as for
irony, a single wall from a high building was standing with empty win-
dow holes among the mass of bricks. Wonderful scenery for a Wagnerian
play! Let them play now! They showed us what they can do to a town.
They showed us Lidice, they burned the town to the ground and now
we proved we can do the same, even far better. Lidice was a small village,
but you can find in Germany big towns crossed out from the map. It will
take generations to build it up again. For years they will be ghost towns
and they should serve as a demonstrative lesson for German future generations. Some of them should be ordered to stay this way and excursions
should be organized as sightseeing trips. . . .

You can easily understand that life ceased to exist in these towns.
The whole population or rather the part that remained alive is gone.
Sometimes we could see a man or woman searching in the fragments
of rocks, which was once their home for something to save. The best
result could be a broken chair or a kitchen pot.

Believe me, Vita, I am not a hard boiled egg and this type of human
annihilation would always touch me very deeply, but not now and not

against German men and women. When I see them pushing on the roads their little carriages with their belongings I am not sorry for them at all. Don't forget, this view is too familiar to me, with the only difference that at that time German flyers, playing heroes, machine-gunned people on the roads of Poland, France, Belgium and other countries. It exists an expression 'the revenge is sweet'. And, I feel it, even if I could not yet personally do my share.

In one respect, I am not yet clear with myself, and this is towards little German children. I like children and with a few I made friends – with the little ones who came to our camps in France and Belgium to get their candy. The American boys are goodhearted and they shared their candy rations with every child [sic] and nationality didn't make any difference. But here [in Germany] we have strict order [sic] "Don't fraternize." The penalty for breaking this rule is very severe. It is easy with the adults. Anyhow, they try not to see us. When they meet us on the streets, they turn their faces or keep their heads down. But the small children don't understand it. They see a soldier. Many times they greeted us with a Hitler-salute. To give you an example – when we ate our rations on the roads we always had children around us. It was this way during the whole trip. Our last meal in Dutch territory, as usual, was shared with little Dutch children. But a few hours later we stopped on German soil to eat our K and C rations and were again surrounded by German children. No one looked at them, at least it appeared this way. No one talked to them.

But, I couldn't eat my whole ration and I don't like to accumulate in my pockets candy and biscuits. I just forgot to pick up [candy and biscuits] from the grass. When I got up, I saw how these poor little children grabbed everything I left. (I see I instinctively used the words "poor little children." I am afraid I will have troubles with myself).

As a German interpreter for the army, Joseph was in a unique position to observe interrogations of Nazi military and high-ranking civilians. In a letter of May 6, he wrote to Vita:

The old Prussian behavior showed up immediately. They showed respect before uniforms and brass and most certainly my carbine. They stood at attention answering my questions and I must say they were most cooperative. In the near future I will have a possibility to see how far this goes. Perhaps they are still under the big shock to see their land conquered and also to find out that all the stories given them by the Hitler-band was only a pack of lies. But it is too late now and now I only hope that besides their present suffering, something will be done to free the world from Prussian militarism with ideas of conquest and despotism from their ruthless practices.

Concerning the Germans for whom he translated, Joseph felt nothing but contempt. In a letter to Vita from Germany, written on May 18, 1945, he made observations about the just-defeated enemy:

> I have the highest antipathy towards these people for how they behave now. Listening to them someone could think Nazism didn't exist at all, that only the Jews and Bolsheviks made up the stories about the atrocities. Everyone tries to hide the true nature of his identity. You will not find one who will confess that he was a member of the Nazi Party, even if he was a leader. They all pretend to be 'good Germans'. They express their dislike of Hitler and his regime. In one word, they pretend to be angels in a human body. I am not talking about little people. My remarks are about statements made by men who sent people into concentrations camps. Those men should have the courage to take responsibility for the things they have done during the past twelve years. At least, I [would still] consider them as murderers, but as men. They are ready to be slaves. They are willing to shine our shoes with their tongues. They are so scared . . . . and the Germans, asked for a list of who was a member of the Nazi Party, immediately have ready list of names. And, I wouldn't wonder whether the list includes his father or mother.

As for Arnold Spitzman, he made a life for himself in Brazil. Judging from a 1983 letter from Spitzman to Joseph, the two apparently had only fragmentary contact over the decades. By then, Spitzman was the father of two daughters and was on his second marriage. There was no discussion of the surreal journey over hostile borders or the flirtation with deportation to Europe.

*   *   *

In a conversation, Chris Browning asked me an obvious yet profound question: "How did your dad rebuild his life after the war?" A narrative of Joseph's escape from Nazi-occupied Poland, and his efforts to free his family, without addressing how Joseph survived emotionally, would leave a monumental gap in Joseph's story. The core question of why or how he was able to reconstruct his life needed to be explored, if not answered. Over the years, I had thought about that fundamental question. I assumed that my father never had an alternative. I regard my father as a truly remarkable man. Perhaps the ability to rebound from tragedy resides deep within the psyche. Joseph clearly refused to slip into despair or emotional paralysis and I learned of his anger only in reading the letters to my mother. Clearly, he treasured his roles as husband, father, and later as grandfather, and enjoyed a wide circle of friends. He was also especially proud to be an American.

Like many Holocaust survivors, my father preferred silence over sharing his ordeal. The personal loss and incalculable pain of saving oneself while failing to rescue those whom he loved so much surely haunted Joseph every day of his life. The topic never came up among family or friends. Whether Dad's failure to discuss his past with me, even when I became an adult, was borne of a desire to sidestep self-pity or guilt, to spare me from exposure to such horrors, or simply to bury the past is not known.

My mother screened books, magazines, and movies for Holocaust themes, to keep the Holocaust at a distance. I recall one occasion when my mother lapsed in her role as gatekeeper. As a child, my parents took me to see Rolf Hochhuth's 1963 drama, *The Deputy*, which accused Pope Pius XII of deliberate silence during the Nazi slaughter. Scarcely ten minutes into the play, Dad quietly got up from his seat and left the theater. I distinctly recall turning to mom and asking, "Why is Dad leaving?" She gave me a reassuring "everything is OK" pat on the shoulder. At intermission, I found Dad vigorously pacing in front of the theater, with an uncharacteristically solemn look.

I remember many occasions when people would share their nighttime dreams. Dad would always say, "I don't dream." As a child that statement was a source of curiosity. Today I know why his subconscious mercifully smothered his dreams, and why the subject of the Holocaust was off limits. Even as a youngster, I knew intuitively that there were boundaries I could not cross and pain I did not want to inflict.

An examination of the letters exchanged between my parents in the spring and summer of 1945, when Joseph was overseas in the army and desperately looking for his family, convinces me that the resurrection of

Joseph's life can be explained through the exquisite love he shared with my mother; marrying my mother saved him.

One week after their wedding, with Dad on his way to the European theater, his new bride wrote: "It is great here tonight and I am alone. My eyes are closed and you are beside me – the touch of your hand, the kiss of your lips. I am going to keep my eyes closed now, dearest – so you will remain the whole night through."

Later that month, Mom wrote: "I shall write just for the sake of talking to you – yet having nothing concrete to say – only repeated words of love. If you were here in a million different ways I could show that love; there would be no need to continually put it into words."

It is easy to imagine Dad as the GI at mail call in Berlin gently opening an envelope reading these words from Vita: "While I inhabit familiar parts, scenes of our year together – you go farther and farther. It is much easier to feel your nearness – a walk, a restaurant, a beach, a river – but for you, as the miles add it must be difficult to realize your wife isn't a myth. There is a glow in my eyes of happiness in having your love. Wake up, Vita! There's still a war on – and work to be done."

What could Dad have been thinking as he walked among the recently conquered Germans – the very people who murdered his entire family and buried a way of life? Rather than allow himself to be consumed by hatred, he treasured the words from his wife. She wrote: "I don't want to indulge in self pity. There will be a tomorrow when these things I just dream of now will be reality. The waiting period isn't too difficult when you believe in tomorrow." The nightmare that surrounded Joseph every waking minute was counterbalanced by his new bride's dream. "Even if someday I wake up and find it a dream," Mom wrote in July 1945, "I'll be waiting for you, because my love is real."

Because of the love of his wife, Joseph was able to incorporate the concept of a new beginning. "I have a wonderful husband," wrote Vita. She added: "Through his sunshining warmth I learned how to smile again – and now there will be no end – for I shall smile without end. They are truly smiles from within – for it is great happiness even to think of him."

Although neither as facile in his new language nor prone by personality to romanticize, Dad certainly echoed Mom's sentiments in his letters to her. After discussing the prospect of a promotion and a significant new assignment, Dad wrote from Berlin in July 1945: "They [the Army] can't offer me anything that would be worth to postpone my return even for one hour, not for one minute."

In April 1945, while in Belgium, Dad wrote this at 5:00 A.M.: "Second anniversary [i.e., two months] of the biggest day in my life and – without you. The whole night passed while I was wide-awake with my thoughts and my love far away.... Everyone is still in deep sleep. It's peaceful around me, but I had to write to you. I wanted to talk to you, to translate into plain words the things I found in you, in your eyes when we smile at each other. Those were wonderful unforgettable days and they will, they must come back again."

Three months later, Dad again reflected on a postwar future: "Dearest, not four months, not even four years nor our whole lifetimes will bring any regrets. Why should it be different? We know what we want and we have been waiting too long for each other not to appreciate the happiness which we can give each other."

More than giving him a reason to rebuild, Mom knowingly or unknowingly created an alternative universe for Dad. In reference to Joseph's ultimately futile search for survivors, Mom wrote: "The news you have been looking for these years might be more obtainable now – whether it be good or bad – at least you will know. We can look forward to and hope for the best – but please, darling, should it be bad – 'take it' and know that you have me to come home to – *in another world*" (italics added).

PART TWO

CRACOW

The Fate of the Jews of Cracow under Nazi Occupation

Christopher R. Browning

T his collection of letters to Joseph Hollander from various members of his family in Cracow is precisely that – a collection of family letters. They were not written to document the sequence of momentous historical events that their writers experienced or to describe graphically the suffering they endured. On the contrary, both fearful of the possibility of postal surveillance and anxious to reassure Joseph, the letter writers were consciously vague in their references to the political events and German policies of the time and understated in describing the immense difficulties of life that they faced during the first two years of the war in which their correspondence still reached the as yet neutral United States. Focused on deep personal and familial concerns, the letters by themselves provide neither a clear narration nor an explanatory context. Instead, many key factors affecting the lives of Cracow Jews are referred to obliquely or not at all. Wishing to be as nonintrusive as possible in annotating such personal letters, the editors have decided to provide two contextual essays – one concerning German occupation policies and the other examining the prewar and wartime situation of the Jews of Cracow, as well as an additional narrative concerning the recipient of the letters, Joseph Hollander.

When the German army began the invasion of Poland on September 1, 1939, the first response of many Poles, whether Jews or non-Jews, was to flee eastward because they could neither imagine the speed with which the advancing German army would overtake them nor foresee that the Soviet army would occupy eastern Poland after September 17, in accordance with the secret provisions of the Nazi–Soviet Non-Aggression Pact. But the vast majority of those who had briefly attempted to flee at the outbreak of war returned within days to their homes under German occupation. Both the homes left behind and refugees wandering the roads were, of course, subject to theft. This upheaval is referred to briefly and circumspectly in the letter of December 9, 1939, when Klara refers to the unfortunate loss of two suitcases "during our trip." It is mentioned once again on April 8, 1940, when Klara again refers to the loss of most of their belongings "during our land exploring journey." During the Jewish high holidays in the fall of 1940, Klara looks back to the "last year, when we all were at the farm for 14 days, sleeping on the ground and hay. The worst was not to know what was happening at home" (Klara, October 15, 1940).

For most Poles, the prospect of living under Soviet rule was even more frightening than that of living under the Nazis, but for Jews, the Nazis represented a distinctly more ominous threat. Thus, even after the end of hostilities but before the new demarcation line between the German and Soviet zones became sealed near the end of the year, there was a second wave of flight, so that altogether between 200,000 and 300,000 Jews from western and central Poland fled to the Soviet zone. It was an option that many weighed but could not talk about openly in letters that might be read under postal surveillance. Klara's husband entertains plans to move "to Aunt Rozia" (i.e., the Soviet zone) despite "certain difficulties," and Dola's husband, Henek, does make it to "Aunt Rozia," in this case, first Boryslaw and then Drohobycz in Eastern Galicia under Soviet rule. Dola briefly contemplates also going to "Uncle Tolstoy" but fears she would receive no moral support from her husband "in a foreign country." (The fear of postal surveillance can be seen again in the veiled reference to the Germans as the "horrible" "old aunt" in Klara's letter of May 26, 1940.)

After the defeat of Poland, the vanquished country was officially partitioned. The eastern half of the country was incorporated into the Soviet Union. The western borderlands were annexed to the Third Reich. The central region was turned into a German colony known as the General Government and divided into four districts: Warsaw, Lublin, Radom, and Cracow. The city of Cracow became the colonial capital of the general governor, Hans Frank, as well as the district governor, Otto Wächter.

Initially, the Jews of Cracow were subjected to the same anti-Jewish measures introduced throughout German-occupied Poland in the fall of 1939 – confiscation of property, forced labor, marking, and the imposition of a Jewish council or *Judenrat* as the conduit for German demands and orders – as well as various rituals of degradation, humiliation, and violent assault. All Jews had to find ways to hide valuables from the freezing of bank accounts, official confiscation, and rapacious freelance pillaging. Faced with an array of intensifying economic constrictions, Polish Jews had to be very adaptable in finding new ways to sustain themselves and their families. Many middle-class Jews, both men and women, faced the prospect of finding jobs involving some kind of manual labor, both to feed their families and to secure the documentation that would protect them from forced-labor roundups that were terrifying, debilitating, and uncompensated. The letter writers feel both pride and relief that they are acquiring "handicraft professions."

Many Jewish businesses, like the travel agency that Joseph Hollander left behind in Cracow, simply were closed and their assets plundered. Others were taken over by non-Jewish owners in an expropriation process euphemistically called "aryanization." The economic fate of those Jews whose businesses were expropriated was fatefully influenced by the disposition of the individual "trustees" who took them over. Some "trustees" kept the former Jewish owners on as employees to utilize their expertise and familiarity with the business and thus permitted them a minimal livelihood from their former possessions; others drove the former owners away entirely. In this regard, Joseph's brother-in-law Salo was among the more fortunate, and he notes that under the new "Aryan" leadership, "we can come to work, while many other business owners lost everything and cannot even enter their old locales" (Salo, February 1940). Dola, who did not immediately accept a position as clerk in the former family business, faces much greater economic uncertainty (Dola, October 28, 1940).

The ultimate goal of Nazi Jewish policy at this time, however, was not simply persecution and exploitation but rather the systematic expulsion of the Jews of the annexed or "incorporated territories" and then of the General Government to a "Jewish reservation" in the Lublin district at the farthest extremity of the German empire. This region was

pronounced suitable for what the Nazis euphemistically called "resettlement" because "its extreme marshy nature" would "induce a severe
decimation of the Jews."[1] In preparation for this vast program of ethnic
cleansing, Heinrich Himmler's deputy, Reinhard Heydrich, ordered that
Polish Jews from the small towns and countryside be concentrated "in
ghettos" in cities to facilitate "a better possibility of control and later
deportation."[2] This process of concentration in larger cities to facilitate expulsion did not initially envisage the creation of long-term sealed
ghettos, although that is what in fact emerged in 1940 in Lodz and
Warsaw when the anticipated expulsions bogged down and the Jews
became stuck.

The fate of Cracow Jews began to diverge from that of other Jews
in Poland in the spring of 1940, when Hans Frank decided his capital
city should not be subject to the same concentration of Jews as other
urban areas in the General Government. As German colonial officials
flooded into the new capital city, the housing shortage became acute.
On April 12, 1940, Frank announced that it was "absolutely intolerable"
that "thousands and more thousands of Jews slink around and take up
apartments" in the city that the Führer had honored by making it the
capital of the General Government. He thus intended to make Cracow
"the most Jew-free" city in the General Government through "a vast
evacuation operation" that would remove 50,000 Jews and leave only
5,000 or at most 10,000 indispensable workers. Once this was accomplished, one could build clean German residences and "breath German
air," he proclaimed.[3]

The Jews of Cracow were given until August 15, 1940, to leave the city
voluntarily. If they did so, they would be allowed to take their belongings
and choose where they wished to settle. Jews who did not leave by August
15 would be subject to forced deportation without the right to take

---

[1] IMT, vol. 30, p. 95 (Nbg. Doc. 2278-PS: Seyss-Inquart report on his trip to Poland,
November 17–22, 1939).

[2] NA microfilm, T175/239/2728524-28 (conference of Heydrich's division heads and
Einsatzgruppen leaders, September 21, 1939).

[3] Hans Frank, *Das Diensttagebuch des deutschen Generalgouverneurs in Polen 1939–1945*,
ed. by Werner Präg and Wolfgang Jacobmeyer (Stuttgart, 1975), p. 165 (entry of April
12, 1940).

property. Ultimately, only Jews who were deemed important to the city's economic life would be allowed to remain.[4]

Frank justified the expulsion on the grounds that the Jewish population of Cracow had increased 50 percent since the conquest of Poland and was the primary cause of the housing shortage. Indeed, some Jews expelled from western Poland were resettled in Cracow, and Mania notes that five people from Poznan are assigned to her apartment (Mania, July 23, 1940). This is such an unwelcome intrusion and loss of privacy that the family chooses to move to a smaller apartment. According to the statistics of the Jewish community itself, however, the Jewish population had risen a scant 1 percent between the fall of 1939 and spring of 1940, from 65,488 to 66,110.[5] Before the mid-August deadline, Frank agreed to allow 15,000 Jews to remain in the city.[6]

Needless to say, German policy set off a desperate scramble among Cracow Jews for the coveted permits that allowed them to remain in the city. Many were unsuccessful, and by the end of September, some 35,000 Cracow Jews had departed the city with what property they could carry rather than face the prospect of arrest.[7] Among those Jews who tried to remain without the required permission, the Nazis sent 500 to forced labor breaking stones as an exemplary warning.[8] By October, the expulsions had not only come to a temporary halt, but expelled Jews also began slipping back into the city of Cracow, the Jewish population of which rose once again to between 50,000 and 60,000. The furious district governor, Wächter, berated the civil administration in charge and transferred authority for further resettlement actions into the hands of the SS and

[4] YVA, O-53/85/738 (Cracow to Lublin Gendarmerie, August 2, 1940) and 752 (Lublin department for population and welfare to Kreishauptleuten, August 9, 1940). USHMM, RG 15.026m, 1/14/23 (draft, Generalgouverneur to district heads, May 1940), 24 (Bekanntmachung des Stadhauptmanns betr. Abwanderung von Juden, n.d.), and 42–3 (Generalgouverneur to district heads, May 25, 1940).
[5] USHMM, RG 15.026m, 1/14/27–29 (report of Jüdische Gemeinde, May 20, 1940).
[6] USHMM. RG 15.026m, 1/14/68–70 (Ragger report on meeting with Frank, August 2, 1940).
[7] YVA, JM 814, Division of Internal Administration's summary of Situation Reports, Cracow, September 30, 1940.
[8] USHMM, RG 15.026m, 1/14/79–81 (Ragger report on meeting of August 19, 1940).

police.[9] The result was a series of brutal police razzias on November 29 and December 3 and 9, 1940, to demonstrate to the Jews "the seriousness of the situation."[10] In February 1941, another 27,000 expulsion orders were prepared, and throughout the month, train transports set out from Cracow to other parts of the General Government.[11]

From the summer of 1940 through February 1941, the looming threat of expulsion from the city is a constant motif in the letters. As Dola writes on July 28, 1940, "The nightmare of deportation looks into our eyes." On the same day Mania confides, "We live in a chaos and uncertainty." In addition to separation, they feared the "Unknown" (Salo, July 28, 1940) as well as the prospect of life in a small town "without any comfort" and "not even running water" (Klara, August 19, 1940). Of course, more than comfort and familiarity was at stake. For all Jews in German-occupied Poland, life was difficult, but the most vulnerable were the uprooted refugees. Displaced from the communities where they had homes, jobs, and contacts (and often non-Jewish friends with whom they had left valuables), forced to travel with little or no property, relocated in unfamiliar, bewildering, and often unwelcoming surroundings, the penniless refugees were almost invariably the first to succumb to epidemic or starvation or suffer yet further deportation. This dread of being expelled from Cracow was instinctively correct, but it also left Joseph Hollander's family seemingly unaware of the frightful consequences of the alternative – the trap of ghettoization.

The great Jewish communities of Lodz and Warsaw had been sealed in ghettos in May and November of 1940, respectively. Jews in the surrounding areas had either been forced into these two ghettos or sealed in smaller ghettos of their own. These ghettoization measures of the Warthegau region around Lodz and the Warsaw district did not yet affect the Jews of southern Poland, stretching from Cracow to Lublin. On the contrary, the German policy in Cracow had been to disperse

<hr/>

[9] USHMM, RG 15.026m, 1/14/101–3 (Wächter to Schmid, November 21, 1940); YVA, JM 814, Situation Report of Krakau-Land, November 8, 1940.

[10] YVA, JM 814, Situation Report of Cracow District, January 27, 1941 (Wächter to Rühler). USHMM, RG 15.026m, 1/14/113–15 (KdO Krakau, Einsatzbefehl, November 27, 1940).

[11] YVA, JM 814, Situation Report of Cracow District, March 13, 1941 (Wächter to Bühler). YVA, JM 814, Lublin District Report, March 6, 1941.

rather than concentrate the city's Jews. That situation changed in March 1941. In part because of the increased demand for housing resulting from the German buildup for the invasion of the Soviet Union, but also fully congruent with the ideological imperative of intensifying separation between Jews and non-Jews, German authorities in these regions not only expelled urban Jews into the surrounding countryside but now also squeezed the remaining urban remnant into pitifully small areas designated as "Jewish quarters" or ghettos. In a domino effect, Poles were then often moved into vacated Jewish lodgings, and the Germans took the best for themselves. The ghettoization decree for Cracow was issued on March 3, for Lublin on March 24, for Kielce on March 31, and for most other cities in the region in early April 1941.

These letters from Cracow reveal the upheaval of the ghettoization process only in the most circumspect and fragmentary way. At the end of February 1941, both Mania's and Klara's families, the Nachtigalls and Wimisners, had to vacate their apartments within twenty-four hours. Dola's husband-to-be, Munio Blaustein, was expelled to Tarnow, and she had either to follow him immediately or a "Chinese Wall" would separate them forever. The others had "either [to] leave or move to the Jewish quarter in Podgorze," the industrial suburb across the Vistula River from Cracow that had been selected as the site of the ghetto. Mania's and Klara's families, along with their mother, managed to find a two-room apartment in Podgorze and thus move together into the ghetto.

In contrast to Lodz and Warsaw, where virtually all economic ties beyond the ghetto walls were severed and the ghetto inhabitants experienced terrible starvation and skyrocketing death rates, the economic noose around the neck of the ghettoized Cracow Jews was not as tight. Thus, Salo, Dawid, and Genka continued to work at their previous jobs, which presumably meant that, along with many others, they were allowed to leave the ghetto for work on a daily basis. Nonetheless, the food situation changed drastically for the worse. As late as February 6, 1941, Mania assures Joseph that "we have enough to eat, nobody is hungry" and pleads "please do not send packages anymore." After ghettoization, however, the small packages that Joseph continued to have sent from neutral Portugal take on great importance and are now received with immense gratitude.

The very fact that Joseph's family in Cracow had an enterprising contact in the United States who was willing to go to extraordinary lengths to help them introduced one very unusual factor into their experience under Nazi occupation – namely, the procurement of some kind of foreign papers. Before the outbreak of war, the Nazis had pursued the goal of a Germany "free of Jews" through making life so miserable and hopeless for German Jews that they would choose to emigrate despite the loss of property left behind. The chief obstacle facing German Jews who wanted to leave was not the Nazi regime preventing emigration but the lack of other countries permitting immigration. In the fall of 1939, German authorities likewise not only permitted flight over the demarcation line into the Soviet Union but in some cases coerced it, until the need for stable relations with their new Soviet neighbor required controlling the border. While the Nazi regime continued to allow Jewish emigration from the Third Reich until October 1941, as long as those trying to leave were not deemed a potential asset to the Allied war effort (such as young men of military age), the number of viable emigration routes steadily shrunk. Jewish emigration through Italy ended in May 1940 and through the Soviet Union in June 1941, and thereafter only the tenuous route through Spain and Portugal remained open. To maximize these limited possibilities for the emigration of Jews from the Third Reich, the Nazis blocked Jewish emigration from or through all other countries under their control, including the General Government. The only exceptions were those Jews who held foreign citizenship and passports and therefore legally were not emigrating but rather returning home.

The impact of German policy governing Jewish emigration is reflected in the letters. With the looming threat of expulsion from Cracow, Salo (August 22, 1940) perceptively realizes that "sooner or later all the Jews will be forced out of here" and that therefore they must contemplate registering for emigration. A month later, Dawid (September 17, 1940) asks Joseph "to arrange the papers for us as soon as possible." Both families register for emigration with the U.S. Embassy in Berlin, only to find themselves behind more than 43,000 others on the waiting list. Then, "like stars from the sky" (Genka, December 9, 1940), papers arrive from the Consulate General of Nicaragua. Clearly, Joseph had arranged, at considerable cost no doubt, for the issuance of entry papers of some kind. Indeed, one must suspect that the willingness of various diplomats to sell such papers increased in inverse proportion to the likelihood that their customers would ever actually arrive at the border to present them. The euphoria is short-lived, as Dola (December 18, 1940) quickly discovers that in reality it is impossible to leave the General Government with such papers. Only Nicaraguan citizenship and passports, which Dawid (April 28, 1941) continues to ask Joseph for even after they have been ghettoized, will bring any benefit.

Aside from family news, the letters from the ghetto become even more cryptic. Following the momentous invasion of the Soviet Union on June 22, 1941, for instance, there are only the briefest but repeated quick assurances from Dola and Munio, who had moved once again from Tarnow to Nowy Sacz, that everyone is "doing well." Postal delivery becomes increasingly uncertain, and Munio's sister in Switzerland, Regine Hütschnecker, becomes a necessary conduit. The last letters from Poland in Joseph's collection date from December 1941, just days after the U.S. entry into the war. Thereafter, Joseph receives only occasional fragments of information passed on by Regine, including news in December 1942 that his mother had died the previous August but that the others were still alive.

What transpired in Cracow and Nowy Sacz after the last letters of December 1941? What was the fate of Joseph Hollander's family? For this, the historian must turn to the postwar memoir literature and court records. Perhaps the single most important memoir of the Cracow ghetto was written by the Polish pharmacist Tadeusz Pankiewicz.[12] His pharmacy Under the Eagle, at the Plac Zgody where thousands of Jewish workers left and returned to the ghetto each day and where those fated for deportation were assembled, was the one non-Jewish business that was allowed to continue operating within the walls of the Podgorze ghetto and provided Pankiewicz with an extraordinary vantage point from which to witness events in the ghetto. By uncanny coincidence, Pankiewicz was also a prewar acquaintance of Joseph Hollander and is mentioned twice in the letters (Dola, May 16, 1940, and Mania, May 5, 1941). He is one of the two Poles mentioned by name from whom the family receives help.

[12] Tadeusz Pankiewicz, *The Cracow Ghetto Pharmacy* (New York, 1987).

Aside from the Germans, four institutions loomed over life in the ghetto in Pankiewicz's account. First was the Labor Office, or *Arbeitsamt*. It provided the identity cards and permits that allowed work outside the ghetto. Second was the *Judenrat* under the chairmanship of Dr. Arthur Rosenzweig that served as the conduit for German orders. Third was the so-called *Ordnungsdienst*, or Jewish ghetto police, under the notorious Symche Spira. He was described by Pankiewicz as "blindly dedicated to the Germans... a megalomaniac, wrapped in fantasy, a classic example of a psychopath, neurotic,... an unthinking robot, carrying out the Gestapo orders as if hypnotized."[13] Finally, there was an unusually large and diverse array of informers, who worked for various German agencies and "infiltrated all the institutions of the ghetto."[14] Unlike Lodz, where the autocratic Chaim Rumkowski controlled all economic activity, the Cracow ghetto more closely resembled the "free enterprise" spirit of Warsaw. The nouveau riche of the ghetto, often smugglers or those with privileged relations with the Germans, could open restaurants, stores, and places of entertainment while others struggled to subsist.

Estimates of the ghetto population of Podgorze vary from a low of 16,000 to a high of 22,000.[15] In fact, the population varied over time as some Jews were expelled from the ghetto into the Lublin district[16] and others slipped into the ghetto illegally[17] or were transferred from outlying communities. The systematic reduction of the ghetto did not begin until June 1942, fifteen months after it was created. Construction of the first Nazi death camps at Belzec and Chelmno had begun in the fall of 1941, and the mass killing of Jews in the Warthegau region around Lodz began soon thereafter in early December. In contrast, mass killing in Belzec did not begin until mid-March 1942. The first victims were Jews deported from Lublin and Eastern Galicia. Within one month, the

[13] Pankiewicz, *The Cracow Ghetto Pharmacy*, pp. 33, 67, 136.
[14] Pankiewicz, *The Cracow Ghetto Pharmacy*, pp. 18–19, 23–5, 35–7, 131.
[15] For the low estimate, Malvina Graf, *The Krakow Ghetto and the Plaszow Camp Remembered* (Tallahassee, 1989), p. 38. Graf's memoir is clearly influenced by Pankiewicz's earlier publication. The high estimate comes from German court officials: Zentralstelle der Landisjustizverwaltungen (hereafter ZStL), II 206 AR 641/70, vol. 13 (Indictment of Rudolf Körner and others by the State Attorney's Office of Hannover), pp. 77–8.
[16] Pankiewicz, *The Cracow Ghetto Pharmacy*, pp. 33–5; Graf, *The Krakow Ghetto*, p. 41.
[17] For example, Graf, *The Krakow Ghetto*, pp. 54–5.

Germans had gassed more than 78,000 Jews in the primitive, small-scale facilities at Belzec. Overwhelmed by the deluge of victims, the Belzec camp was closed for five weeks from mid-April until late May while new, enlarged gas chambers were constructed. Meanwhile, an additional death camp at Sobibor was opened in early May 1942. After the new facilities at Belzec began functioning in late May, the Nazis in the General Government then had the capacity to expand the killing operations to encompass the Jews of the Cracow district in addition to those of Lublin and Galicia.

The ghetto deportation operations in the Cracow district were coordinated by the SS and Police Leader Julian Scherner, his chief of staff Martin Fellenz, and the head of the Jewish desk of the Gestapo, Wilhelm Kunde. In May 1942, they summoned the heads of the various SS and police formations in the district to plan their first major deportation action from the ghetto in Podgorze. On the night of May 28–29, the ghetto was surrounded by Reserve Police Battalion 74 and units of ethnic German police known as the *Sonderdienst*. On the following morning, it was announced that all Jews of the ghetto would have to register, under threat that one inhabitant of each apartment house would be killed in which any other inhabitant of the apartment house evaded registration. For two days, a team of Gestapo officials, along with officials of the Labor Office and *Judenrat*, manned twelve registration desks. A cursory glance determined which Jews and their families received yellow identification cards, indicating capacity for work, and which did not. Two days did not suffice to process the entire ghetto, when the registration was broken off on the evening of May 31. Nonetheless, all Jews who did not have yellow cards were ordered to report to Plac Zgody the following morning for resettlement and work in the east.[18]

When insufficient numbers of Jews reported on June 1, German and Jewish police sealed off various streets and seized all Jews found without yellow cards until the day's quota of 2,000 had been reached. They were then marched from the ghetto to the Plaszow train station and embarked for Belzec. A horse-drawn wagon followed the column to pick up the

---

[18] For the planning and registration, see Judgement of Martin Fellenz, State Court of Kiel, 2 Ks 6/63, pp. 12–13, 15–17; Indictment of Rudolf Körner and others, pp. 81–2; Indictment of Wilhelm Kunde and others, State Court of Kiel, 2 Js 858/64, pp. 75–6.

bodies of those shot along the way. Another 2,000 Jews were seized and deported in the same way on June 4. On June 7, the Jewish police, on orders from the Germans, announced another check of identity cards. All Jews who passed inspection were then given blue cards. More than 1,000 Jews who did not were marched to a nearby factory and kept overnight before they were deported to Belzec on June 8.[19] Among the first deportees were the former head of the *Judenrat*, Dr. Rosenzweig, and his family. Deemed inadequately obsequious for German purposes, he was replaced by the more compliant and unsavory David Gutter.[20]

Following the first Cracow deportation, the SS and Police Leader Julian Scherner coordinated a sweep of death across his district, beginning in Tarnow in June; Rzeszow, Debica, and Przemsyl in July; and Jaroslau, Krosno, Jaslo, and finally Nowy Sacz in August. From August 15 through 19, 1942, Jews in surrounding towns were either shot en mass or marched to Nowy Sacz, the Jewish population of which swelled to 15,000 or 16,000. A long, twenty-five-car train shuttled back and forth from Belzec, departing Nowy Sacz on August 24, 26, and 28 and taking one third of the Jews each time. Only the *Judenrat* and 500 Jewish workers were temporarily spared.[21] The sweep of the district continued through Novy Targ, Sanok, and Miechow, and then Tarnow once again by mid-September.

After a six-week pause, the ghetto liquidators then returned to Cracow. On October 17, 1942, the ghetto was surrounded, and Symche Spira was ordered to designate 4,000 to 5,000 nonworking Jews for deportation. The compilation of lists produced inadequate results, however, and the following day, German units entered the ghetto to carry out the roundup and selection. In addition to selecting at will from among

---

[19] Fellenz Judgment, pp. 17–27.

[20] Pankiewicz, *The Cracow Ghetto Pharmacy*, pp. 39–48. Pankiewicz gives a slightly different sequence of events and estimates the total number of victims at 7,000. Graf, *The Krakow Ghetto*, pp. 43–8, estimates 7,000 deportees and some 1,000 killed on the spot. These estimates may be closer to the truth than the German court estimate of 5,000, for German courts tended to gravitate to the lowest estimates to avoid disputes over numbers.

[21] Judgement against Heinrich Hamann and others, State Court of Dortmund, 16 Ks 1/65, pp. 247–315.

the work groups, the Germans rampaged through the ghetto, searched houses, and emptied the hospital, old people's home, and orphanage. Hundreds of Jews were shot on the spot, and 7,000 were deported to Belzec.[22]

Incredibly, after this vast decimation of the Jewish population of the Cracow district, the families of Joseph Hollander's three sisters were apparently still intact. On December 5, 1942, Regine Hütschnecker wrote to him of the death of his mother the previous August but noted that she was "always happy to hear about Dola and the others." Apparently, Munio and Dola, due perhaps to the former's position as a minor functionary in the Jewish community, had been spared along with the *Judenrat* and a small number of Jewish workers at Nowy Sacz. Virtually all the outlying remnants of Jews in the General Government who had survived the great deportations of 1942 were concentrated in a handful of labor camps, transferred to a handful of "remnant" ghettos (such as Cracow), or murdered in the spring of 1943.

For at least some of the Jews of Cracow, where the population had swelled once again to 20,000, the terrible ordeal and struggle for survival continued longer. The ghetto was divided into two sections, A and B, for working and nonworking Jews, respectively. On March 13, 1943, the working Jews of ghetto A were assembled for selection and told to send their children to the reopened children's home. Those selected for further work were marched to the nearby labor camp of Plaszow, and the others were transferred to ghetto B. On the following day, March 14, ghetto B was ferociously liquidated. Many Jews, perhaps as many as 2,000, including those in the children's home and hospital, were shot on the spot. Another 3,000 were deported to Auschwitz, where they were among the very first victims of the newly operational Krematorium II in Birkenau.[23] Members of the *Judenrat* and Jewish police remained in the ghetto for several more weeks before being transferred to Plaszow

[22] Pankiewicz, *The Cracow Ghetto Pharmacy*, pp. 67–82; Indictment of Körner, pp. 95–6; Indictment of Kunde, pp. 79–81.

[23] Pankiewicz, *The Cracow Ghetto Pharmacy*, pp. 106–20. Indictment of Körner, pp. 115–16. Indictment of Kunde, pp. 81–2. For the fate of the Auschwitz deportees, see Danuta Czech, *Kalendarium der Ereignissen im Konzentrationslager Auschwitz-Birkenau 1939–1945* (Hamburg, 1989), pp. 440, 442.

as well.[24] Those who managed to survive the terror regime of Amon
Goeth, the notorious Plaszow commandant, were then – following the
evacuation of the camp before the advancing Red Army – subjected to
the ordeal of the death marches in the last months of the war.

Joseph never learned when and where his sisters, Dola and Mania,
and his brothers-in-law, Munio and Salo, perished. He did gather fragments of information concerning the fate of Klara, Dawid, Genka, and
Lusia, however. On December 26, 1944, he heard from Regine: "As
to your family I only can inform you of this.... In March [1943] they
wrote they [received] permission to live in Cracow.... The last letter I
received [was] dated 10 August 1943. There they wrote that they are
alright, but that they have to go by a transport to an exchange" (Regine
Hütschnecker, December 26, 1944). On July 20, 1945, Joseph wrote to
his new wife from Germany about what he had learned from a concentration camp survivor who "had traveled with my sister and her family
from Cracow to Belsen" and who "was together with my sister Klara, her
husband, their two daughters and a child they adopted in camp Belsen
until May 28, 1944." Then Klara and her family were deported on one
of "two transports each of 150 persons with the best documents... to
an unknown destination for exchange against German citizens" (Joseph
Hollander to Vita Fischmann, July 20, 1945). It would appear that in the
chaos of broken and destroyed families resulting from the Holocaust,
Klara and Dawid, like Joseph, had taken on responsibility for another
child. But what can one make of such seemingly implausible traces? Did
the Wimisner family actually survive until May 1944 by virtue of the
Nicaraguan documents Joseph has procured for them? It is, in fact, very
possible.

In the first years of the war, the Germans had negotiated a limited
number of civilian prisoner exchanges, including the exchange of some
Jews for Germans who had been interned in Palestine. In 1942 and early
1943, as the Germans sought to deport all Jews from various countries in
Europe, they encountered the problem of Jews holding the citizenship
of countries that, for diplomatic and strategic reasons or fear of possible
retaliation, they did not wish to offend. Such Jews were temporarily
exempt from deportation to the death camps in the east, but the Germans

---

[24] Pankiewicz, *The Cracow Ghetto Pharmacy*, p. 131.

did not want to leave them in the countries they were trying to make "free of Jews."[25] Thus, in June 1943, one section of the concentration camp at Bergen-Belsen was designated as a "resident camp" (*Aufenthaltslager*) for civilian prisoners being held for possible "exchange," and among those sent to this section of Bergen-Belsen were Jews claiming citizenship from a list of sensitive countries.[26]

Particularly interested in extracting Germans from Latin America, the Foreign Office pressed the SS to exclude from its common measures against Polish Jews those who held even dubious papers from Latin American countries. Despite what they had witnessed and experienced in the Polish ghettos, they were to be sent to Bergen-Belsen, where the validity of their papers and their potential for exchange were further examined. After being held in various Gestapo prisons, such as Montelupich prison in Cracow, as well as in the Hotels Royal and Polski in Warsaw during the final liquidation of the ghettos, 2,283 Polish Jews with some kind of papers promising future citizenship in Honduras, Paraguay, Chile, Guatemala, Ecuador, Mexico, Haiti, or Nicaragua were transported to Bergen-Belsen between July and September of 1943. These Polish "exchange Jews" were kept separate from other exchange prisoners because of what they had seen. Their papers were examined, and when inquiries to the Latin American countries in question produced no confirmation of their validity, they were gradually transferred to Auschwitz. The last such transports departed in late May 1944.[27] In the end, only fifty holders of dubious Latin American papers remained in Bergen-Belsen, from where they were transferred to Theresienstadt in the last weeks of the war and survived. It would appear, therefore, that Joseph Hollander's procurement of Nicaraguan papers for the Wimisners came agonizingly close to saving his sister Klara and her family.

---

[25] On German diplomatic sensitivity concerning certain categories of foreign Jews, see Christopher R. Browning, *The Final Solution and the German Foreign Office* (New York, 1978), pp. 102–8, 154–8.

[26] The definitive work on the Bergen-Belsen exchange prisoners is Alexandra-Eileen Wenck, *Zwischen Menschenhandel und 'Endlösung': Das Konzsentrationslager Bergen-Belsen* (Paderborn, 2000). For the Polish Jews in Bergen-Belsen, see especially pp. 138–63.

[27] Wenck, p. 154, refers to one such transport on May 24, 1944. Joseph Hollander's survivor spoke of two such transports, each of 150 prisoners, on May 28, 1944.

Through the Eyes of the Oppressed

Nechama Tec

Under the oppressive German occupation, private correspondence was guided by the need *not* to reveal forbidden and potentially damaging information. This was particularly true for groups such as the Jews. Because they were targeted for persecution and eventually annihilation, Jews had to be careful not to reveal forbidden and potentially damaging information through their personal correspondence. Yet, even though hidden meanings in wartime Jewish correspondence are hard to decipher, careful scrutiny can yield valuable information. Such carefully extracted data offer evidence about the evolving history of this period. Potentially, too, this evidence can provide new insights into personal feelings and coping strategies of these wartime letter writers.

Mutual correspondence more precisely reflects the dynamics of inter-actions than do official wartime reports. Inherent wartime instabilities in themselves, however, undermine the possibility of a two-way corre-spondence. The set of letters that inspired this book represents only one side of a correspondence. Even though no answers to these letters sur-vived and parts of this one-sided correspondence were lost, the available letters can enlighten us about that historical period and about the letter writers' individual responses to the circumstances around them.

Written in a politically coercive, cruel environment, the content of these personal communications grew out of a discrepancy between what the writers may have wanted to convey and what they actually said. Prac-tically all that could be said openly were expressions about the pleasures of receiving mail and hopes for future meetings. Most other personal experiences and observations, when communicated, had to be disguised, often in ingenious ways.

Conspicuously absent from these writings are realistic descriptions of changed and changing conditions. Direct and clear references to the Germans and their collaborators are rare. These purposeful omissions, in turn, suggest that Jews had quickly learned about German demands and German reactions. Concurrently, they also confirm that these Jewish letter writers valued the exchanges and were both dependent on and eager to continue these fragile channels of communication. I believe that beyond the information to be decoded from these letters, singly and collectively, they do offer some unanticipated fresh insights about the Holocaust and, more generally, about life in extremis.

I begin by asking how the Hollander family, including those who married into it, fit into prewar Polish Jewry?

Of all the European countries, pre–World War II Poland had the highest concentration of Jews. The estimated figure for prewar Polish Jewry was more than 3.3 million. They made up about 10 percent of the country's population. As the largest community of Jews in Europe, Polish Jews were also the least assimilated. The majority of Jews looked, dressed, and behaved differently from Polish Christians. Some of these differences can be traced directly to religious requirements that called for special rituals and attire. Others were accentuated by the urban concentration of Jews. More than 75 percent lived in urban settings, whereas the same was true for only 25 percent of the Polish Christian population. Urban–rural differences were magnified by occupational differences. Of the Jews, only 4 percent were engaged in agricultural pursuits, whereas 79 percent were employed in manufacturing and commerce. In contrast, for the gentile population, more than 60 percent lived off agriculture, and 25 percent were employed in manufacturing and commerce.[1]

Educational background further exaggerated such existing distinctions. In prewar Poland, more than half of the Jewish children attended special Jewish schools. Enrollment in religious schools, in which Yiddish was spoken, in turn discouraged mastery of the Polish language. In response to a 1931 census inquiry, the overwhelming majority of Jews reported Yiddish as their native tongue (79 percent), and only

[1] L. Lifschutz, "Selected Documents Pertaining to Jewish Life in Poland, 1919–1938," in *Studies on Polish Jewry*, ed. Joshua A. Fishman (New York: YIVO Institute for Jewish Research, 1974), p. 280.

12 percent gave Polish as their first language. The rest chose Hebrew.[2] Jews and Poles lived in separate, different worlds, and their diverse experiences made for easy identification. It has been estimated that more than 80 percent of the Polish Jews were easily recognizable, whereas fewer than 10 percent could be considered assimilated.[3]

The Hollanders belonged to this assimilated minority. Jews identified in this fashion were not homogeneous. Some had tried to conceal their Jewish origin. Others would have liked to do so but for a variety of reasons were unable to. Still others had no problems identifying themselves as Jews. The assimilated that admitted to being Jewish can also be differentiated by the degree to which they maintained Jewish traditions and religious practices. The Hollanders as a group selectively adhered to some Jewish traditions.

For example, in a letter dated May 16, 1940, the matriarch of the family, Berta Hollander, reminds her son, Joseph, to say Kaddish (prayer for the dead) for his deceased father. She concludes this with: "May the Almighty grant that you meet only with the best." Not surprisingly, with growing anxiety and uncertainty, references to God appear more frequently.

Following the 1935 death of the relatively tolerant founder of modern Poland, Józef Pilsudski, the position of Polish Jews began to deteriorate. By 1937, Poland installed a new government, and the Camp of National Unity became the main base for this semidictatorial regime. It aimed at solving the country's problems by openly supporting anti-Semitism in social, cultural, economic, and political spheres.[4] This policy, in turn, led to a proliferation of anti-Jewish measures, which extended to most societal realms.[5]

---

[2] Antony Polonsky, *Politics in Independent Poland, 1921–1939* (Oxford: Clarendon Press, 1972), p. 40.

[3] Celia S. Heller, *On the Edge of Destruction* (New York: Columbia University Press, 1977), p. 69.

[4] Edward D. Wynot, Jr., "A Necessary Cruelty: The Emergence of Official Anti-Semitism in Poland, 1936–1939," *The American Historical Review* 76/4 (October 1971), pp. 1035–58.

[5] Heller, *On the Edge of Destruction*, p. 57. The Versailles Minority Treaty and the 1921 Constitution guaranteed the rights and freedoms of the minorities, but these measures never became laws. This treaty was ineffective. Edward D. Wynot, Jr., *Polish Politics In Transition* (Athens: University of Georgia Press, 1974), pp. 16–18.

In the economic sphere, these restrictions led to a variety of concrete actions. One of them prevented Jews from holding civil service jobs. Another barred them from employment in the state-owned monopolies, such as the liquor and tobacco industries. The government also introduced examinations for artisans that were specifically designed to fail Jews. Because those who could not pass the examinations were barred from employment, this measure posed a serious threat to the livelihood of Jewish artisans.[6] Finally, through special pressures, Polish unions succeeded in limiting Jewish employment even in the textile mills owned by Jews.[7]

The National Democrats, in particular, were also in favor of boycotting Jewish businesses, and other political leaders went along with their demands. Anti-Semitic youths stood in front of Jewish stores barring customers from entering. Vandalism and beatings often accompanied such measures.

Sometimes what had begun as a business boycott would evolve into a general pogrom. This was indeed the case with the 1936 Przytyk pogrom, which led not only to property destruction but also to loss of life.[8] Less direct boycotts of Jewish businesses were supported through a proliferation of propaganda leaflets, placards, and posters, all of them condemning Jewish business.

Discriminatory practices were not limited to employment and commerce. Institutions of higher learning also became battlegrounds for anti-Semitism as both quotas and ritual harassment restricted or eliminated Jewish participation. Universities, which accepted a limited number of Jewish students into their medical faculties, reserved separate benches for them, on the left. Prohibited from sitting anywhere else, unwilling to use the assigned spaces, Jewish students stood in protest during all lectures. Regardless of the subject of study, some students who

---

[6] Lestchinsky, "The Industrial and Social Structure of the Jewish Population of Interbellum Poland," *YIVO Annual of Jewish Social Science* 11 (1956–7), pp. 243–69; Emmanuel Ringelblum, *Polish-Jewish Relations during the Second World War* (Jerusalem: Yad Vashem, 1974), pp. 10–22.

[7] Lifschutz, "Selected Documents," p. 279.

[8] During this pogrom, two Jews and one Pole died. See Pawel Korzec, "Anti-Semitism in Poland as an Intellectual, Social and Political Movement," *Studies on Polish Jewry*, p. 87.

were identified as Jewish were physically threatened and abused. During the period 1937–8, some universities had to suspend classes solely because of the violence committed against Jewish students. Between 1925 and 1939, the proportion of Jewish students at Polish universities dropped from 21.5 to 8.2 percent. This decline grew more precipitous in the later years. In the last four years preceding the outbreak of World War II, the number of Jewish university students dropped by 3,000.[9]

The Jagellonian University in Cracow was an active supporter of anti-Jewish restrictions, both officially and informally. This made Jewish recipients of Jagellonian University diplomas particularly rare. As a lawyer and Jagellonian graduate, Joseph Hollander automatically became a member of a very select minority. Subsequent business successes further cemented his high social position. In view of Joseph's accomplishments, his decision to leave Poland was exceptional. In some ways, this move must have haunted him for the rest of his life.

Even though a university education had eluded the rest of the Hollander family, all of them appear to have benefited from secular and "higher" schooling. In prewar Poland, education that reached or came close to the high school level was appreciated and uncommon. Only an elementary education was open to the general public. For Jews, a secular high school education put them almost automatically into the assimilated category. Higher education of the Hollander family is reflected in their fluency with the Polish language. The matriarch, Berta, wrote in German. Not only this choice of written language but also her style of handwriting attests to her German schooling in the Habsburg Empire, prior to World War I.

Letter references show indirectly that at least part of the family tried to flee eastward at the outbreak of war. They lost some of their personal possessions and were forced to return to Cracow. Why other family members either did not choose or were unable to join Joseph when he made timely prewar preparations to escape abroad is not clear.

Danger signs were there before the German occupation of Poland. Specifically, in 1937 Polish politicians began to search for a so-called

---

[9] Jacob Lestchinsky, *Crisis, Catastrophe and Survival: A Jewish Balance Sheet, 1914–1948* (New York: Institute of Jewish Affairs of the World Jewish Congress, 1948), p. 33.

Jewish solution.[10] In 1937, Józef Beck, the foreign minister, speaking in the Polish parliament, insisted that Poland had space for only half a million Jews. This meant that more than 2.5 million would have to leave.[11] The Poles showed great interest in an early version of a Madagascar Plan, aimed at removing Jews to that island off the east coast of Africa.[12] The government's desire to be rid of the Jews and the seriousness with which this goal was pursued were shown in a Polish exploratory mission to Madagascar in 1938.[13] Polish hopes in this regard were an eerie anticipation of a far vaster and more coercive Madagascar Plan devised by the Germans in 1940.[14]

As ideas about Jewish emigration were gaining momentum, realistic chances for their fulfillment were becoming more remote. Barriers to Jewish emigration had emerged from a variety of directions. Already by 1924, the United States' traditional receptiveness to immigrants underwent a drastic change, making it the last year for open immigration. In the late 1930s, the United States accepted fewer than 7,000 immigrants from Poland, a figure that included Poles as well as Jews. A white paper promulgated by the British severely limited Jewish influx into Palestine, an action taken in part as a gesture of goodwill toward the Arabs.[15] Largely because of an international economic crisis, many other countries also introduced immigration restrictions.[16]

Polish Jews thus faced a difficult situation. Impoverished, unwanted, with no choices and no places to go, they continued to stay. Time was working against them, against all of them, including Joseph's relatives. When the Germans conquered Poland, the estimated number of Jews

[10] Carole Fink, "Germany and the Polish Elections of November 1930: A Study in League Diplomacy," *East European Quarterly* 15/2 (June 1981), 181–207; Wynot, *Polish Politics*, p. 21.

[11] Korzec, "Anti-Semitism in Poland," p. 91.

[12] For a historical account of this plan, see Philip Friedman, "The Lublin Reservation and the Madagascar Policy," *YIVO Annual of Social Science* 8 (1958), pp. 151–77.

[13] Bernard D. Weinryb, "The Jews in Poland," in *The Jews in the Soviet Satellite*, ed. Peter Meyer et al. (Westport, CT: Greenwood Press, 1953), pp. 207–326.

[14] Christopher R. Browning, *The Origins of the Final Solution* (Lincoln: University of Nebraska Press, 2004), pp. 81–93.

[15] Bernard Wasserstein, *Britain and the Jews of Europe, 1939–1945* (London: Institute for Jewish Affairs, 1979), p. 19.

[16] Lestchinsky, *Crisis, Catastrophe and Survival*, pp. 20–21.

in Cracow was 60,000, one third of the city's population. As usual, the German occupation of Cracow started with brutal assaults against Jewish property and lives.

On September 21, 1939, Reinhard Heydrich, head of the Reich Security Main Office, ordered that a "Council of Jewish Elders is to be established in every Jewish community which as far as possible is to be created from the leading persons and rabbis. Up to 24 male Jews (depending on the size of the Jewish community) are to belong to the Council of Elders. It is to be made entirely responsible, within the literal meaning of the word, for the exact and prompt fulfillment of all instructions which have been or will be given."[17]

To be made up of prominent prewar communal leaders, these newly created *Judenräte*, or Jewish Councils, were to function as administrative bodies for the transmission of German orders. In reality, this process departed from the initial plans. Before and following the early stages of the German occupation, some prominent Jewish leaders managed to escape to safe havens. In addition, a large proportion of the Jewish male elite was murdered in the months following the German takeover. Still, some other Jews at various stages refused to identify themselves as potential leaders because they rejected all cooperation with the occupational forces. The initial murder of the Jewish male elite, the escapes of prominent leaders, and the refusal to work with the occupational forces created a serious gap within the higher echelons of the Jewish male leadership. Specifically, this meant that authorities charged with the task of creating *Judenräte* had to rely on second- or third-rank leaders.[18]

The history of the Nazi-appointed *Judenrat* is filled with many unsettled debates.[19] The character, function, and fate of these wartime councils were in a continual flux. Displeased with any sign of independence, the Germans would execute some or all members of an entire *Judenrat* and replace them with new members who were expected to be more compliant. As a result, the composition of the Jewish Councils kept

[17] J. Nooks and G. Pridham, eds., *Nazism, 1919–1945*, vol. 3, *Foreign Policy, War and Racial Extermination* (Exeter: University of Exeter, 1988), pp. 1050–1053.

[18] Lucy S. Dawidowicz, *The War against the Jews* (New York: Holt, Rinehart and Winston, 1975), p. 224.

[19] Jacob Robinson, "Introduction: Some Basic Issues That Faced the Jewish Councils," in *Judenrat*, ed. Isaiah Trunk (New York: Stein and Day, 1977), pp. xxv–xxxv.

changing, often as many as seven to eight times. With each change, the moral makeup of the *Judenrat* heads usually worsened. Shortages of leaders and the fact that decent men in increasingly larger numbers refused any *Judenrat* connections changed the quality of these leaders.[20] Over time, those who rose to the position of *Judenrat* heads increasingly lacked the inner resources necessary for dealing with the extreme and unprecedented demands.[21]

Among the so-called second-rank prewar leaders was the newly appointed head of the Warsaw *Judenrat*, Adam Czerniakow. Even though most saw him as decent and honest, some leaned toward the assessment of Czerniakow "as someone whose modest talents had enabled him to play a modest role in the prewar Jewish community." Those who saw him as a man of limited talents felt that he hardly qualified for the grave burdens imposed on him by the oppressive German regime.[22]

On July 23, 1942, Czerniakow committed suicide. This act coincided with his refusal to cooperate in the deportations, which eventually reduced the ghetto population by about 90 percent. Czerniakow's suicide has been interpreted in contradictory ways. Without going into too much detail, here I lean toward two closely related interpretations. Czerniakow's suicide reflected his refusal to collaborate with the enemy in handing over his people to their death.[23] A closely related second view expressed by Jonas Turkov states that Czerniakow's suicide "... left an indelible impression on everyone ... and served as the best illustration of an utterly hopeless situation."[24] Indeed, Czerniakow's wartime diary attests to his anguish and the supreme efforts he made on behalf of the Warsaw Jewry.[25]

---

[20] Phillip Friedman, "Social Conflicts in the Ghetto," *Roads to Extinction, Essays on the Holocaust* (Philadelphia: Jewish Publication Society of America), pp. 131–52.

[21] Phillip Friedman, "Jacob Gens: Commandant of the Vilna Ghetto," *Roads to Extinction, Essays on the Holocaust*, p. 379.

[22] Lucy Dawidowicz, ed., *A Holocaust Reader* (New York: Behrman House, 1976), p. 236.

[23] Israel Gutman, "Adam Czerniakow – The Man and His Diary," in *The Catastrophe of European Jewry*, eds. Israel Gutman and Livia Rothkirchen (Jerusalem: Yad Vashem, 1976), p. 486.

[24] Gutman, "Adam Czerniakow," p. 486.

[25] *The Warsaw Diary of Adam Czerniakow: Prelude to Doom*, ed. Raul Hilberg et al. (New York: Stein and Day, 1982).

A similar yet different example comes from Lodz. Leon Minzberg, the prewar Lodz community leader, escaped before the Germans conquered the area. The authorities appointed in his place Moredchai Chaim Rumkowski, a much less prominent leader but one who was available and eager to serve as the head of the *Judenrat*.[26] Rumkowski was probably propelled by a desire for power and status. In addition, his behavior, particularly during the first phase of his service, suggests "a profound feeling of historical mission, which only a few chosen ones merit and which he was obliged to fulfill. The madness of the Nazi policy regarding the Jews was still not clear to him nor to the rest of the Jews."[27]

In Cracow, Dr. Arthur Rosenzweig, a jurist, was a highly respected, prominent member of the local Jewish elite. Rosenzweig assumed the leadership of the *Judenrat* after the German authorities had eliminated the first Jewish Council. He agreed to this position reluctantly. Rosenzweig's sense of duty and courage subsequently led to his brutal removal from this position.

By April 1940, the authorities issued an order that required most Cracow Jews to vacate the city.[28] This order was a part of an effort to push as many Jews out of Cracow as possible, but it never precisely specified which Jews would have to leave. Fear, anxiety, and endless rumor spread among the Cracow Jews. The 1940 Hollander correspondence is filled with expressions of dread about the unpredictable and unknown future. A few examples consistently illustrate the worries caused by the looming orders of deportation. Niece Genka writes on July 21, 1940: "I would like to sleep during this time. You cannot plan anything ahead of tomorrow. It is really hot here now but nobody goes away. I don't know what to write."[29]

"If there will be a break in our correspondence please don't worry. Just wait until we let you know where we are. Maybe God will help us stay. But it is war; we live like on a volcano and an order is an order."[30]

Salo, the brother-in-law, suggests a tentative relief. "As I wrote to you a couple of weeks ago, we thought that we belong to this group of people

[26] Phillip Friedman, "Pseudo-Saviors in the Polish Ghettos: Mordechai Chaim Rumkowski of Lodz," *Roads to Extinction, Essays on the Holocaust*, pp. 333–52.
[27] Friedman, "Pseudo-Saviors in the Polish Ghettos," p. 336.
[28] "Cracow," *Encyclopedia Judaica*, vol. 5 (Jerusalem: Keter), p. 1038.
[29] Letter by Klara's daughter, Genka.   [30] Letter by Klara dated July 28, 1940.

who will be forced to leave Cracow. In the meantime, as a result of my intervention I was told, I got a temporary permit to stay. We don't know it for sure yet, and we don't know for how long. I don't have anything on paper in my hands yet, so I cannot be sure of anything."[31]

Berta, the respected and admired matriarch of the family, voiced relief and concern: "Dear child, we are staying in the apartment temporarily until January 31. The gods know what will be then. The main thing is that, praise God, we are all well."[32] Expressions of anxiety and fear cross generational and gender lines. Nor were these emotional reactions confined to the Hollander family.

Felicja Schachter-Karay, a member of a large Jewish family in Cracow, six daughters and one son, was thirteen at the time. She explains: "When in 1940 the Germans were about to throw the Jews out of Cracow we left for a small town. We went to Brzesko . . . on our own." To my question about why they went to Brzesko, came the answer: "My father knew many people in that town, we thought that it would be safer . . . it was very small."

In this new place, her father's efforts to earn a living were continually frustrated. Felicja's mother was resourceful; she stepped in and helped support the family. When asked how her mother helped the family, Felicja said: "My mother was mostly trying to pass for a Christian, she would sell and buy and this is how she supported the family. We children helped her a little . . . she was actually doing the most. From the economic perspective our situation was continuously deteriorating. But we were not yet starving. At this time, my father could not do anything. He was just staying home. He was very depressed, more and more depressed. But, my mother was trying to earn some money. Mother even managed to return to Cracow, for a while. . . . We had some connections with the ghetto in Cracow, one of my sisters was there. . . . She refused to come with us to Brzesko, she died in the Cracow ghetto. . . . I remember that when my sister was sick in Cracow, my mother took off the band (with the Jewish identification). . . . somehow she entered the Cracow ghetto and stayed with my sister until she died. Only then did mother return, she was completely white, with all gray hair. . . . She was fifty-three at the time. This broke her completely . . . my sister's death. . . .

[31] Letter dated August 22, 1940.   [32] Letter dated December 28, 1940.

"There was tension in our ghetto, it was mounting and mounting...but we had no place to go....The liquidation of the Brzesko
ghetto began at night....all of us ran away because it happened at
night....My mother and father went to a Polish peasant, my two sisters
went to a Polish woman to hide, one other sister went to hide near the
river. There was an old tool shack near the river....Most of the Jews
who initially escaped were captured. The peasant threw out my parents.
The recaptured Jews, probably including my parents, were taken to a
forest near Miechow. They were all shot. One of my sisters and I were
on the run, still coming back to this old shack near the river. Policemen
were constantly looking for runaway Jews."

For quite a while, neither Felicja nor her sisters gave up their struggle
to remain free. Sometimes they would part company for safety, but after
many unsuccessful attempts at finding semipermanent shelters, Felicja
and two of her sisters reconnected again. With no place to go, they
smuggled themselves into the Cracow ghetto. During the last "Aktion"
in Cracow, the Germans transferred them to the Plaszow concentration
camp. Later on, with two of her considerably older sisters, she was sent to
Skarzysko Kamienna, a camp that murdered its prisoners by debilitating
slave labor, starvation, illness, and executions. Toward the end of the war,
the three sisters ended up in a Hasag munitions factory in Leipzig. Their
imprisonment ended with the arrival of the Soviet Army.[33]

The Cracow ghetto was created on March 21, 1941. In contrast to
their variously expressed fears of expulsion, the Hollander correspondence offers only a few vague allusions to the ghetto. For supplementary
information, we must turn to other sources. One of them is the important memoir of Tadeusz Pankiewicz, the Polish owner of the Cracow
ghetto pharmacy. From the unusual perspective of a non-Jew inside the
ghetto, Pankiewicz captured the evolving history of the Cracow ghetto.
A sympathetic observer, he painted vivid pictures of the progressively
brutal circumstances under which the Cracow Jews were forced to live
and die.

---

[33] Felicja Karay, personal interview (Chulon, Israel, 1995). For more extensive information, see Felicja Karay, *Death Comes in Yellow: Skarzysko Kamienna Slave Labor Camp*
(Amsterdam: Harwood, 1996).

He was sensitive to the courageous struggles of the Jews, their grow-ing humiliations, loneliness, and devastating losses. Not limiting himself to recording his observations, he was also actively involved in diminish-ing Jewish suffering caused by the German assaults. Among the many recipients of his generosity was also the Hollander family.

After the war, the state of Israel honored Pankiewicz with the Yad Vashem recognition as a "Righteous among the Nations of the World." Yad Vashem was established in 1953 in Jerusalem as a memorial to Euro-pean Jewry murdered during World War II, a historical event that only later came to be known as the Holocaust. This memorial also pays trib-ute to gentiles who saved Jews during that period. The formal Hebrew title for these saviors is *Hasidei Umot Ha-Olam*, literally translated as the Righteous Ones of the Nations of the World. Attached to the Yad Vashem institution is a special committee that deals with requests for this distinction. As a rule, it is next to impossible to receive this title without a request from Jewish beneficiaries; survivors usually petition the committee to honor their protectors. In addition, to qualify for such a Yad Vashem distinction, the actions performed by these gentiles had to involve "extending help in saving a life; endangering one's life; absence of reward, monetary and otherwise; and similar considerations which make the rescuers' deeds stand out above and beyond what can be termed ordi-nary help." In part ambiguous, these criteria leave little doubt that those who saved Jews solely because of payments do not fit into the definition of "righteous Gentiles."[34]

Almost exclusively, the Hollander letters focus on family life. They mention neither the German assaults nor the roles played by the *Judenrat* as a whole or its specific members. In contrast, Pankiewicz describes the Cracow *Judenrat*, which, as in other parts of Poland, was composed of twenty-four members, with the attorney Dr. Arthur Rosenzweig as president. This group served as the official representative body of the Jews. Its offices were located in the main police station.

Activities of the *Judenrat* were primarily concerned with carrying out the orders of the Gestapo. These orders included challenging

[34] Nechama Tec, *When Light Pierced the Darkness* (New York: Oxford University Press, 1986), pp. 3–4.

administrative tasks, such as preparation of the statistical data, lists of
residents, registration of stores, and distribution of food and fuel for the
inhabitants. With time, German pressures and demands were expanded
to include the physically and morally impossible challenges. Dr. Rosenzweig was among those who refused to become a part of the murder
process.

Pankiewicz reports about Rosenzweig's rough dismissal by the SS and
his arrest. The Rosenzweig family was "transported to Belzec, . . . perished in a gas chamber. Undoubtedly, he was not useful to the Germans.
An exceptionally decent man, with an impeccable reputation, a lawyer by
profession, he was able to reason and think critically. He [Rosenzweig]
was not overwhelmed by the honor thrust upon him by the Germans –
it was a burden – as was any managerial position in those days, especially
for a man of honor and dignity."[35]

A slightly different story comes from Miriam Akavia whom I interviewed in Israel in 1995. Miriam was born in 1927 into a warm, well-
to-do family in Cracow. At the start of the occupation, her family suffered heavy financial losses, including blackmail and public beatings of
the father. Miriam explains: "My father was an independent man who
made all the decisions. He was at ease with himself . . . but at the start of
the war he broke down. . . . This is when my mother took hold of things.
She took control, he was a broken man, and he who had been so decisive
could not do it any more. . . . My mother was wonderful. . . . Still, we had
many, many problems . . . felt very powerless."[36]

As for most Jews and so for Miriam's family, a move to the Cracow ghetto only compounded their problems. She explains that Arthur
Rosenzweig was a family friend and also her father's lawyer. When he
became the head of the *Judenrat*, he invited Miriam's father to accept a
position on it. The father did. Miriam refers to the father's job as very
difficult. She continues, "When the Germans asked Rosenzweig to make
up a list of Jews who should be deported, he put only himself on the list.
So they took him. That was the last we saw of him. People don't know

[35] Tadeusz Pankiewicz, *The Cracow Ghetto Pharmacy* (New York: Holocaust Library, 1987),
pp. 46–7.
[36] Miriam Akavia, personal interview (Tel Aviv, 1995). See also Miriam Akavia, *An End to
Childhood* (Ilford, United Kingdom: Vallentine Mitchell, 1995).

about him, how he sacrificed himself for us. After him, there was a terrible Jew who was head of the *Judenrat*. His name was Gutter. I'm not sure. But my father resigned when his friend went away.

"After that my father had to do unskilled labor, heavy work. My brother worked in some kind of a factory. We had to move because they decreased the size of the ghetto, and a friend of mine joined us. More people came later. We were fourteen in one room. It was terrible, there was a big line in the morning, to the bathroom, to the kitchen."[37]

Pankiewicz does not judge the *Judenrat* of the Cracow ghetto harshly. He concludes that the early and later *Judenrat* members "simply did not really know the true character of the Germans and the occupation from personal experience. I am unalterably convinced that were it not for the fact that there were so many decent and honorable members in the *Judenrat*, the fate of the ghetto dwellers might have been much worse. . . . Many people who lived through the war outside of Poland did not realize what surviving in the ghetto entailed."[38]

In contrast, Pankiewicz sees the Jewish police of the Cracow ghetto in a different light. Known as the *Ordnungsdienst*, or OD, it was headed by Simcha Spira, a man dedicated to carrying out German orders – "wrapped in fantasy, a classic example of a psychopath . . . a semi-illiterate, spoke Polish and German poorly, an unthinking robot, carrying out the Gestapo orders as if hypnotized."[39]

About his pharmacy and the role it played in the ghetto, Pankiewicz notes that "in the opinion of most of the people, [it was] a sort of embassy, a diplomatic station, representing the world, singularly free, within the walled and imprisoned city.

"It became a daily meeting place for a variety of interesting people. Here, one could find assembled at certain hours of the day, people of all ages and in all walks of life. Here, from early morning on German newspapers and the underground press were read, the latest war communiqués could be studied and commented upon, and the political situation assessed. Here, also, the daily problems and worries were discussed. Conversations continuing far into the night weighed the future

---

[37] Miriam Akavia, personal interview.
[38] Pankiewicz, *The Cracow Ghetto Pharmacy*, pp. 62–3.
[39] Pankiewicz, *The Cracow Ghetto Pharmacy*, p. 31.

prognostications. 'Let something happen, finally,' they were saying. It seemed that this inhuman time had halted, that the clock of history stopped at the fatal hour . . . perdition!"[40]

The pharmacist recalls an evening attended by Mordechai Gebirtig, a well-known popular Yiddish poet. Gebirtig recited his compelling and captivating poem, "Es Brent" (The World Is Burning). This song was this poet's response to the 1936 pogrom in Przytyk, in Poland, in which several Jews were killed. About this special evening, Pankiewicz recalls: "Even today I still hear the melodic murmur of the poet's words, 'Zun, zun, zong,' full of lyricism and musing. . . . 'I wrote this poem with tears moving,' said the poet to me. 'Because in writing it I cried like a baby!' Somehow this poem, expressed the prophetic vision about the ultimate disappearance of the Jews. 'Es Brent' was often performed at different gatherings. By 1943, it became the battle song of the fighting Warsaw ghetto and the Jewish rebels fought and perished singing this song."[41]

Gebirtig was born in Cracow in 1877. This poet supported himself and his family by carpentry because he was unable to do so from his poetry. He was nevertheless greatly appreciated by the Jewish people long before he was noticed by the literary critics. The first collection of Gebirtig's poetry was published twice, in 1942 and in 1948. The Germans murdered Gebirtig during the June 1942 deportations from the Cracow ghetto. Halina Nelken, a teenager and an inmate of the Cracow ghetto, had known Gebirtig since early childhood and was shaken by the poet's murder.[42]

Warmly remembered by Pankiewicz is another evening, an evening to which he brought his dear friend Kocwa, a professor of the Jagellonian University. Upon entering the pharmacy, they found the pharmacist's coworkers and two gifted Jewish musicians, the Rosner brothers, a violinist and an accordionist. Pankiewicz recalls:

> At the table set with delicacies from a Jewish kitchen, immersed in the enchanting melodies of Viennese waltzes, we completely forgot the passage of time, the curfew, the war, the walled-in little town and the

---

[40] Pankiewicz, *The Cracow Ghetto Pharmacy*, p. 11.
[41] Pankiewicz, *The Cracow Ghetto Pharmacy*, pp. 21–2.
[42] Halina Nelken, *And Yet, I Am Here* (Amherst: University of Massachusetts Press, 1999), p. 172.

fate of its inhabitants sentenced to so much humiliation and tragedy. The dinner extended into the wee hours of the morning. It was an unforgettable night, one that we recalled many years after the end of the war.

Despite these rare escapes, time seemed to move the hands of the clock faster and faster. People who, not so long ago, could not conceive how one could live under such conditions were getting used to them, giving up the most primitive demands of civilization and beginning slowly to forget even the recent past. The daily worries – about a piece of bread, fighting to keep one's job in the city, producing practically no income but providing a possibility of leaving the ghetto – occupied the lion's share of one's free time. The *Arbeitsamt*, under the direction of a Viennese named Schepessy, kept office hours from morning until late night. German, Polish, and Jewish clerks were busy preparing files on the workers, made job assignments, supplying contingents of people for work outside of the ghetto at each demand of the German authorities.[43]

Except for a veiled allusion to help received from Pankiewicz, the Hollander correspondence is silent about illegal escapes into the forbidden Christian world, the so-called Aryan side. In Poland, on October 15, 1941, a new law made any unauthorized Jewish presence outside the ghetto a crime punishable by death.[44] The same punishment applied to Christians who helped Jews enter or leave the forbidden Christian world.

Widely publicized, this law became well known, and transgressions were promptly followed by executions, which were also widely publicized.[45] The Germans were efficient. To their continuous anti-Semitic propaganda, they added rewards for those who would denounce a Jew. The nature of these bounties varied depending on the locality and the demand for certain goods. They might have included rye flour, sugar,

---

[43] Pankiewicz, *The Cracow Ghetto Pharmacy*, pp. 8–9.

[44] Dawidowicz, *A Holocaust Reader*, p. 67; Wladyslaw Bartoszewski, "Egzekucje Publiczne w Warszawie w Latach, 1943–1945," *Biuletyn Glownej Komisji Badania Zbrodni Niemieckiej w Polsce* 6 (1946), pp. 221–4.

[45] Philip Friedman, *Their Brothers' Keepers* (New York: Holocaust Library, 1978); Kazimierz Iranek-Osmecki, *He Who Saves One Life* (New York: Crown, 1971); Szymon Datner, *Las Sprawiedliwych* (Warsaw: Ksiażka i Wiedza, 1968); Tec, *When Light Pierced the Darkness*, pp. 52–69.

vodka, cigarettes, clothing, and, in some instances, half the property of the apprehended fugitive.[46]

Over time, the search for escaping Jews and their Polish rescuers was stepped up, and the terror became ever greater. As the pace of Jewish extermination increased, so did the need to pass into the Christian world. Neither the presence of the law nor its strong enforcement prevented some Jews from trying to pass and some Poles from helping them.

Figures about the number of Jews who tried to survive this way are elusive. One prominent historian is of the opinion that of the 100,000 Jews who tried to live on the Polish side, 20,000 perished, an estimate that leaves 80,000 who survived by passing.[47] Others find this figure too optimistic, putting the number, more realistically, at 40,000 to 60,000.[48]

The experience of Miriam Akavia, the teenager from the Cracow ghetto, illustrates how shaky and complex life in the forbidden Christian world was. "I looked like a Christian and so did my brother who was tall, blond with blue eyes. My father got Aryan papers for me and my brother. First my brother went to Lwow. Why there, I don't know, and how he got the papers, I don't know.... At the end of 1942, there was another Aktion, we were hidden.... A few days later, I left the ghetto.

"I was bewildered, like in a dream. I didn't know what was happening to me. I went to a certain woman in Cracow and she told me not to worry, that she would take care of things. This woman's husband helped. He took me to the train, and I joined my brother in Lwow."

For brother and sister, life in Lwow meant horrible living quarters, blackmail, near-denunciations, and continuous uncertainty. Then disaster struck. Her brother was caught trying to help a Jewish woman enter the Lwow ghetto. Miriam is still haunted by the telephone conversation she had with her father right after this happened: "Father started to cry on the phone, and he said, 'Come home. Come to Cracow.' I felt so

---

[46] Zygmunt Klukowski, *Dziennik Z Lat Okupacji, Zamojszczyzny* [Wartime Diary from Zamość] (Lublin: Lubelska Spółdzielnia Wydawnicza, 1958); Stanislaw Ziemiński, "Kartki Dziennika Nauczyciela w Łukowie z Okresu Okupacji Hitlerowskiej" ["Pages from a Teacher's Diary"], *Biuletyn Żydowskiego Instytutu Historycznego* 27 (1958), pp. 105–12; Tec, *When Light Pierced the Darkness*, pp. 40–41.

[47] Personal communication by Szymon Datner during a seminar at YIVO, New York, 1980.

[48] Weinryb, "The Jews in Poland."

horrible. . . . I said yes. I wanted to be with them. Whatever would be, I wanted to be with them."

Leaving all her belongings behind, Miriam boarded a train. As promised, her father waited for her. "When I saw him I realized that he looked worse than before. He took me back to the ghetto. I cared for the small children. I cleaned them from lice . . . [these children had been left in their care by relatives]. . . . I became hysterical when a letter arrived from my brother. He wrote that he had been caught and taken to prison."

After an escape and an unsuccessful search for shelter, he reentered the ghetto in Lwow. The family wanted Miriam to go to Lwow to help him. Miriam refused. She thought that she would not even know how to find him. After this letter, they never heard from the brother again.

Miriam describes the mounting difficulties. "There was a denouncement in the ghetto. They came and searched for my Aryan document, and found it. They wanted to know who was its owner. My mother did not tell. So, they took my sister instead, and a neighbor girl. My fingerprints were on the document. . . . we had to bribe people to release the two girls. . . . I felt so guilty that I had left Lwow but my brother hadn't. I felt extremely guilty that my sister had been arrested instead of me. I was so depressed."

Miriam could not face the prospect of a return to the Aryan side. Her family, particularly her energetic mother, would have liked her to try again. In the end, Miriam was taken from the ghetto and interned in a series of concentration camps. Of the entire family, only she and her sister survived.[49]

As the Hollander letters show, this family hoped to join Joseph in the United States or somehow to reach South America. The letters written to Joseph consistently express hope that they would be reunited in a better world. Joseph was relentless in his efforts to accomplish this, ready to spend whatever money it took. Knowing how devoted and accomplished Joseph was, they continued to trust in his ability to rescue them. Perhaps this basic trust prevented them from considering the option of an illegal life in Poland. Ironically, as assimilated Jews whose command of the Polish language was good, they had an advantage over the majority of

[49] Miriam Akavia, personal interview (Tel Aviv, 1995).

unassimilated Jews. Because this issue was never mentioned, we can only speculate about it.

In addition, the two teenagers in the Hollander family, Genka and Lusia, with their brief additions to the letters, convey a growing sadness. There is no mention of young friends. Probably they did not belong to any of the youth groups. We know that, particularly in large ghettos including Cracow, there were youth organizations. Before the war, these organizations, affiliated with both Zionist and non-Zionist movements, covered the entire political spectrum from left to right. At the beginning of the German occupation, many of these youngsters saw the war only as a passing phase. Within the youth organizations, members concentrated on their own education and that of others, hoping to diminish the demoralizing effects of the deteriorating situation. They were preparing for a better, more just future.

With the worsening of ghetto conditions, these youth group members implemented their educational plans by devoting themselves to the teaching of children, lecturing adult audiences, and advancing cultural activities, including the production of theatrical events. From there, quite naturally their efforts expanded into the promotion of social welfare. These young Jewish activists seemed at once more daring and more realistic than many of the older generation, including the prewar leaders of the political parties.

By 1942, members of various political youth groups recognized that the Germans aimed at the total annihilation of the Jewish people. When they reached this conclusion, many of their leaders began to prepare for different forms of resistance. Initially, the Jewish public was to be educated about their impending fate through the preparation and distribution of illegal publications. These activities were accompanied by the collection of arms. Although eager to fight the Germans, youthful resisters were realistic about the inevitable outcome of any armed encounters. Knowing well that they could not stop the destruction of Jewish lives, they wanted only to salvage the honor of the Jewish people through the ghetto fighters' armed resistance.[50]

---

[50] Israel Gutman, "The Genesis of Resistance of the Warsaw Ghetto," *The Nazi Holocaust*, ed. Michael Marrus, vol. 17, *Resistance to the Holocaust* (Westport, CT: Meckler, 1989), pp. 180–84.

In large ghettos in particular, preparations for resistance often led
to the cooperation of various political groups on matters such as timing and location of future confrontations. Around 1942, rumors about
forest partisans began to circulate. In ghettos surrounded by forests,
such news suggested a choice: one might fight inside the ghetto, or one
might try to join the partisans. Most of the underground youths were
reluctant to leave the ghettos. They felt responsible for their imprisoned communities and feared that by leaving they would be abandoning their people. They also feared that their departure would trig-
ger the immediate destruction of the ghetto. The Germans relied on
the principle of collective responsibility. This meant that any number of Jews were responsible for the "crimes" committed by any other
Jews.

Not surprisingly, some fellow Jews were afraid of underground activities. Occasionally, then, the attitudes of the general ghetto popula-
tions toward young resisters could tip the scale in favor of staying
or leaving a ghetto. Older, more traditional ghetto inmates, including some members of the *Judenräte*, were suspicious of the young.
Many of them thought that Jewish contributions to the German war
economy could save, if not all, at least the working part of the Jewish population. For them, the prospect of a fight in the ghetto or of a
mass escape into the forest would portend the destruction of an entire
community.

To be sure, plans about the place, form, and timing of resistance
changed often. Some leaders of the underground compromised and made
accommodations. Despite all these obstacles in Poland and other parts of
Eastern Europe, Jewish underground organizations were set up in seven
major ghettos (Bialystok, Cracow, Czestochowa, Kovno, Minsk, Vilna,
and Warsaw) and in forty-five minor ghettos.[51]

When I asked Miriam Akavia if she knew about the existence of an
underground in Cracow, she mentioned her older sister who "was somehow connected through a boyfriend of hers with the Underground, the
Jewish resistance group in the ghetto, but I didn't know anything about it.
Gusta Draenger was an important person in the Underground. Through

[51] Israel Gutman and Shmuel Krakowski, *Unequal Victims* (New York: Holocaust Library,
1986), p. 106.

my sister and the Underground, we were told that they were going to destroy all the Jews and we should try to save ourselves."[52]

As with other resistance movements, the Jewish underground in Cracow consisted of a coalition of youth organizations. A strategic partner in this assemblage was Akiva, a politically moderate Zionist group initially dedicated to nonviolence and cultural pursuits. Following a common pattern, the Cracow Jewish underground first concentrated on its own members' self-improvement. Eventually, these efforts came to include involvement in the cultural and welfare activities of the ghetto. Soon they turned to the collection and dissemination of information and the printing of illegal newspapers. They also forged documents, including passes and train tickets.

By 1942, young underground leaders in Cracow and elsewhere became convinced that all Jews were destined for destruction. This led to the procurement of arms and to closer ties with the Polish Underground, especially the more accessible Communists, Polska Partia Robotnicza (PPR), who demonstrated greater willingness to cooperate with Jews than the National Polish Underground (AK). Among the dedicated leaders of Akiva were the couple Szymek Draenger (Marek) and Gusta Draenger (Justyna), as well as Aaron Liebeskind (Dolek).

The fate of the Cracow Jewish underground was dictated partly by its failure to gain widespread acceptance among the ghetto population and its desire not to endanger the very existence of the entire ghetto. Through its cooperation with the PPR, Akiva obtained the underground's first two pistols and ammunition. They tried to establish contact with forest partisans but failed. Out of the six men who left the ghetto for the forest, only one returned. The failure of a forest option tipped the scale in favor of urban operations. Among their daring accomplishments was the December 22, 1942, grenade attack on Cyganeria, a Cracow coffee shop frequented by Germans. The shop was damaged, and several Germans were killed or wounded. This operation went off smoothly and was assessed as a success. Denunciations followed this attack, however, which led to the arrest of many Jewish resisters. Among them were Gusta and Szymek Draenger and Aaron Liebeskind. Liebeskind was executed. Gusta, Szymek, and the rest were imprisoned. During her incarceration,

[52] Miriam Akavia, personal interview.

Gusta recorded on toilet tissue the history of the Cracow ghetto underground.

This fragile document was smuggled out of the prison. It became one of the most important primary sources for our understanding of these events. On April 29, 1943, husband and wife staged separate escapes that also freed other comrades. After the prison escape, the group published and distributed the magazine, *Hehalutz Halohem* (The Fighting Pioneer). They also resumed urban sabotage actions. But their idealism and courage in these clandestine operations were outweighed by their inexperience. In the fall of 1943, the Draengers were caught again. Nothing else is known about them. By November 1943, the Cracow Jewish underground ceased to exist.[53]

Among the few Akiva underground survivors is the courageous courier from Cracow, Hela Schüpper-Rufeisen. I interviewed Hela several times in Israel. She became an underground courier around 1941 and felt compelled to engage in practically uninterrupted travels. She often moved between Warsaw and Cracow, smuggling documents and arms and accompanying male resisters to the forests and to various places on the Aryan side. Despite her Aryan looks and command of the Polish language, she was caught several times and interrogated, but she miraculously regained her freedom. Occasionally, the Polish police who interrogated her suspected her of being a Pole and a member of the Polish underground and therefore let her go.[54]

She shared with me some of her experiences: "One day when I ran away from the ghetto in Warsaw the Germans shot after me and I was injured. I simply ran into a ruined house.... The Germans looked for me, but did not find me, it was all due to chance.... I was at Mila 18 during the uprising in the Warsaw ghetto. At that point, I was given a letter by Anielewicz to Antek Cukierman asking for help because the uprising was in full swing. This was the 8th of May 1943, very early in

[53] Gusta Draegner, *Pamietnik Justyny* (*Justyna's Diary*) (Cracow: Wojewódzka Żydowska Komisja Historyczna, 1946; Gusta Davidson Draenger, *Justyna's Narrative* (Amherst: University of Massachusetts Press, 1996). This and most other publications about the Jewish underground in Cracow rely on Gusta's diary written in prison.

[54] Hela Schüpper-Rufeisen, personal interview (Bustan Hagalil, Israel, 1989, 1995). See also Hela Schüpper-Rufeisen, *Pożegnanie Mileji8* [Goodbye to Mila 18] (Cracow: Beseder, 1996).

the morning. I left the ghetto together with eleven other people. We went through the sewer system. None of the eleven made it to the end of the war."[55]

Hela had difficulties finding a place to live. Exposed to constant threats, she moved to Hotel Polski where many Jews who had false South American passports stayed. They had paid money for a false promise of emigration to South America. One day, all these Jewish hotel dwellers, without any warning, were picked up. Most of them ended up in concentration camps. Hela, as part of this large group, was transferred to the Bergen-Belsen concentration camp. There she stayed for one and a half years until she was liberated in 1945.[56]

Active in the Polish underground, Pankiewicz was well informed about the Jewish resistance in Cracow. About this issue, he concludes, "The Cracow Jews perished without achieving a libertarian revolt on the scale of the Warsaw Ghetto Uprising, but they died with dignity, honorably, and without abasing themselves before the enemy. With the exception of a small number of those who sold out to the enemy, all who worked in various capacities engaged in deliberate and effective sabotage. Everything possible was done to slow the tempo of the assignments, to fail to meet deadlines and, in the ghetto, to remove valuable objects, destroy and burn them, so that they would not fall into German hands."[57]

He pays tribute to Jewish resisters by expounding on their anti-German operations and by mentioning many more of their participants by name. Some of the men were his personal friends, some he only heard about. One of those he knew well and was particularly eager to remember, "Szai Dreiblatt is inextricably linked with the active conspirators. He lived in the ghetto and devoted all of his spare time, from the start, to construct a bomb, using only the most primitive of tools in a locksmith's shop. Of course, under such circumstances, the attempt failed. The only thing smuggled out of the ghetto was his detailed design, which was used later in the production of a bomb. His conception was used in

---

[55] Hela Schüpper-Rufeisen, personal interview.
[56] Hela Schüpper-Rufeisen, personal interview. For an account of the Hotel Polski, see Abraham Shulman, *The Case of Hotel Polski* (New York: Holocaust Library, 1982).
[57] Pankiewicz, *The Cracow Ghetto Pharmacy*, pp. 78–9.

preparing the munitions for the attack on the premises of Cyganeria in Cracow."[58]

In retrospect, the German destruction of European Jewry proceeded along the stages of identification, expropriation, and removal from gainful employment; isolation; and annihilation. Complex and often overlapping, these stages aimed at the victims' degradation before their murder. To facilitate the process of destruction, the Germans established special settings for the Jews. The Nazi-created ghettos were a part of the stage of isolation, whereas concentration camps paved the way for the final stage of Jewish murder. Faced with a system of ruthless destruction, some Jews relied on their own self-created emergent responses or settings. These emergent settings were semi-autonomous reactions to the German process of Jewish annihilation. Collectively, they reflect Jewish efforts to retain their humanity. Examples of these emergent settings were Jewish underground movements and resistance activities, the establishment of havens in forests, and illegal attempts at hiding or passing in the forbidden Christian world – the so-called Aryan side.[59]

Coming back to the Hollander correspondence, one of my earlier assertions suggested that these letters may contain unanticipated findings that could lead to new insights about life in extremis. This correspondence covered somewhat more than two years, from the fall of 1939 to the end of 1941. Central to most of these communications are hopes that Joseph, the son and brother, will rescue the family. With these hopes came anxieties that letters will go astray and that the entire correspondence will stop. Despite the ever-present concerns, the hopes continued, mainly because Joseph tenaciously pursued all available avenues of rescue, even those that included only tentative, vague promises. Perhaps Joseph's lifelong, spectacular achievements in themselves refuted the likelihood of failure.

Anxiety about letters going astray was also realistic. Many of them disappeared without a trace. Their indirect, laborious journeys through the United States, Switzerland, Portugal, and other places increased the chance of loss. Eventually, all cooperative efforts to keep this

[58] Pankiewicz, *The Cracow Ghetto Pharmacy*, pp. 79–80.
[59] Nechama Tec, *Resilience and Courage; Women, Men, and the Holocaust* (New Haven: Yale University Press, 2003), p. 18.

correspondence going were overwhelmed by history. With the end of 1941 and the U.S. entry into the war, all direct communications between Joseph and his family stopped.

Revisiting this correspondence, I first ask if and how the content of these letters varied with generational and gender distinctions of the letter writers. Next, I examine these letters from an inductive perspective. That is, looking at a few consistent changes in the content of these letters, I try to ascertain to what extent they originated in the activities of the letter writers and to what extent they grew out of the politically coercive environment that was forced on the Jews.

A closer view of these letters suggests some generational divides. The oldest family member, the matriarch, Berta, expresses her continuous devotion to her only son, Joseph. A typical example of her way of writing to her son follows: "How I wish I were a fly so that I could fly to see you, my dear child. My only wishes are to know that you are happy and content. What good fortune it is for a mother to have such a dear son, everyone envies me. I do not tell anyone, but strangers talk about you. May the Almighty grant you that you are well and happy and able to do your work. I go to bed and get up with thoughts of you, my love."[60]

Such approximate beginnings are more often than not followed by anxious expressions of fears that the letters would be lost. A rather frequent comment reads: "I am sad about one thing that I have no letter from you. The last letter was No. 14. . . . Letter 13 has not arrived. Are you at least receiving my letters. I write every week."[61]

Berta's remarks reveal that the Hollanders devised a system of numbering letters, designed to keep track of lost mail. Berta is not the only one concerned about mail going astray. Other family members also check whether letters had reached their destination. Whether this knowledge reduced their anxiety is not known. Probably it did. Besides, the very presence of a letter-checking system supports the cliché that necessity is the mother of invention. Filled with painful threats and deprivations, the Holocaust often led to unusual ingenuity.

Notable is the correspondence of the youngest generation, the two teenage nieces, Genka and Lusia. Their letters are less frequent and much shorter than those others wrote. Somehow they appear to be both different and similar. To illustrate, a part of Genka's letter says: "I am not

[60] Letter dated November 12, 1940.   [61] Letter dated January 8, 1941.

happy. I don't go to the beach, or to the movies, I don't read and in general I feel not alive." Lusia writes: "I see – thank God – everything in bright colors; I feel good and comfortable in the world, I have enough joy of life for this whole highly respected family of ours. But now seriously: about my profession, I have all the papers ready. I got my exam which I passed very well. When I will have an opportunity I will look for some nice job. In the meantime I send you thousands of kisses and hugs. Lusia"[62]

The mood of each letter is different; one gloomy and one upbeat. Yet both are self-centered. A preoccupation with self is somehow expected from teenagers. The depressing tone of the one and the cheerfulness of the other probably reflect personality differences. In fact, scattered remarks by various family members describe the two nieces as different. Genka is perceived as the brooding and dissatisfied type; Lusia as an easygoing, positive person.

Along with the variations in the responses of these two sisters is a basic similarity in their assessments of ghetto life. The two teenagers' comments suggest an absence of and a longing for youthful social activities. However, other sources paint a different picture of the Cracow ghetto young. Particularly during the early stages of the ghetto, other accounts show how the Jewish youths met in each other's homes, how they spent time dancing, flirting, and in general entertaining each other. Occasionally, their social gatherings spilled into the coffee shops that sprang up in the ghettos. Also, the ghetto had all kinds of theatrical and musical events. Frequently, "profits" from these cultural activities were used for ghetto welfare.[63] The serious, intellectual Halina Nelken, also a teenage inmate of the Cracow ghetto, weaves into her fascinating ghetto diary vivid descriptions about youthful entertainments.[64]

Somehow, Genka and Lusia did not benefit from these opportunities for entertainment and cultural activities. Perhaps these two teenagers were totally absorbed in their desire and need to escape from the ghetto surrounding into a better future that their absent uncle was trying to accomplish for them.

---

[62] Both letters dated July 1, 1940.

[63] Katarzyna Zimmerer, *Zamardowany Świat: Losy Żydów w Krakowie 1939–1945* [The Murdered World] (Crakow: Kraków Wydawnictwo Literackie, 2004), pp. 84–7. Tec, *Resilience and Courage*, pp. 64–7. An article about Mordechai Gebirtig's life also appeared in the *Encyclopedia Judaica*, vol. 7, p. 35.

[64] Nelken, *And Yet, I Am Here*, p. 89.

Between the oldest and youngest generation are the three sisters, Dola, Klara, and Mania. In their correspondence to Joseph, each expresses warm feelings toward him and special concerns about his well-being. But neither the depth of their feelings nor the kinds of concerns about their brother's welfare comes close to those expressed by the mother. When communicating with her son, it is as if Berta wanted to envelope him with all the love and devotion she can muster. These differences in the brother–sister and mother–son attachments are not surprising.

What seems more unusual is how this traditional, generational diversity continued to operate in a political system determined to destroy all Jewish traditions and ultimately the Jews themselves. Some of these traditions seemed surprisingly resilient, as they continued to exert their influences. Closely intertwined into Jewish lives, perhaps these traditions shielded the Jews from personal disintegration.

Efforts to retain certain traditions were not limited to generational patterns. Gender distinctions and patriarchal principles continued to color Jewish lives under the German occupation. Comparative cross-cultural research shows that most people live in patriarchal, male-dominated, male-identified, and male-centered societies. That is, in most societies, including Jewish communities, men are traditionally defined as dominant, competitive, and rational. In contrast, women are viewed as submissive, cooperative, emotional, and nurturing.[65] These distinct societal role models translate into asymmetrical female–male relationships, in which men officially wield more power.[66] As the subordinate partners

---

[65] A few examples of cross-cultural publications about the universality of patriarchy are Bronislaw Malinowski, *Sex and Repression in Savage Society* (Chicago: University of Chicago Press, 1927); Bronislaw Malinowski, *The Sexual Life of Savages* (Boston: Beacon Press, 1987); Margaret Mead, *Male & Female* (New York: William Morrow, 1949); George Peter Murdock, *Social Structure* (New York: Macmillan, 1949); Peggy Reeves Sanaday, *Female Power and Male Dominance* (New York: Cambridge University Press, 1981). One more example that focuses on the centrality of the patriarchal Jewish traditions is Erich Fromm, *Love, Sexuality, and Matriarchy: About Gender* (New York: Fromm, 1997), pp. 46–75.

[66] For theoretical discussions on the effects that differential power has on the interactions of different role partners, see Robert K. Merton, *Social Theory and Social Structure* (Glencoe, IL: Free Press, 1957), pp. 370–79; Kurt H. Wolff, ed., *The Sociology of Georg Simmel* (Glencoe, IL: Free Press, 1950), pp. 181–300.

in male–female relationships, women tend to react rather than initiate actions. Responding to rather than initiating behavior, women are more likely to satisfy their needs and wishes in indirect ways.

With some exceptions, the two men who corresponded with Joseph were Dawid and Salo. Each was married to one of Joseph's sisters – Dawid to Klara and Salo to Mania. Occasionally, parts of Dawid's and Salo's letters mention their involvement in the collection of documents and transfers of information for the procurement of immigration visas for the entire family.[67] The women rarely contributed to these tasks.

Dawid's and Salo's help in taking care of formal documents that would improve the fate of their family conform to the traditional male role of protector. Traditional patriarchal principles assign to men two major roles: family protectors and providers. When the Germans implemented their policies of Jewish persecution and annihilation, they deprived Jewish men of their ability to perform these traditional male roles. Dawid's and Salo's efforts to gather and organize documents for emigration are exceptions.

Additionally, in somewhat twisted ways, patriarchal principles continued to affect the lives of the Hollander family. In 1939, after Poland's defeat, the Germans fulfilled their treaty obligations to the Soviet Union by allowing the Red Army to advance to the so-called Molotov–Ribbentrop line. Concretely, this meant that the Germans turned over to the USSR more than 50 percent of prewar Polish territory. To the Third Reich, this arrangement promised peace on its eastern borders and offered freedom to wage war against Western Europe. Jews who lived in the parts newly annexed to the Soviet Union were automatically shielded from the German invasion. Jews who lived under the German occupation saw in these Soviet-annexed parts of Poland a possibility for safety. Lured by such possibilities, an estimated 200,000 of them crossed the German–Soviet border and settled in the freshly annexed Soviet lands.[68]

Henek, Dola's husband, was among the refugees who reached the Soviet zone of Poland. Henek and his family settled in the town of Drohobycz. His wife, Dola, stayed with her family in Cracow. Scattered

---

[67] Two examples of such discussions are contained in letters written on June 2 and August 22, 1940.
[68] Israel Gutman, personal communication.

comments made by members of the Hollander family describe Henek as
a selfish, unreliable man who failed to make his wife happy. Dola agrees
with these negative assessments. Although estranged, the couple occasionally exchanged letters. Here and there, Henek, assuring his wife of
his love, would invite her to join him. Dola dismissed his love procla-
mations and invitations as insincere, empty gestures. She did not even
consider the possibility of re-creating their problematic, shaky marriage.
Time only increased the emotional divide between the couple.

Possibly Dola's friendship with Munio, a man she met, contributed
to her growing estrangement from her husband. Gradually, Dola and
Munio's friendship turned into deep love. Their attachment continued
for a year and a half. Under the German occupation, this time span
approached eternity. However, for quite a while, Dola and Munio hesitated to make the depth of their feelings public. They were aware of
obstacles. Dola's marriage would have to be dissolved before she could
marry the man she admired and loved.

The world around the Hollanders, as for the rest of Cracow Jews,
continued to crumble. The Germans were progressively more determined to shrink Cracow's Jewish population. One way they set out to
accomplish this was through different "deportations." Concretely, this
could have meant a variety of assaults: forceful removal to concentration
camps, direct executions, and transfers to other ghettos. With the looming threats of deportations came fears of separation. The Jews believed
that being married reduced the chances of separation. Up to a point,
these expectations were valid.

Pankiewicz, the keen observer of the Jewish plight in Cracow, points
to additional reasons for marriages and remarriages among the besieged
Jews. He describes one of his Jewish friends, a man he greatly admired.
This friend experienced two consecutive tragedies, the loss of a wife and
the loss of a son. Although shaken to the core, after a while the friend
remarried in a secret ghetto ceremony. Pankiewicz comments: "People
enclosed in the ghetto did not like to be lonely, did not want to go for
the resettlement alone, and did not want to die in loneliness."[69]

In Dola and Munio's case, all these reasons converged, with some
additions. In principle, the Hollander family approved of the couple's

---

[69] Pankiewicz, *The Cracow Ghetto Pharmacy*, p. 22.

attachment. With time, Berta and her two other daughters concluded that a divorce from Henek and a marriage to Munio would be the right solution. As a family, they also felt that divorce and remarriage were serious steps that ought not to be taken lightly. This meant that Dola would have to consult her brother Joseph. Not only would she need his consent but also his blessings, particularly for forming a new marriage.

The youngest among his siblings but the only man of the family, Joseph automatically became the family head. Neither the distance that separated him from the others nor the oppressive political system under which most of them lived posed a challenge to the brother's authority. In the rather lengthy correspondence that concentrates on the issues of Dola's divorce and remarriage, no one questioned the fact that Joseph was in charge of the traditional, moral issues affecting the family. Patriarchal principles, following the established traditional pattern of male dominance, were firmly entrenched.

In fact, the main player, Dola, supports fully this reality. Uncertain about her brother's reaction, anxious that he might not approve of her intended divorce, she sent him several letters. She waited for answers. In the meantime, Dola took no steps in the direction of a divorce. She only continued to build her case by underscoring again and again the loveless conditions of her marriage. She adds to her correspondence a copy of Henek's letter to her, as proof of his lack of sincerity and how this has continued for the duration of their marriage.

Soon the mother and sisters start to plead for Dola's case. Each explains the situation, each asks for Joseph's consent and blessing over and over again. Undoubtedly, these letters moved slowly. Some never reach their destination. The family must have taken this into consideration, by writing more letters. In a September 18, 1940, letter, Dola asks her brother, "Do you think that it is a good time now to resolve my marriage?"[70] She explains her plight more extensively in a lengthy letter on November 5. By 1941, letters describing Dola's dilemmas multiply. In one of them, she asks Henek for a divorce. Instead of a divorce, she receives news about her husband's death. There was no gloating, only sadness.

[70] Letter dated July 24, 1940.

Then more Jews were forced out of the Cracow ghetto, which the Germans had created in March 1941. According to a newly introduced German order, those who were transferred to ghettos outside of Cracow could take their spouses with them. Munio, a relative newcomer to the city, was among those who had to relocate. For Dola and Munio, this meant that unless they married, they would be separated and probably unable to reunite in the future. In a letter to Joseph, March 15, 1941, Dola wrote that she and Munio would be married on March 18. Munio wrote explaining the situation to Joseph and reassuring his future brother-in-law: "My heart is full of the best gifts for her [Dola]. Your family knows me for 18 months now, they gave us their blessings."[71]

What is especially surprising is that the correspondence over Dola's decision to marry Munio continues even after they were married. On March 22, 1941, the mother writes to her son asking him not to be surprised by Dola's decision to marry. Berta is clearly not yet convinced that Joseph approves of the match. Part of this letter explains and pleads: "As her mother I encouraged her, since she could not do anything else. She could not get support from anyone and she did not want to be a burden to the brothers-in-law. She was a thorn in the side, not everything she did was right, for this reason we suffered, because we were tired of her. You know that the sisters are fond of each other, so they encouraged her. It was not so easy to say goodbye, but we realized that it would be better for her. She ought to be happy, since she has had a hard time for ten years. I ask you, my dear child, do not be angry with her and think about her." Berta finishes by enclosing Dola's address in Tarnow in the hope that Joseph will write to her. Does this mean that she is still not sure that he will approve?

As if this were not enough, Berta's next letter to her son was dated only one day later (March 23, 1941). In it, she assures him that Dola is very happy with her husband. She then offers another elaboration: "she [Dola] just frets that you, my dear child, should not be angry with her because of this step she has taken. For 18 months, we saw her husband often. He is a good-looking hardworking man and gets along with everyone. Write to them so that she can be assured that you will not hold this

---

[71] This letter is from Munio, written on March 6, 1941, to Dola's mother asking the mother for Dola's hand. It also reached Joseph.

against her. You know how she suffered for 10 years." A letter from Dola to her brother dated April 27, 1941, in which she sends him birthday wishes, touches on the warm relationship that they continue to have. Probably the slow and unreliable mail contributed to the long time it took to receive Joseph's approval.

Quite independently of that, however, it is amazing how much attention the Hollanders devoted to Dola's divorce and marriage. That is, the efforts invested in supporting the traditional male authority of the family were enormous. What are the implications of these efforts? What do they mean? After all, the world as those who participated in this correspondence knew it was shattered. In Cracow, this family was surrounded by humiliating, devastating oppression, imposed by overpowering evil forces.

The exaggerated wish for Joseph's approval seems to express a hunger for tradition. Could it be that while so desperately trying to retain a part of their past, the family members were also asserting their basic humanity? Was this one of their ways to retain the human spark that the Germans had so brutally tried to extinguish? The Hollander family, as so many other Jews under this occupation, tried to protect some of their traditions through cooperative efforts. In a real sense, these cooperative efforts must have reminded them of life as it was. In part, too, cooperative efforts to retain some remnants of tradition might have served as a defiant gesture against the German determination to humiliate, degrade, and annihilate them.

In addition, for the Hollander family, and probably for most other cooperative groups, involvement with Dola's divorce and marriage distracted them from the devastating surroundings in which they had to live. Put another way, preoccupation with these issues lessened awareness about the oppressive German occupation. This in itself must have acted as an improvement in the quality of their lives. To be concerned about the welfare of those one cares about, to love and be loved in itself, promotes quality of life.

In the end, Dola and Munio were victims of the murderous policies of the Third Reich. But we know that when they were together, they were happy, they felt fulfilled by their mutual love. Somehow, early on, Dola knew what this marriage to Munio would mean if it happened. She writes to her brother, before her attachment to Munio was openly discussed. "I envy the wives who can count on their husbands' support – even if it is long distance support. . . . Life plays tricks – I found this support outside of the marriage – if I were free, who knows? Maybe I would risk. But it's war, can one think about the future now? Forgive me this egocentric letter, and that I take your attention away from everything else. I agree to make sacrifices for the happiness of the family. It is very hard to live surrounded by hatred. In order to handle this, one needs some support and love. Up till now I have felt betrayed by life but I love it anyway, and maybe with my thirty nine years I still can think about a joyful future?"[72]

The Hollanders were a warm and caring family. For historical accuracy, however, it is important to note that here and there some tensions appeared, occasionally directed at Genka, Dawid, Dola, and others. But these scattered expressions of disapproval did not amount to serious conflicts, nor did they undermine the firm solidarity that was so characteristic of this group. As a unit, they relied on each other for concrete as well as emotional help. Even though separated from Joseph by impenetrable barriers, his distant presence gave them courage, concrete aid, and, most important, hope for a better future. Similarly, this brother and son was totally committed to his relatives and never wavered in his determination to rescue them. Joseph, too, might have also derived some comfort from his relentless efforts.

What is exceptional is that this total preoccupation with saving the family left room for helping others. The Hollander correspondence includes attempts to aid others in a variety of ways. To illustrate, in an August 10, 1940, letter, Dola writes, "Mrs. Spitzmann asks you for help since her son didn't honor her with even a letter." The way in which Dola asks for a favor shows that she knew that her brother would welcome this request. Nor was this an isolated instance of Joseph aiding nonfamily members in need.[73]

Nevertheless, much of the Hollander correspondence was filled with assurances that their situation was not bad. More often than not, when a complaint slipped in, it was followed by a denial that the situation was actually as terrible as it seemed. Often it included an assurance

---

[72] Letter dated July 24, 1940.

[73] One clear example that shows this family's willingness to help others is in the letter written on September 25, 1940, by Dola.

that they could handle the situation. Again and again, they emphasized that being together gave them strength and eased the difficulties. Some of their problems were only alluded to, others might have come out inadvertently.

Decency, compassion, and care with which the Hollanders acted toward each other and toward nonfamily members created a protective barrier against the continuously growing assaults against the Cracow Jews. Inevitably, some cracks appeared. These cracks were exceptions to the usually guarded manner of communication. Some of them came across as outbursts of a suppressed anguish. A few brief illustrations follow.

Klara: "I ask God to help us to be together. . . . Those who are alive often envy the dead ones now. But a man is stronger than it seems and lives with the hope that it will be better. The only comfort are your letters."[74]

Dola: "I am trying to stay strong. Unfortunately, one gets more and more emotionally exhausted."[75]

Klara: "I would like to hibernate this winter like the bears do to see nothing and to hear nothing."[76]

Mania: "We all sit like on a volcano, our nerves are almost used up."[77]

The spontaneity and sincerity of these outbursts tend to enrich and validate the evolving Holocaust history. Moreover, when researchers compare the contents of the Hollander correspondence over time, they are bound to confront findings that suggest changes in attitudes and behaviors. Unlike the writers of these letters, we as observers have the advantage of looking at several sources of information. At the same time, we can compare them to each other in a variety of ways. The frequency with which certain issues are mentioned and how they are mentioned in themselves have the potential to offer insights into the lives of the letter writers. Findings signaling changes, in particular, have the potential to provide historical evidence about attitudes and behaviors because these had been emerging under the German occupation.

Without imposing their own values, researchers ought to look at these letters in an inductive way. Thus, the questions with which one would

[74] Letter dated August 9, 1940.
[76] Letter dated October 22, 1940.
[75] Letter dated August 1, 1940.
[77] Letter dated October 30, 1940.

start depend on the topics these letter writers focus on. Here and there, I have alluded to some of these pervasive concerns: the maintenance of close ties despite the actual separations, efforts to retain some traditional continuity, and the value of cooperative efforts.

A rather obvious preoccupation woven into these letters was food. For Jews in particular, food allotments became a problem shortly after the Germans conquered Poland. Severe food shortages led to long bread-lines. Jews were routinely and forcefully removed from these lines. With the help of local Poles, Germans made sure that those identified as Jewish were denied access to the meager food supplies. Already at the outset of the German occupation, the Jews as a group suffered from special food shortages.

With time, increasingly severe food shortages overshadowed virtually all aspects of Jewish life. On balance, despite variations, forceful transfers into Nazi-created ghettos made hunger a constant companion of Jew-ish ghetto dwellers. By controlling food deliveries, the Germans often turned the closed quarters of the ghettos into death traps. Around 1942 and beyond, the authorities became determined to do away with "use-less" ghetto Jews. This was translated into the murder of unproductive people, the old, the sick, and children.

A substantial portion of the Hollander correspondence deals with food. This information is expressed in the attitudes and reactions to food packages that Joseph kept sending in a continuous flow. Many of these packages were lost. Specifically, from the beginning till the end of 1940, the letters that mention packages ask Joseph to stop sending them. These letters correctly argue that it is a waste of his money, particularly because so many of them are lost. Besides, they emphasize that they have food and manage quite well. He is asked not to worry. Of course, they always politely thank him for any packages they get. Sometimes they point out that a package was damaged – some things might have been stolen. All this was to discourage Joseph from incurring additional future expenses.[78]

---

[78] A few examples of letters that urge the brother not to send packages are February 11, 1940; May 30, 1940; July 28, 1940; August 9, 1940; August 22, 1940; and September 18, 1940.

With time, assurances that food packages are not necessary became less frequent. Eventually, they disappear, only to be replaced by grateful thanks. These thanks are followed by detailed, glowing descriptions of the contents of each package that did reach them. More specifically, following ghettoization in 1941, the amount of attention devoted to food grows, reflecting an intensifying preoccupation. For example, in a June 9, 1941, letter, Berta expresses special thanks for packages she and other family members received. A package seemed to have arrived from Lisbon and the mother specifies its content – "coffee, tea, sugar, soap, three boxes of tinned food, powdered chocolate, which tasted especially good to me." She continues by telling who else received a package and how grateful they were.

An appreciation of packages has implications beyond the much-needed provisions they contain. This is particularly evident from a letter written by the couple Dola and Munio. Dola comments: "I thank you very much for the packages. Munio expressed already his gratitude. I am so touched that I still have in you my old good dear brother – it's more important than the content of the packages. I left for myself some cocoa which substitutes chocolate. . . . I really miss you. Now I understand you missing home and Dear Mother. I am healthy, and in normal conditions, I would be happy. Stay well."

From the middle of 1941, there is hardly a letter that does not include some mention of food. What is interesting is that hardly any of these comments suggest that no packages should be sent. Instead, the recipients of these parcels show their approval by specifying each item and by telling Joseph how important each parcel is and how glad they are to have these items. What is also different by 1941 is that the men of the family become involved in writing and commenting on the food packages. For example, in one of his letters, the brother-in-law Salo on May 9, 1941, writes: "We have already written to you that we all . . . have received the packages you sent to us with mostly tea and coffee, I keep repeating that because we are never sure if the letters reach you. Therefore, I am saying it once more that the bigger packages haven't arrived – maybe they will still come – but you should perhaps make some inquires at the company you sent them with, and request your money back. You are trying to help, spend your money and by doing this you always risk that it won't reach us.

So before you receive a confirmation from us that your package arrived, please don't send anything. Thank God we are all together. We are waiting for the documents; I know that you are doing everything you can. You will receive the pictures in the meantime."

Salo's letter differs from the rest of his correspondence in the amount of attention he gives to food. This preoccupation with food may reflect a blurring of gender roles. In addition, it shows the growing food shortages that the Jews, including the Cracow Jews, had to endure. As he continues to dwell on the contents of these parcels, he offers advice on how to make these transfers of food more efficient and less costly. Such advice may also express Salo's need to be useful. It takes place, as we know, in a political system that closed off all avenues for acting in prewar, traditional ways. For Jewish men, in particular, the German occupation created a definite rupture between their prewar and wartime roles. Men could not protect the family from German assaults.[79]

In yet another part of this letter, Salo returns to his earlier preoccupation and mentions the family's emigration documents. Could this attention to bureaucratic arrangements reflect a tentative move toward the masculine role of family protector?

I agree with Browning that this collection of letters "focuses on deep personal and familial concerns." Moreover, because the content of these communications is often hidden, it requires careful decoding. On the other hand, precisely because these writings focused on personal familial concerns, they contain potentially important historical evidence about the Holocaust. There is a shortage of evidence about Jewish perceptions of the horrendous circumstances they had to face, especially as they moved toward the final stages of their lives. Relevant here are Primo Levi's observations that the survivors who tell about their experiences are the exceptions. After all, most Jews perished, and those who managed to escape being murdered cannot tell us what being murdered meant. Accordingly, Levi explains, "the job completed was not told by anyone, just as no one ever returned to describe his own death."[80]

---

[79] Examples of letters that thank profusely and specify the contents of the food packages are May 9, 1941; June 12, 1941; June 17, 1941; June 26, 1941; July 8, 1941; July 9, 1941; and July 17, 1941. Tec, *Resilience and Courage: Women, Men and the Holocaust*, pp. 346–7.

[80] Primo Levi, *The Drowned and the Saved* (New York: Summit, 1986), pp. 83–4.

Levi's comments point to the potential significance of the Hollander correspondence. The entire family perished. Through their letters, they left information about their personal experiences, feelings, and reactions to the events around them. This correspondence serves as additional evidence about the evolving history of the Holocaust, from an unmediated perspective, untouched by survivors' postwar experiences. I have no intention of placing a different research value on data provided by those who perished and those who survived. I only welcome letters and writings that resemble them as another source of data. More sources of data offer more opportunities to validate research findings.

For years, my research has concentrated on the voices of the oppressed, voices that originated in a variety of sources, such as wartime diaries, postwar memoirs, a range of archival materials – and my direct interviews with Holocaust survivors. Singly and collectively, these data include the victims' vivid accounts of their personal experiences. Mixed with their personal stories are equally vivid observations about the fate of their families, friends, and communities. These rich Holocaust materials have both weaknesses and strengths. Puzzles remain.

Some weaknesses and strengths apply to letters, postcards, and hastily written notes by Jews on their way to concentration camps. To such additional sources of data, the same care and attention must apply as to all other voices of the oppressed. Treated as an additional source of evidence, letters enrich our knowledge about the Jewish perspective of the Holocaust. Just as in all other sources of qualitative data about the Holocaust, so here there is always the danger of reading too much into these letters. There is sometimes the temptation of building castles in the air.

To avoid distortions, one simple rule a researcher has to follow is never to dismiss contradictory findings. That is, if we treat seeming contradictions with respect and care, they often lead to a broadening of the earlier findings and/or to alternative interpretations. Either outcome is welcome. When relying on letters, just as with other sources of qualitative data, the "what" and the "how" are intricately related to each other.

The research value of wartime letters, postcards, and notes dropped from cattle cars that transported Jews to various concentration camps was earlier recognized by Emmanuel Ringelblum, the initiator and organizer of the archival collection known as Ringelblum Archives, Oneg Shabath, or ARG. A part of these important archival materials include personal communications, collectively referred to as Letters.[81]

Independently, the Hollander correspondence supports Ringelblum's position. Throughout their letters, Berta Hollander's daughters spoke about her lovingly. Occasionally, their love is expressed in a worry about Berta's ill health. This is evident already from letters written in the summer of 1940. One of them reads: "Mother works like an ant, tries to take care of everything, although the current events really affect her, which combined with her age and longing for you leave their marks on her." Additional letters, dated September 17 and 18, speak about Berta's gall bladder problems. Yet, at the same time, the sisters reassure Joseph that her condition is not serious and that he should not worry.

The last letter Joseph received from his mother was dated December 23, 1941. About a year later, the only communication dated 1942 came to him from a relative by marriage, Regine Hütschnecker. She wrote: "Unfortunately I have to inform you that your Dear Mother died peacefully and without pain on August 28, 1942. It is unfortunately God's will and we humans cannot help it."[82]

What this warm letter failed to mention was that, for that time and place, Berta Hollander's natural death was a blessing in disguise. It most probably spared her experiencing a humiliating and cruel death.

In closing, I wish to shift focus and ask what the authors of these letters might have gained from their wartime correspondence. We know that the final fate of the Hollander family was most probably a cruel and debilitating death. Yet, from their letters, we learn that intricately mixed with their fate were also emotionally and morally uplifting experiences. At the core of these positive experiences was a continuous awareness that Joseph, from a distance, unconditionally cared for and loved them. They expected all kinds of sacrifices from Joseph, whom they loved and esteemed. This knowledge in itself must have lifted their spirits and improved the quality of their lives. Considering how strong their attachments to and trust in Joseph were, all these positive feelings must

---

[81] *Archiwum Ringelbluma: Konspiracyjne Archiwum Getta Warszawy*, tom 1, *Listy o Zagładzie* [Ringelblum's Archives, vol. 1, Letters about Destruction], ed. Ruta Sakowska (Warsaw: Wydawnictwo Naukowe PWN, 1997).
[82] Letter dated December 5, 1942.

have helped them retain hope that he would not give up trying to save them.

These hopes must have diminished some of their sufferings as they were approaching death. Indeed, scattered throughout the Hollander correspondence are expressions of joy, love, and gratitude to Joseph, whom they believed would not abandon them. They were right. He never did. Long after his family perished, Joseph's silent involvement with their fate mirrored his unfaltering, profound commitment to all of them.

Comments on Joseph Hollander's Speech

Christopher R. Browning

Sometime after his arrival in Europe in 1945 but still shortly before the war was over, Joseph Hollander was apparently asked to give an inspirational or motivational talk about the nature of the German enemy. The text of his talk was eventually found not alongside the collection of letters from his family, but elsewhere in his personal papers. It is remarkable that even though he did not know the "vocabulary" of the Just War Tradition or the term "genocide" recently invented by Raphael Lemkin, a Polish lawyer of Jewish descent, he understood clearly that Hitler's war was not a "normal, regular" (i.e., conventional) war waged against enemy combatants but rather was a war fought "abjectly" against unarmed civilians (i.e., non-combatants). And better than even many historians for several decades after the war, he already understood in 1945 – before the Nuremberg Trials – that the Nazis' "big game of mass murder" was epitomized above all by their attempt "to destroy and annihilate all European Jews" and that this was most graphically demonstrated in the "massacres in the ghettos of Poland" where two million Jews had perished, 360,000 from Warsaw alone. The only point at which his knowledge was still blurred was the actual mechanics of the killing in the death camps. He knew that Jews were deported from the ghettos en route to their deaths under the pretext of being sent off to labor. And he picked up rumors about killing by "fumes" and "burning," which he mistakenly attributed to lime in railroad cars, not the assembly-line mass murder of gas chambers and burning pits or crematoria. That seems to be the only aspect of the Nazi genocide of the Jews that was still beyond his capacity to fully grasp.

The Nazi Mind

By Tec 5 Joseph Hollander, 32 863 494

Know your enemy! Every one of us, during his training period has heard many times this expression. Our War Department, through training films, different booklets and posters does the utmost to familiarize every member of the armed forces with the enemy and his military equipment, with his weapons of war. We learn how to recognize an enemy plane, an enemy tank, and to know the difference between their military machines and ours. We understand how this is important. Many times the difference is "to kill or be killed."

To know your enemy and to know him well means to know how to fight him and how to defeat him. But to know his skill and to know his tools of war, does not give us the whole picture, and the whole knowledge. We must know as well his mind, his mind which is behind his weapons; we must know his real character; we must even know his soul. We must know him through and through.

Fighting and wars are as old as the world and will exist as long as men will exist. It's true that the character of wars changed with the centuries, with the always rising culture and mechanical inventions. Each succeeding war is on a higher standard of killing. The human mind works to find ways of quickest and most wholesale killing.

I would like to make clear, I am not a pacifist nor a peace monger, especially when I am on the side which is not an aggressor.

We all know that almost every second generation engages in war. But as long as the fight is a fight between men who face each other armed, it can be called a normal, a regular war. But this war which we are now fighting is not a normal war. Our enemy started a new system a new way; he fights abjectly. He does not like to face an armed opponent.

I like to talk right now about the German nature as it happened that I know much more about them than I know about their partners the Japs.

My personal experience which authorizes me to state this goes back to the unforgettable 17 days from 1 to 17 September 1939 that I spent in Poland and saw how the brave German fliers machine-gunned innocent, unarmed, weaponless, completely defenseless women, children, and aged men, who were fleeing from cities which had been destroyed by bombs and set afire; looking for refuge in the woods. You could see with what personal satisfaction and joy a German flier – after having unloaded his bombs and already on his way home – lowered his plane over roads crowded with civilian figures and started his game. He machine-gunned everyone and everything.

I don't even like to describe what I saw as I arrived on one road a half hour later after this kind of game was played. And this happened in September 1939 all over Poland. Later we knew the same play was repeated all over Europe. But this was only the beginning, this was only a rehearsal, a practice before the big game of mass murder, which started later. You all know that one of the Nazi commandments is to destroy and to annihilate all European Jews. You surely heard about the methods which they are using to achieve their goal.

For personal reasons I watched closely during these past five years of war the German atrocities, especially persecution of Jews. I watched this infernal machine, whose horrible sounds reach our ears every day from martyred Europe and above all from Poland.

It may seem superfluous to speak of these miseries because we pretend to ourselves that we are very well acquainted with them, and because after having read so many "black books" and so many terrifying accounts, after having seen so many horror films out of Hollywood, it seems to us that we know everything about martyred Europe. And – what is worse – some of us even suspect that they have been taken in by exaggerated propaganda, and that after all European air must be more or less breathable as so many millions of people are still breathing there.

If you would like to listen I will try to describe just as an example how Nazis managed to annihilate 400,000 Jews in Warsaw. This will be perhaps the best "practical" lesson in the cycle under the title "Know Your Enemy."

I once read a report about life under the German heel. The title of this article was "In the Depths of Hell." This is the right name to describe the tragedy, and the massacres in the ghettos of Poland.

There are some further facts to be added to what you think you know of the martyrdom of the countries occupied by Nazis and of the fate of the most unfortunate of all unfortunate peoples, the inhabitants of these countries. There are some scenes which have been acted out in reality and before which even the most audacious imagination would fail. Goya was not pessimist enough to paint such scenes and Dante did not surpass them in the most infernal visions of his "Inferno."

Let's take as an example the Warsaw Ghetto. Of the four hundred thousand Jews who were confined in the Warsaw Ghetto, only forty thousand are alive at this time. This is a single statement which should make even the most indifferent shudder. The Warsaw Ghetto was nothing but a gigantic prison, and the inhabitants were condemned to death.

I would like to cite the story of the president of the Jewish Council in Warsaw whose suicide revealed to the Polish Jews that they were already before the gates of Hell. On the eve of that day the Gestapo asked him to choose seventeen thousand inhabitants of the Ghetto to be transported to the East, to do some work for the Nazis. He understood that this was a simple sentence of death, and he killed himself rather than betray his people.

In the Ghetto the next day there began a man hunt, always under the pretext of drafting labor for the East and every day from that moment on, hundreds and thousands of Jews passed through the gates of the Ghetto and went off to trains whose true destinations no one knew. The Ghettos were being gradually emptied by murder.

Thanks to the courageous souls who made their way among the unhappy Jews, we know in what unspeakable conditions, by what terrifying procedures, by what new diabolic inventions the Germans succeeded in liquidating the Polish ghettos. They massacred over two million of the Jewish population of Poland. We have learned with horror that thousands of these condemned people were forced to watch the mass executions. We now know to what use the railroad cars were put; that their floorboards were covered with lime which burned the feet and whose fumes caused death. We now know that thousands of men were deprived of life simply by herding them in masses on the floor-boards which very quickly became the base of a pyramid of corpses. How simple their methods!

I gave you only a short picture what went on in Warsaw. But it was not better in any other place where the professional murderers "The Gestapo" could lay their bloody hands and their degenerate minds. Nothing is sacred for them, nothing is taboo. Volumes of books and millions of words could be written to describe their atrocities and a voice of a prophet would be necessary to express it all.

Only after this war will be over will we hear how many millions of people have disappeared during these five years, were shot, hanged, or kicked to death by the guards in the concentration camps.

I would like to spare you, as I think that you already know whom we are fighting, you already know their criminal madness, you know the real Nazi mind, which is behind the German weapon.

But their reign will be short and their end is already sighted on the horizon. We all hope that we have now started the final chapter of this war of liberation.

Finishing this description of the Nazi mind and character I'd like to add one more observation.

Not since the Thirty Years' War of the seventeenth century had Germany seen the real face of war in its murderous ugliness. The German armies were always sent to fight their battles on foreign soil; if they could not win the war in other lands they surrendered rather than have it carried into their own country. And – I am sure – that this time they will surrender unconditionally.

PART THREE

THE LETTERS

Annotated by Craig Hollander and Christopher R. Browning

Letters without Reply
November 1939–May 1940

O n September 1, 1939, Germany launched its invasion of Poland. Apparently having long anticipated the outbreak of hostilities, Joseph Hollander and his wife Felicia (Lusia) had already departed Cracow and were residing in the town of Zaleszczyki in the southeastern corner of Poland on the Romanian border. On September 6, Joseph procured a visa from the Romanian consulate in Lvov to enter Romania and, still far from the advancing German army, returned to Zaleszczyki to await further events. On September 17, in accordance with the Nazi–Soviet Non-Aggression Pact, the Red Army entered Poland from the east to secure those territories of Poland promised by Hitler to Stalin as the price of the latter's neutrality. The zone soon to be occupied by the Red Army included the region of Eastern Galicia and the border town of Zaleszczyki. On the following day, September 18, Joseph and Lusia promptly crossed into Romania, leaving Poland forever.

The rest of Joseph's family – his mother, his three sisters and their husbands, and two nieces – had remained in Cracow until the outbreak of the war. The German army reached their city on September 6. Like so many others, they apparently attempted a panicked escape (in contrast to the well-laid plans of Joseph) ahead of the rapidly advancing German army but were almost immediately overtaken by events and had to return to the city. Several of their subsequent letters referred obliquely to this failed escape attempt. Klara noted that "during our 'trip' we lost two suitcases with dresses" and then again later that "during our land exploring journey we lost most of our belongings."[1] But no other details

---

[1] Klara to Joseph, December 9, 1939, and April 8, 1940.

of this chaotic period of Polish military collapse and the early German occupation were narrated in the letters, even though the Jews of Cracow were subjected to arbitrary rituals of humiliation, unfettered violence and pillaging, and an endless array of discriminatory edicts that forced them to wear a Star of David marking, made them vulnerable to forced labor roundups, and froze their financial assets. As one survivor subsequently recalled, the Cracow Jews "found themselves outside the law, a free prey" to the German occupiers.[2] And another that "By the winter of 1940 the world had turned upside down."[3]

Aside from discretion about putting such experiences in writing, Joseph's extended family in Cracow initially had no address to write to him. It would appear that their first word from Joseph was a postcard from Rome, dated November 3, when Joseph and Lusia – having made their way from Romania through Yugoslavia to Italy – were awaiting a ship to Lisbon. Apparently, Lusia's relative Paul Schreiber in Vienna had also heard from Joseph and Lusia, for the family in Cracow received news from him in postcards dated October 31 and November 10. Noting that "nothing from here can be sent out," they asked Paul to relay news to Joseph. It was this news via Paul Schreiber, finally catching up with Joseph after it was forwarded to Lusia's brother Jan Schreiber in New York, that constitutes the first letter of Joseph's collection.[4]

Evidently, Joseph must have sent additional correspondence from Italy, informing the family that he was traveling on to Lisbon. They then began to write him at poste restante (general delivery) in Lisbon, not knowing that he would be denied entry there on November 29, 1939, and forced to sail on to New York, where he arrived without an entry visa on December 6. On the contrary, they assumed all was well in Portugal, for Dawid congratulated Joseph on getting "a permanent stay permit and work permit" in a letter mailed from Cracow to Lisbon on the first day of the new year.[5]

[2] Miraiam Peleg-Marianska and Mordecaii Peleg, *Witnesses – Life in Occupied Krakow* (London: Routlege, 1991), xiii.
[3] Janina Fischler-Martinho, *Have Your Seen My Little Sister?* (London: Valentine Mitchell, 1998), 34.
[4] Dola to Paul Schreiber, November 20, 1939, and Paul Schreiber to Joseph, no date.
[5] Dawid to Joseph, January 1, 1940.

The first word to the contrary was a postcard mailed by Joseph from Ellis Island on January 16, 1940, that reached Cracow in mid-February. This was apparently the first direct word the family had from Joseph since his departure from Italy for Portugal the previous November. Thereafter, the family letters to Joseph were sent to the address of Lusia's brother in New York, Jan Schreiber. Incredibly, the family letters to poste restante in Lisbon (from November 1939 through January 1940) were forwarded to Jan's address in New York and eventually reached Joseph as well.

If Joseph began to hear from the family in Cracow on a regular basis, much to their frustration, his replies were not reaching them. On April 8, 1940, Salo wrote to inform Joseph that they had had no news "directly" from him since the postcard from Ellis Island, and they were "waiting for news as if for salvation." Could he please send a telegram. At the same time, Dola wrote that they had only heard indirectly through others with contacts in New York that Joseph and Lusia "couldn't go to Lisbon and are being held in the harbor of NY.... We keep waiting for the news from you. The last card was from Ellis Island."[6] In late April, Joseph's mother learned indirectly through Lusia's relative in Vienna, Adele, of Joseph's plans to travel to Mexico.[7]

Finally, on May 4, the family in Cracow received a telegram from Joseph, probably in response to Salo's plea one month earlier. This was the direct word that they had been waiting for "with longing."[8] Then, as if a dam had burst, Joseph's replies arrived in a bunch. On May 16, they received postcards of February 23 and March 6 and a letter of February 28.[9] The many months of the family's sending letters from Cracow without reply finally came to an end. Thereafter, a real exchange began.

The family in Cracow heard little from Joseph, but he was hearing from them. Although their letters were cautious and made virtually no mention of the hardships they were suffering, Joseph was well aware of their plight. "I keep receiving letters from my sister and my brother-in-law in Kraków, and from the content, I can easily guess that the situation over there is terrible," he wrote to a Haifa lawyer on March 4, 1940. Unable to secure his own entry into the United States, he was already struggling to arrange their emigration to Mexico or Cuba, for which he

[6] Salo and Dola to Joseph, April 8, 1940.   [7] Berta to Joseph, May 1, 1940.
[8] Berta and Dola to Joseph, May 5, 1940.   [9] Mania and Salo to Joseph, May 16, 1940.

needed money that his brother-in-law Dawid Wimisner had invested in Palestine. "I don't believe I have to stress that the life of this family depends on how soon this matter can be solved. . . . I am awaiting your response with impatience since the situation is burning and any delay may be catastrophic."[10] Over the next months and years, the plight of Joseph's family in Cracow would only get even more desperate.

November 20, 1939

From Dola to Paul Schreiber (Relative of Joseph's Wife):

Dear Paul,[11]

Now you are our good angel, you paid us back more than we could expect. Simultaneously with your two postcards (from October 31 and November 10) we received a card from Józiu from Rome (with the date of November 3). Unfortunately nothing from here can be sent out.

We have no choice but to ask you to get in touch with him. We know that you will lovingly do that. We all are healthy and together, except for my husband who left to live in Drohobycz[12] with his family. Józiu's mother-in-law lives with her sister Mrs. Horowitz. She is healthy and optimistic.

Mania and Klara live with the dear Mother at the old address. I went through lots of changes, I live already in the third apartment, and soon I have to move to a fourth one.

Dear Paul and Adele, we thank you so much! You don't even know how much better our lives are when we have the news.

Dola

On the other side to Joseph (Józiu) from Paul Schreiber:

Dearest Józiu,

I hope you received my card. Today I got a letter from Dola and answered her immediately. Everything is well, everybody is healthy, that's the most important. I wrote to Dola but at the old address. I doubt that she will receive my card. Please send me the addresses of Mania and Klara

[10] Joseph to Samuel Spann, March 16, 1940.

[11] This letter was sent from Poland to Paul Schreiber in Vienna, then forwarded by him to Lisbon, and forwarded once again from Lisbon to Joseph in New York c/o Jan Schreiber.

[12] In Eastern Galicia, the part of Poland occupied by and annexed to the Soviet Union.

immediately. I hope this letter will comfort you. With deepest respect for you and your wife.

Paul

November 24, 1939

From Dola:

Dearest Józiu[13]

Thank God we all are healthy and we work. Henek left to live with his family. Your mother-in-law feels well and is even joyful, she lives with her sister Mrs. Horowitz. Lusia's father and relatives stay where they used to be. Dear Mother is always so happy to hear from you. I write the same to Adele in case you don't receive this card. I wish you and Lusia much much happiness. Lots of luck from Klara, kisses from Genka.

Dola

From Berta:

My dear and beloved Children

Words cannot express my happiness over receiving a letter from you. When will we see each other? Your Mother Berta

Undated letter, probably late November or early December 1939

From Berta:

Much loved children!

I received the card you wrote to Malcia.[14] You write that you were happy to have a letter from us. Now imagine my joy that you write you are both well. I wish you much good fortune wherever you turn; I can't express myself with words. I wonder if I can still hope to see you again.

I must be content with your letters, only please write me your news often, since I am always thinking about you. When one suffers, I say at least it is not my son. I am content with everything, I only ask God to give me life to see you again.

---

[13] This letter and all the following letters through January 1940 were originally sent to poste restante, Lisbon, and then forwarded to Joseph in New York, c/o Jan Schreiber.

[14] Berta's affectionate nickname for Mania.

You are sent affectionate kisses from your Mother, who wishes you blessings and good health.

Berta

From Dola:

Our only joy now comes from your letters. I live with a great quandary, for I too intend to go to Uncle Tolstoy.[15] But do not worry about us. We all are healthy and this is the most important thing. When you write please let me know if you have heard anything about the kids of Spilimann since they are not in Kraków.

Greetings for Lusia,

Dola

From Klara:

My dear,

We all are OK. I just want this winter to pass so the sun can warm us up again. Mania lives with the kids in a studio at Ebersohns. Uncle with his business partners are with Aunt Rózia. Lusia takes private sewing lessons and Genia got a job at my husband's business where she gets a salary and is very proud of that. They come home together, our biggest pleasure now is to sit at home.

Stay well.

Klara

From Mania:

To this family letter, I will add a few words. As for now we are doing quite well. From tomorrow we will wear uniforms, I suspect we will look good in them.[16] We have become something like a herd of chickens now, we just sit and warm our butts at the stove. Lots of happiness and luck in your travels.

Mania

---

[15] Klara is referring to the Soviet-occupied zone of Poland because her husband Henek had fled to Eastern Galicia.

[16] If this is an oblique reference to marking with the Jewish star, ordered by the General Governor Hans Frank on November 23, 1939, that would date this letter to late November or early December 1939.

December 2, 1939

From Salo:

My Dearest Ones!

We have already received three cards from you, but we are unable to establish direct contact with you. There is not much to relate about the business; it goes on slowly and in small steps. Most important is that the sisters and mother are all here together and are in good health. With that one must now be content. All the best to both of you, and please keep us happy with further reports. Thousands of kisses.

Salo

From Mania:

My dearest ones,

Your card brought so much joy that I am unable to express it with words. We are all healthy. Dola lives with me. Klara didn't change her address yet, and dear Mother lives with her. I expect the best news from you.

Mania

December 9, 1939

From Berta:

My much-loved Children

Today I received your letter and card, and I am in a hurry to give you news. We are all comfortable. If only winter were over. The main thing for me is to get a letter from you. I read your letters several times so that I remember them. I think about you day and night, so, my dear ones, write us often.

Dear Józiu,

Adele wrote that she had sent you my letter. She is completely beside herself about Kurti's proceeding. If it is possible, please write to her. Otherwise, I have nothing more to write you than affectionate kisses.

Your Mother Berta

From Genka:

My very dear ones,

You won't imagine how much I would like to be with you. This climate makes me feel very bad. I am sitting all day long in the store, and I really want to learn some profession. I think about photography or retouching. How do you like this idea? I would so much like to meet with you and talk. Write back to us a long letter since we are so curious how you are doing.

Kisses,
Genka

From Klara:

Our neighbors are horrible people; they make lots of noise not only during the day but they also don't let us sleep at night. My husband has announced he is moving to Aunt Rózia,[17] but there are certain difficulties connected with that. Lusia sews really nicely now. We need it badly because during our "trip" we lost two suitcases with dresses. We greet you warmly. Stay well and happy.

Klara

From Dola:

A hundred times a day I thank God that you are where you are. I am breathing but I am not alive. Did you get the letter where I asked if you knew anything about the children of Spilimanns from Kraków? Lusia's bedroom and dining room are being kept in good condition.

Bye, Dola

Undated letter (postmarked January 1, 1940, in Cracow, to Lisbon, received by the U.S. Postal Service on January 9, 1940)

From Berta:

I am writing you only a few lines, so that you will have news from us, that we are all in good health. I would like so much to have a letter

---

[17] Again, a reference to the Soviet-occupied zone in eastern Poland.

from you. We sent a letter for you to Adele. It is unpleasant for us to trouble her so often, as I do not know what sort of business her husband has. I have decided to write you only cards, which you surely will receive.[18] Otherwise I have nothing to tell you except to kiss you and Lusia affectionately.

Your Mother Berta

From Dola:

Dearest Brother,

I also want to add some lines to this family letter. Accidentally, I learned that Mr. L. from Bulonia lives in G . . . [illegible]. Unfortunately he left the day before our arrival there (the shop assistant from the store of Mrs. Spilimann told us about him). Also your letter was delivered to us on the last day of Mr. L. staying in Kraków. We regret very much that we couldn't meet with Mr. L. in person.

I already wrote to you that I live at Mania's place – she made me a place to sleep where it was available. I have news from Henek from people who are returning. It's so cold this winter, I mostly sit at home. You know how sensitive I am. We miss you very much, but we are happy that you succeeded in getting there. Greetings for Lusia. I am just about to go to her mother.

Kisses,

Dola

P.S. I got a card from Adele (Paula is already in New York). Adele says that she hasn't received an answer from you yet.

From Mania:

Dear, beloved Brother,

We were really surprised that you left us without news for so long. We wrote two letters to Portugal, for which we didn't get any answer. I am very happy because of the last news. May God help you to find a good place for yourselves.

I had no doubts that you forgot about us. I remember our last conversation before you left. It's not about me and Salo but about Klara with

---

[18] This remark probably reflects an assumption that postcards would be less delayed than letters in censorship.

her family and Dola. As I already wrote to you I had to close the business. I had to pay for two months; also to put a heater over there.

The Knopfs come often to me, as well as many other people. I feel sorry for the Knopfs, but unfortunately I can't help them. I gave them back everything they had left in the office. A clerk from Cook's office told me that the central office "Poltow" burned down. Salo wrote to some clerks in Warsaw but we didn't get any answer.

I wish you all the best, peace and happiness.

Mania

From Klara:

Dearest Józiu,

Your letters are our great and only joy. I don't even have to write to you how we hope you will write often and good things. We all are healthy, we do have enough to eat. I hope that we will survive somehow and stay on the surface without drowning; my husband works in the store. It's hard to get the goods but we do manage somehow. Do not worry, God is with us.

I kiss you and Lusia very warmly.

Klara

From Dawid:

Dear Józiu,

I am very happy because of what you write. It's great that you got a permanent stay permit and work permit. Since you are over there please don't forget us and try to help. My daughters have handiwork professions: Genka learns photography and Lusia is a tailor; Klara learned how to cut and sew shirts and pants, and I can do everything.

Greetings for Lusia from all of us.

Dawid

February 12–13, 1940

From Genka:

Dearest Uncle,

I am very happy that you are over there. I really wish to be there with you, and hope that one day I will be there with you. So I ask you

Dear Uncle to pick up my stuff from Mr. Rosner and to take it to your place.

I surprised the whole family one night when I had appendicitis and had to have surgery. Now it's all over and I can walk again. I really hope that soon I will be there with you.

I am surprised that you didn't get any news from us; we sent several letters.

Lots of kisses
Genka

From Klara:

Beloved Józiu,
For two months we have been waiting for news from you. Now we are finally comforted knowing that you are already there. We thank God for every night we can sleep and for every day we live through. My husband as a war veteran has all kinds of privileges. Please write often since Dawid has different plans and ideas every day.

I kiss you and greet Lusia
Klara

From Dola:

Dearest Józiu,
Finally we got news confirming what we heard. I live in a rented furnished room.

Henek is still with his family, he doesn't have anything to come back to.

If I could trust that he would take care of me I would leave. I wouldn't be afraid to start from zero and would probably find some work to do. But I am afraid of lack of moral support in a foreign country. I wish you and Lusia lots of the luck and happiness.

Dearest brother, when will we see each other again?
Dola

From Mania:

Dearest, beloved Brother,
I know that you know your letter brought much joy to us. I am sorry that you haven't received the letters written to Portugal.

I would give my life away to know if you are doing well. Will your travels end at this point? Dearest Józiu, I don't even want to think about the fact that we are really separated. Will life be so cruel for me this time too and won't I see you again?

I needed to close down the business. It would be impossible to keep it.

Dearest Brother, please write to us often. Greetings to Paula. Kisses for Lusia. She should thank God that she is so lucky and doesn't have to share our destiny.

Lots of happiness to both of you.

Mania

From Salo:

Dear Jazek!

We have just received your delightful card from America and wish you above all good fortune, good health, and happiness. Even if we had no direct news, still we received hints from the family letter that you probably went to America. Adele wrote us a few days ago that you were in America. We wrote four letters poste restante to Lisbon but received no answer. Your last card was from Rome. Thank God we know you are in America, hopefully in good health. There is not much to report from here. The main thing is that we are healthy. We were not able to keep the business going. Details about this another time.

It is premature to ask now about your intentions in America, but I want to hope we will see each other again. I would really like that very much. We did not say a proper goodbye. Here huge . . . [illegible] hold sway, that was . . . [illegible] necessary. Each member of the family will write separately.

We send warm regards. Write us the most detailed letter you can. Greetings to Lusia and everyone. God grant that we will have the joy of seeing one another again and be able to take pleasure in each other's company.

With an affectionate hug and many kisses

Your

Salo

From Dawid:

I am very happy that you are in NY. I hope you feel well over there. Thank God my family and I are well. Uncle asked through Switzerland how we were doing. Please greet him warmly from all of us. Greetings to your wife.

Dawid

From Berta:

My dear and beloved Children!

I have no words to write of my joy that I know where you are. I am well thank God but my only wish is to see you. Whether I can expect that is God's affair nevertheless I have hope. My dear children, I really do not know what I should write you, in the next letter I will have my wits more about me and will write more.

I kiss you affectionately,

Your Mother

Kindest regards to Paula, Leo and wife as well as both sons

Berta

Undated Letter

From Salo:

Since the card sent from Ellis Island on January 16, we haven't received anything from you.[19] I hope that your trial time in Kessegarten went well and you are already on your way to NY or somewhere else in America.

Immediately after receiving your card we sent a long family letter which we hope you have already received. We can never be sure, we send everything to the address of Jan Schreiber.

Here everything is more or less like it used to be; the family stays healthy. Mother and your sisters always wait with nostalgia for your letters. In times like these, it really means a lot.

Business still exists under an Aryan leadership. We are not better or worse off than thousands of others in similar situations and relationships. But we can come to work, while many other business owners lost everything and cannot even enter their old locales. That's so to say a plus for us. There is very little being done though. Henek is in Boryslaw.

---

[19] This letter was presumably sent shortly after those of February 12–13, 1940, earlier in the chapter, that were sent in response to the first news from Joseph from New York.

Hopefully you have received other letters from us. We can never know and we feel helpless in this aspect. We have to patiently bear all the good as well as bad.

We are very curious about your destiny, please send us news.

I greet you warmly and wait for good news from you. Lots of hugs.

Salo

From Mania:

Dear brother,

I would like to ask you countless questions, but not this time. I am just asking you to write often, it's going to be the only pleasure for us in these difficult times. Let me reassure you that up till now we don't suffer any hunger. Dola used to live with me, but now she has moved to a studio apartment. It would be great if you received all the letters where I described everything.

Stay well and happy.

Mania

March 4, 1940

From Berta:

Dear Mr. Schreiber!

Please excuse me for turning to you, but I do not know my son's address, as he has not yet written to me. I am very concerned about him. And so I am enlisting your kindness and hoping that you will answer my letter right away. Thank you in advance. Yours truly, B. Holländer.

Should Józiu read the letter, I ask him to write to me himself and give me his exact address, and I will write him a long letter. I send kisses to both. Lusia can also write me a few lines. I will be very happy if she is content.

Your Mother

From Dola:

To Mr. Schreiber –

When I signed up on an emigration list at the American Consulate, I wrote your name as one of my relatives in the US. It doesn't oblige you to anything of course, and it may be to my advantage. I also wrote the name of the cousin Hollander and my brother.

Kisses for him and Lusia.

Dola

P.S. We are in possession of a postcard of 16.I. [January 16] of this year from Ellis Island. We wrote a detailed letter in reply.

March 16, 1940

Letter from Joseph Hollander to Dr. Samuel Spann, a lawyer in Haifa

I am a brother-in-law of Dawid Wimisner from Kraków (Gertudy Street 7) and I am writing on his behalf.

I left Poland right before the war, and I have been in New York for a few weeks now.

I keep receiving letters from my sister and my brother-in-law from Kraków, and from the content, I can easily guess that the situation over there is terrible. I have to do absolutely everything in order to help them to leave.

I have an opportunity to arrange their emigration to Cuba or Mexico. It will require a very significant amount of money. I also have to purchase four ship's tickets (my sister has two daughters).

I know from my brother-in-law that he gave you 'Power of Attorney' to collect the money he had in the Chankin Society from the land he bought from them. My brother-in-law also informed me that this money was due to be paid by the end of June or in the beginning of July last year.

Could you please let me know what amount of my brother-in-law's money you have at your disposition at this point for my brother-in-law so I have an idea what I can do. According to him you shouldn't have any trouble getting a permit for passing this money to me. He claims that the English government in England doesn't cause any problems regarding the sending of money to Polish citizens if one can prove that the money belongs to them. This you can easily prove. I don't believe that you would encounter any difficulties with that from the Palestinian officials.

Please send me as soon as possible all the necessary information about the amount of money my sister Klara and her husband can dispose of. I am in a rush since I know that recently some changes were introduced due to the division of the Polish Bank.

I don't believe I have to stress that the life of this family depends on how soon this matter can be solved. Knowing you from Poland I have no doubts that you will do everything in order to help me to save my sister and her family.

I am awaiting your response with impatience since the situation is burning and any delay may be catastrophic.

April 8, 1940

From Salo:

My dear ones!

We keep hearing that you are already in NY but we don't have any news directly from you, we only got one postcard from Ellis Island. We are waiting for news as if for salvation. We don't understand why we haven't heard from you for so long. I already wrote several letters. Please write soon. If it is not too expensive, please send a telegram.

We all are well.

Salo

From Berta:

Today I turn 74; I am not lucky enough to have all my loved ones near me today. You are not here. But everybody was especially warm this year; even Dawid behaved nicely. I know it will make you happy therefore I am writing this to you.

My dear child, can I still hope to take you in my arms? I live only with this hope to see you again.

Every day I believe that at least I will have some mail from you but unfortunately nothing comes. I wrote a letter to Mr. Schreiber asking him to write something about you to us.

I am, thank God, healthy. Please greet everybody from me. I hope to get a letter from you really soon.

Your old mother

From Klara:

My dear!

During our land exploring journey we lost most of our belongings but may this be our only sacrifice. I thank God that we are all together and we all help each other as much as we can. We all work and this is good since we don't have too much time to think, and time runs quickly. I don't have to write you that your letters are our joy, but we don't get too many of them. Are we going to see each other? Write me if it is possible.

Warm greetings from Dawid and the kids.

I wish you luck and send lots of love,

Klara

Berta again:

Beloved Son,

Since I know for certain that the letter will come to you, I will make you aware that Jahrzeit[20] is on May 16. But should the letter come too late, be calm because I will have Kaddish said and will light the candle. Just one more thing, dear child, why don't you write to Vienna so that Adele will send to us, as well as Bula.[21]

From Dola:

Accidentally, I learned that you are already in NY. Ms. W. wrote to her aunt that she met Lusia on the street. Thank God for that! We got one card from Aniela where she tells us that you couldn't go to Lisbon and are being held in the harbor of NY.

Don't worry about us, we are healthy and have enough to eat. I believe that we will survive. Henek is still with his relatives, the last message I received was in January. In the New Year my business does not enjoy much prosperity. Salo is doing well as a clerk. I rent a small room where I live now. I learn English; I signed up for lessons. And I cut fabric if there is anything to cut. And I wait. I must start from scratch with a single pot, not to mention the furniture.

Everybody is asking about you, everybody admires and envies you. We keep waiting for the news from you. The last card was from Ellis Island.

I wish you luck from the bottom of my heart.

Dola

From Mania:

My dear,

I don't want to repeat all the same again; just letting you know that I did write to you several times, and reported about closing the office and

---

[20] The anniversary of the death of Berta's husband and Joseph's father.

[21] This is the only reference in the letters to Bula, who is otherwise unknown.

other things. But maybe you already have our letters? May God help at least you and make you be the lucky one. There is not a single hour when I wouldn't think of you. I know you didn't forget us. Stay well and I wish you luck.

Mania

P.S. Greetings for Janek.

April 10, 1940

Postcard reply from the Haifa lawyer, Spann

Dear Doctor Holländer,

Replying to your letter from March 16, 1940, which I just received, I rush to inform you that according to your brother-in-law's wish I sent the whole amount (253,230.00 zl) to Rosner and Son in London.... As a matter of fact, there are difficulties in getting asylum here. Best regards, Spann

May 1, 1940

From Berta:

Beloved only Son,

Although I have written you a long letter, I delivered it to your mother-in-law since she had the opportunity to give it to a woman to take with her. I hope you will receive it. It was written on April 29. Adele sent me the postcard you wrote to her, and she told me you have plans to travel to Mexico. Please write me.

On April 28, Mr. Mirisch was here, and he had received a letter from his daughter-in-law. She wrote that you are living in a house. When I received your letter, I was at their house.[22]

Dear son, what kind of boy did you take with you? Out of curiosity, I am asking you who the boy is. Beloved child, tell me if you have any business, write me any details. What is Lusia doing? Is it possible that I will still see the two of you? I had a lot to write, but words fail me. I am not able to put everything on paper. I just want to hear good things

---

[22] This reference to "your letter" is unclear because all the other letters indicate they have not in fact received any letter from Joseph since the January 16 postcard from Ellis Island.

from you. Since I know where you are, I am relieved. Since you are with family, I would like to believe you are close to the ones from Vienna. I close with affectionate kisses for you both. Your Mother Berta

Dear Józiu,

I am adding a few lines to Paula since you are corresponding with her. Dear Paula,[23]

Adele writes me that you are not feeling well. What is the reason? I think you should be very content since you and your dear child are together. Is the work you are doing to blame? Be cheerful and happy, you can calmly move about. How much we all would like to be there. Write me a few lines when you have time, you know how much I always liked having a letter from you. I do not have much to write about myself. Affectionate kisses for you and your son. Please give Leo and his family my kindest regards. I remain your Aunt Berta.

From Klara:

My dears. Because I have no space, I am just writing you very warm greetings, also from Dawid. Klara.

From Salo:

My dear ones!

A few days ago a detailed letter was sent to you by private mail in which I communicated everything of importance. I will therefore now limit myself to only a few lines and wish you both the best one can imagine for your new path in life. Stay well. Kind regards,

Your

Salo

From Mania:

My dears! We also sent a letter to you through Adele, upon which Adele brought to our attention that we should write in German because of the censor. Very hearty greetings and kisses and best wishes for the future.

Mania

[23] Paula (abandoned by her husband and trying to raise a difficult son) and Leo (married with one child) are cousins of Joseph living in New York.

From Dola:

Dear Jóizu! I am doing as well as I can, but unfortunately with every day one becomes more nervous. I am happy to know you are there. Much luck. Greet Lusia.
Dola

May 5, 1940

From Dola:

Dear Brother. We received your telegram on the 4th and will act accordingly. We have learned that you have taken the Spitzman son with you. Mrs. Spitzman has asked that I visit. Her husband left together with Henek. We are curious whether you have your things with you. A few days ago I sent off a family letter by express. Greet Lusia. I wish you much good fortune on your birthday. Greetings
Dola

From Berta:

Dear Children
I am in a hurry to let you know that on May 4 we received your telegram, which we have awaited with longing, which put you to expense, and was for us a treasure. We are already writing to you every week, we even wanted to write you on Sunday. Perhaps you will receive our letter on your birthday, so, dear son, we all wish you a happy sojourn and the best of health, so that I may yet experience joy from you. Since Lusia also has her birthday around this time, I also wish for her all the best and that you should be happy together. My dear only one, I have nothing to write you about me except that I am well, so I close with affectionate kisses to you both. Your mother.
Greetings to Paula, Leo, son and family.
Dear child, since I have a sister in New York and she has four married daughters, perhaps it is possible for you by means of radio to learn where she is. The sister's name is Rosa Kohn, maiden name Weiss. A woman visited you who brought us greetings from her. Maybe you will recall that one daughter is a milliner. Maybe by chance someone will contact you. Try to find out for us.

From Klara:

Dear Joizu! I don't have much to write you. The main thing is that we are all healthy. Feliks from your office lived with us in Debnik and often helps us.[24] He sends his regards. Heartfelt greetings to you and Lusia. Klara

From Mania:

Knowing you I am sure you wouldn't feel hurt if I hadn't congratulated you on your birthday. I am not sure if this letter will reach you in time anyway.

But you know that my thoughts are always with you. My dearest brother I wish that it were possible to see you and your Lusia soon so I can express directly all my feelings to you, my very dear brother. Mania

May 16, 1940

From Mania:

Dearest brother,

Today is May 16, and we received two cards of February 23 and March 6 from you. Dear Brother, today we celebrated the anniversary of the death of our Dear Father. May God allow us to celebrate the next one together. It's awful that you are not getting our letters. We do write every week. Last week we wrote a letter via Vienna, this week directly to you. I will look for the marriage certificate. It took us half an hour to look through everything that was in the office. I have Lusia's certificates at my place. Dearest Józiu I could ask you so many questions but I know that you won't answer me. So just write if you both are healthy and well after such long trip? How do you support yourselves? Does Janek support you? We struggle but it's our destiny as it seems. Maybe we will survive somehow. Dear Mother is well; even if we try hard we cannot replace you for her. Write postcards, maybe they will arrive faster? Stay well, I wish you lots of luck. Hundreds of kisses.

[24] Feliks Palaszek, a Catholic Pole and Joseph's former business associate in Cracow.

From Salo:

My dears,

We just received your two cards of February 23 and March 6, and a few minutes ago Klara brought us your letter of February 28. So as you see we must reckon with a travel time of 8 to 10 weeks and that our letters to you must take just as long. We can't do anything about this. We do write every week. I hope that this card will still find you in New York. Mother and the rest of the family are healthy so please do not worry. We also hope that you will be fine after all the struggles you went through. We will look for the required papers, and if we don't find them we will request duplicates. We will send them to you as soon as we possibly can. Greetings from all of us to both of you.

Salo

May 16, 1940

From Berta:

Dear only Son,

We received your dear letter on May 16. I do not know if I should be happy or if I should think about it again, since you are leaving your present residence. I was so happy that you are together with the Vienna children, and now you are saying goodbye and traveling so far. But I hope you have given the matter a lot of thought before deciding to leave. May the Almighty grant that you meet with only the best. I am informing you as I let you know in a letter to you that Jahrzeit was on May 16. I did not know if you received the letter, so I had Kaddish said. When we came home from the cemetery, we received your letter, after waiting a long time to hear from you. Dear child, you do not need to be concerned about my illness, since I have been very well for a long time, and as the saying goes, better to have been sick than to have been rich. For this reason, dear child, be reassured about me, I am not alone. Malcia and Dola are here every day. So my sweet son my thoughts are always with you. Please be entirely reassured and do not think about me, everything will be fine. I close with affectionate kisses for you as well as for my dear daughter-in-law. I was at the Mirisches' and will go there again and deliver greetings. I would like to write to you all day long, I believe I am talking with you. I don't know what words I can say to you. I wish you much happiness and health.

Your Mother,

Berta

From Genka:

Dearest Uncle,

I think that Grandma didn't leave much to write for us but I can assure you that we are doing well. Like we used to be, we are strong, physically and mentally.

Kisses for both of you.

Genka

From Klara:

My dear ones,

I see from your letters that you worry about us too much. I wrote you in many letters that we do have enough to eat, and that we are healthy. You know that dear Mother was sick but you don't need to be surprised by this. Now we can write that we were very worried. At first Dr. Leinkram came but then I took Dr. Wasserberg. She went to see her everyday. I did everything I could and now she is well again.

Dawid has a very good boss, goes to the store every day, and gets some income. Genka works there as well. Dawid got back his old energy. You know him well and you know how he likes taking care of everybody. We are not lacking anything.

My dear ones can you stay over there? We were already so happy. Don't you want to stay? Anyway wherever you'll be, whatever you'll do, have lots of luck.

I wish you that from the bottom of my heart.

Klara

From Dawid:

Dear Józek,

Thanks for the news. God help us to share only good news. I work in the store.

Greetings to both of you, and don't forget us.

Dawid

From Dola:

Dear Józiu,

Because Salo wants to write more, I need to restrict myself. Henek is still at his mother. I live in a rented room and wait for the end of this war. I eat dinners at Klara's. She also took two children of refugees who come for dinners. We do have some advantages from your Feliks and Tadeusz.[25] If I knew that I could be back with my family whenever I wanted to I would have gone to the Aunt Rózia. I am sure I would find work over there. The kids of Kaufmann are there and they write good letters. Be well and happy. Greetings to Lusia.

Dola

From Salo:

My dear Józiu,

Affirming your airmail letter of April 17, we were looking for the marriage certificate among the papers here, but unfortunately we didn't find it. We will ask for a duplicate and send it to you as soon as we can by airmail to Janek's address. We were at your mother-in-law's. She was very touched by the letter from Lusia. It's good that she is so busy with the business and doesn't have much time to think. We also talked a lot with Franka, your sister-in-law. She is doing well, has her own department in the business, so in this aspect it's going quite well. She misses her kids and her husband very much, which is very understandable. Henek is away for 6 months already, Dawid is back with his family for 7 months. In the factory I am alone. Franka asks you to send an affidavit to Warsaw. My previous postcard is hopefully already in your possession. Warm greetings and do not worry about us.

Salo

Greetings from Mania

[25] Probably Tadeusz Pankiewicz, the pharmacist, who is referred to later (see the letter of Mania to Joseph, May 5, 1941). As the only Pole operating a business in the ghetto (his pharmacy), he was in a position to observe events at close range and write one of the most important postwar eyewitness memoirs of the Cracow ghetto.

May 23, 1940

From Salo:

My dear,

We went through all the papers we have at home, but unfortunately we didn't find the requested documents. We asked to make copies and we will send them by official way on May 25 or 27 to the address of J. Everything in duplicate because you will need it that way.

Our last letters will reach you probably faster than this card although one cannot know, sometimes we get your letters after 10 weeks, and sometimes already after 4 weeks.

In your first card of February 2, you mentioned that Leo visited you in your office. What do you think of that?

Mania is not at home right now; please accept our best greetings and wishes that whatever you undertake will bring only prosperity and happiness. At home everything is well in respect to our physical well-being. The whole family sends love.

Salo

[2]

Separation Anxiety
May–August 1940

The threat of expulsion was the most serious challenge confronting the Jews of Cracow in 1940. The trouble began in October 1939, when the Nazis appointed Hans Frank to the post of governor general of occupied Poland's General Government (*General Guberniya*). Believing that Cracow was "an old German city," Frank made the city the territorial capital.[1] He felt, however, that Cracow's large Jewish population was unbecoming of a Reich capital.[2] Consequently, in the spring of 1940, Frank began the "dejewification" process of Cracow, mandating that no more than 10,000 Jews could remain in the city.[3] On May 18, 1940, the Nazis issued a decree giving the Jews three months to "voluntarily" leave Cracow and move elsewhere within the territory. As an incentive, the Nazis announced that those who left by August 15 would be allowed to take all their possessions. The Jews who remained at the deadline risked expulsion and would only be allowed to leave with 25 kilograms of baggage per person.[4]

Although thousands of Jews left Cracow "voluntarily," there were far more than 10,000 Jews remaining in the city on August 15. In accordance with his threats, Frank established a joint Jewish–German eviction committee, which was responsible for expelling Jews from Cracow. The committee was authorized to issue permits, or "postponement documents," for Jews to stay in the city. To Frank's dismay, the

---

[1] Eugeniusz Duda, *The Jews of Cracow*, trans. Ewa Basiura (Cracow: Argona-Jordan Bookstore, 1999), 62.
[2] Gustavo Corni, *Hitler's Ghettos: Voices from a Beleaguered Society 1939–1944*, trans. Nicola Rudge Iannelli (London: Arnold, 2002), 29.
[3] Duda, *The Jews of Cracow*, 62.   [4] Duda, *The Jews of Cracow*, 62.

number of permits that were issued far exceeded what he considered desirable.[5] Nevertheless, more than 3,700 Jews were forced to leave Cracow in 1940.[6]

The family informed Joseph about the "dejewification" directive in the early summer. Yet, the expulsion crisis did not become a dominant topic until late July (ironically, just when they learned that Joseph no longer faced deportation to Mexico). Considering that it took weeks for a letter from Cracow to reach New York, it seems peculiar that the family refrained from discussing the German edict in any detail with Joseph until the deadline was merely weeks away. Perhaps the family did not take the German threat seriously. To that effect, on July 28, Dola remarked that "there are still some optimists who think that Jews from Kraków will be able to stay."[7] With two weeks remaining until Frank's August 15 deadline, however, she acknowledged that "the nightmare of deportation looks into our eyes."

Mania refused to leave Cracow voluntarily. But, true to form, she prepared for the worst. On August 9, she informed Joseph: "I sold the bedroom [furniture] in order to have less things that I will take with me." Explaining Frank's "incentive" for Jews to leave of their own accord, Mania wrote that "whoever leaves voluntarily can take his possessions." She ended her letter by stating: "Try not to worry about us. Maybe God won't forget those who faithfully believe in Him."[8] Throughout the crisis, the family continued to hope that God would ensure their safety, even if they were forced to leave Cracow. "If there is a break in our correspondence please don't worry," wrote Klara in late July. "Just wait until we let you know where we are. Maybe God will help us stay. But it is war, we live like on a volcano and an order is an order. Anyway," she asserted confidently, "God won't abandon us. We are in good spirit!"[9]

As the deadline ominously approached, Salo and Dawid were notified that they would be allowed to remain in Cracow with their families. On August 10, Dola informed Joseph that "Salo's and Dawid's cases were reconsidered and they can stay."[10] Dola, however, realized that she would most likely be expelled from the city. She wrote: "I am going through

[5] Duda, *The Jews of Cracow*, 62.   [6] Corni, *Hitler's Ghettos*, 29.
[7] Dola to Joseph, July 28, 1940.   [8] Mania to Joseph, August 9, 1940.
[9] Klara to Joseph, July 28, 1940.   [10] Dola to Joseph, August 10, 1940.

awful times connected with deportations. . . . Because the elderly 70 and up can stay I am trying to be considered with Dear Mother, who is 74 and needs a caretaker." "Dear Mother" was not convinced that the Nazis would be sympathetic to the needs of the Jewish elderly. "Be concerned for Dola," wrote Berta, "as she will be the first one to go. . . . I know that it may be wrong for me to write you such a thing, but a drowning person grabs at a straw to save himself, my heart is full, my eyes fill with tears, we are in front of water."[11] Yet, Dola somehow maintained her positive mind-set, even facing the prospect of being forcibly separated from her family. She exclaimed: "If I don't get the permit, I will be forced to go into the world all by myself, into the unknown. I will manage but everybody here is really worried."[12]

The family had ample reason to worry in general and about Dola in particular. "In these days," wrote Klara on August 9, "decisions will be made who can stay and who must leave. Many of our friends had to go. I pray to God that we won't be separated. . . . Our lives are being decided in these days. I ask God to help us to be together."[13] Under such duress, even Klara seemed to lose her faith. She asked: "When will God send us the desired peace? Those who are alive often envy the dead ones now." Mustering her strength, Klara reassured Joseph that "man is stronger than he seems, and lives with the hope that it will be better." She hesitantly concluded that "it will be better next year. I am praying for that. It seems we sinned really much."[14]

In the end, the Jewish–German eviction committee permitted Dola to stay in Cracow and care for her mother. But after witnessing his neighbors stripped of their property and deported, Salo realized that the Germans would not be satisfied with simply imposing racial divides on the city. He knew that, one way or another, the Germans wanted to rid their territory of Jews. "As it seems now," wrote Salo on August 22, 1940, "sooner or later all the Jews will be forced out of here." Sensing that greater trouble lay ahead in the future, he stated: "Many people register themselves for the emigration overseas. In order not to blame ourselves later we are thinking about doing the same."[15] Genka, in contrast,

[11] Berta to Joseph, August 16, 1940.
[12] Dola to Joseph, August 10, 1940.
[13] Klara to Joseph, August 9, 1940.
[14] Klara to Joseph, August 9, 1940.
[15] Salo to Joseph, August 22, 1940.

emerged from the expulsion crisis believing that the family had dodged the bullet. Convinced the worst was now behind them, she confidently boasted to her uncle: "We are strong, together, mobilized, and ready for everything."[16]

May 25, 1940

From Mania:

Dearest, most beloved Brother,

I am writing this letter to the address of Paula for two reasons: first I don't want Lusia to criticize my orthography and second because of what I am going to write. Maybe it's not so important for you at all, but I have to inform you about this anyway. It's about the secret that was told Mr. W. from Katowice. The circumstances forced me to reveal it to Salo. I was also forced to lie to him that you gave me permission to tell it to Dola if necessary. Now as I am writing this letter there is no need for that. I can still wait but you never know. . . . So please don't be angry with me but write to me about that, okay?

Adele wrote that Lusia works. What kind of job does she have? If I know you well, you probably suffer because of that since you cannot support her totally and fulfill all her wishes.

Dola wrote to you that if she had freedom to be back with us at any time she would leave.[17] She fools herself that over there she would find a job. That's wrong. She is not made for working. She doesn't have a profession or qualifications; and it's difficult to start something new when you are 40 years old. She wrote to you that she is learning how to cut fabric for shirts but she started it as everything else. I do not blame her, she had honest enthusiasm but there is nothing to do at this time. There is simply no work. It was a private job, so Dola did it with the help of Mrs. W. It is so. She has an idea about that but not much more. If she had enough practice, maybe she would learn but there is nothing to do. At this point she wouldn't be able to cut fabric for a shirt. The worst is that dear Mother worries about her so much. She has little news

---

[16] Genka to Joseph, August 28, 1940.

[17] This is a reference of Dola's continued toying with the idea of going over to the Soviet zone, where her husband Henek lived. In reality, this was no longer possible.

from Henek, he writes only about himself. He doesn't even ask how she is doing and how she supports herself. She learned from somebody that he is doing very well over there.

I often visit your mother-in-law. She is doing well, and the business prospers well. She has a clothing store on the same street where Anda Brone had her fashion business.

We write every week. Stay well, I wish you luck.

Mania

May 26, 1940

From Berta:

Much-loved Children!

I would not like to neglect writing you since I know how much it means to you to have news of us. Now I will tell you which letters we have received from you. This week those from February 2, 19, and 20 all arrived at the same time. So I hope that our letters also get to you, since we write you every Sunday. Yesterday I was at your mother-in-law's with Malcia. She is in good health. I was also at the Mirisches'. I did not see the man at the house, only the parents, everything is all right with them. Dear son, when do you think you will travel again? Or have you already left, where my letter can be forwarded to you. I am well, thank God, I wish to hear good news from you. Otherwise I have nothing to write except I kiss you affectionately and [want] to have letters often so that I can read a lot.

Your Mother,

Berta

From Klara:

My dearest,

Now you probably get our letters regularly, we do send them every week.

This old aunt of ours is horrible. Thank God you don't know her personally. She was always impossible, but now one has to be very strong minded around her, in order to tolerate her demands. I feel sorry for the people she lives with. Thank God that she doesn't visit you. I hope she won't come to you. It's too far away and she is too old for that, she cannot walk so far.[18]

Here everything is all right.

Klara

Greetings from Genka and Lusia, and Dawid. Dola sends kisses.

From Mania:

I cannot really write about anything because before this will reach you it's not going to be true anymore. We do have very warm days but we sit at home, since nobody likes to walk in Kraków anymore. Just to the post office and back.

Lots of luck. I did write to Paula.

Right now the mailman brought two cards from April 4 for us. Hundreds of thanks!

Mania

May 30, 1940

From Salo to Leo Holländer (Joseph's Cousin)

Dear Mr. Holländer,

Yesterday I received a letter from my brother-in-law in which he communicates that his departure to Mexico will probably take place by the end of this month. Two weeks ago he asked me to send him his marriage certificate that he will need in Mexico. Because we were unable to locate it, I made duplicates and sent them to the address of Jan Schreiber, 320 Central Park West.

Everything seemed to be okay but Jan Schreiber as my brother tells me has now left New York and will spend the summer somewhere else. The documents didn't reach him, and it is impossible to track them down at this point. Since I don't know what else I could possibly do I am asking you to be so kind and try to take care of this matter. From here I cannot do anything more. I doubt if this letter will reach you on time.

[18] "This old aunt" is clearly Klara's coded reference to Nazi Germany. Her use of coded language in this manner shows that she was aware of the possibility of censorship and the need to avoid any overt reference to, much less discussion of, political matters.

I thank you in advance. I send warm greetings to you and your wife.
Yours truly,
Salo N.
Time has unfortunately caused all family ties and affiliations to be torn
apart, the one closest to us is also gone, and when will there be a reunion?

From Mania:

Dear Leo,
Hopefully you still remember me although you wouldn't probably
recognize me any more. I still have red hair.
I wish you all the best. Please greet your family from me.
Mania

From Salo:

Dear Józiu,
I was just about to send the letter when I just received your letter from
May 17, quite unprecedented that it came in only 12 days! First of all I
ask you in my own and Mania's name not to send anything any more. I am
giving you my word that we have everything that we need to sustain our
well-being. The packages are not reaching us anyway. It's questionable if
they will arrive at all. Also for other reasons I don't think it's a good idea
to keep sending packages and in this quantity. So please for the moment
do not send anything anymore: neither to us or to anybody else.
    We sent a letter last week, we attached a letter from your mother-in-
law, who is doing quite well. She misses you both of course, but otherwise
she is okay. Your documents, as already noted, were sent on Monday,
May 27 to the address of Janek. All the other questions were already
answered by Dola, Mania and the Dear Mother.
Warm greetings to you and Lusia.
Salo

From Dola:

Dearest, most treasured Brother,
I was very happy receiving your postcard from April 4. Always when
we get news from you we have a celebration here.
    You are right that I need to learn something, some profession, but
what could it be? I don't know how to sew, and I don't have enough
patience to do many things with my restless spirit. I am still learning the
language, and intend to attend a workshop on making leather clothing.

I want to learn something which will help me survive over there, but I have to have a convenient job in the heavy traffic that we do have here now. I am learning how to cut and sew men's clothes; I work with our tailor here.

I had the last news from Henek on February 7.

I had to move out from Mania. It was not a big deal for me. It took me half an hour to pack my clothes, I just had a few dresses and some other clothes. I live in a furnished room, and feel well there. May God help me to be able to pay for this room for some time. I do not suffer hunger and I am healthy. That must be enough for one. I only feel sad in the evenings, when I have to sit all by myself, while I used to go to the last show in the movies. I started a "washing clinic" but don't have much success yet. Maybe with time it will improve.

My dearest, I will survive until we will be together again, that keeps me here, otherwise I would be far away. I don't want to leave the family. I have only one prayer now, wherever you go, whatever you do, may the lucky star always be above your head.

Since I had not yet sent the letter and Mania delivered your letter number 17, I will tell you that up until today we have received nothing, and we ask you, at least for the time being – nothing more at all – we have... [illegible] and, secondly, we could have guests, and these days guests are unwelcome. Are you not angry that I gave Henek's family your address? What kind of people are the Americans? If I had to emigrate, then without... [illegible].

Dola

Additional Note from Adele:

13/6 Also from me heartfelt greetings
Your Adele
For my dear little sister, many greetings and kisses
Received your letter No. 18 today.

June 2, 1940

From Berta:

Dear only Son,
You are my treasure and lucky star. When I get up and go to bed, my thoughts are of you. Why should I not be happy to have such a child, and

I am proud of you. I would like to know only that you are happy, what you want is the important thing. You deserve to be happy and content. How happy I am to read your sweet lines. I cannot so quickly part from your dear letters. I always carry them with me, and when I am anxious, I reach for your letters. Then I imagine that you came to us with your dear stories that we had all forgotten. Dear good child, this week we again received 3 cards and 2 letters all at once.

One was sent to us by Adele, in which you write that you have sent things to us. That was not necessary, we have everything, but I thank you, and do not send more until you have a letter from us. Until now we have not received what was sent. I was at your mother-in-law's. In the last letter, a letter to you both was included. She is very well. She is anxious without the two of you, just like me, today I will go to see her, then I will write you. We wanted to send something to Adele, unfortunately it is not possible. I am sorry for her that she was alone, there is just one thing. She has a good, hardworking husband, she can feel happy with him. You will surely have a letter from Dola before you have my letter. Since I do not have something to write, I will close with affectionate kisses for you and also for dear Lusia. Kindest regards to Leo together with his wife and son, also to Paula and son.

Your Mother,
Berta

From Klara:

My dear!

I had a dream that you came and tears of joy were floating down my cheeks. God allows that we will see each other in happiness.

Here are the birth dates.[19] David 8/XI 1890 in Tarnow. Klara 27/IX 1893 in Wieden. Eugenia 28/III 1921 in Kraków. Dola[20] 19/V 1924 in Kraków.

I wouldn't like Henek to learn your address. When he was leaving he took exactly to the penny his part, and cashes it where he is now.

Greetings,
Klara

---

[19] Presumably this is in response to a request from Joseph and would indicate his first attempt to seek immigration papers for the family.

[20] Lusia Wimisner's legal surname.

From Dawid:

Dear brother-in-law,

As you wished, I have spoken with the sister and promised my help. At the moment she does not need anything as she has income from the house. She and the child are doing well. Klara gave the dates we are responsible for all Kraków? I thank you very much for thinking of us and I hope you will succeed in taking care of that for us. Lusia and Genia ... [illegible sentence].

Greetings to you and your wife.

Most cordially, Dawid

From Genka:

My dear,

You asked how am I doing after the surgery. Very well. After two weeks I could already play football. I only have an ugly scar but it doesn't matter. I usually don't walk around with this part of the body exposed. We have a beautiful summer but I don't go to the swimming pool for obvious reasons.[21]

Kisses for both of you,

Genka

June 16, 1940

From Berta:

My dear beloved Children!

Today I am just writing a card, since I wanted to let you know that Klarcia[22] had received the package you sent, for which she sincerely thanked you, only leave off further shipments, we have everything. But Malcia did not receive her package yet, she has also had everything up until now. Keep trying, we are expecting good news from you. Last week I sent you a letter by Adele, I have not had a letter from you for a long time. Please write, it is my joy. A thousand kisses to you from me and from everyone.

Your mother Berta

---

[21] The "obvious reason" is that Jews were forbidden from swimming in public pools.

[22] Berta's nickname of endearment for Klara.

From Dola:

Dear Brother,

My mending business is getting better. There is something out of it every day. I only suffer from a constant congestion I have pus in my head. I am taking care of that. Maybe when you receive this card I will be okay again. Henek calls me to come to him. But it is impossible.

Kisses,
Dola

Undated Letter

From Dola:

Dearest Józiu,

I answered you for the card addressed to me. Hopefully you have already received it. I received two cards from Henek (since February) both in very different moods. In March a really sad one, in May a very joyful one. He writes which I would expect the least that I should come to him. This is impossible since the commission[23] is gone, and I have for myself quite different hopes now. Only in the worst case, when I don't have a choice, I would do it.

We talked a lot about you on your birthday. The family keeps close together, and that gives us great comfort. There are days when I give up all my hopes but I always get them back somehow. May God give you a lot, lots of happiness dear brother.

Kisses for you and Lusia,
Your Dola

June 23, 1940

From Berta:

Dear beloved Children

I do not have much to write since everyone is going to write you. We received the May 29 letter from Adele, and I am happy that you are

[23] The "commission" refers to those in charge of administering the population exchange agreed on between Nazi Germany and the Soviet Union, whereby ethnic Germans could be repatriated from Soviet-occupied territories of Poland to the German zone and people with family or ancestral ties in the Soviet zone of occupied Poland could be repatriated eastward from the German zone.

doing well. I wish always to hear only good news from you. Dear child, I am enclosing a letter for you from Feliks. He came to see us just as I was reading your letter. He was very happy that you are thinking about him, and he showed all of Debnik that he had gotten a letter from you. Because I will write only a few more lines, it will be that I am happy that you will take pains to look up my sister, Rosa Kohn, maiden name Weiss, born in Chrzanow. I am closing with

Thousands of kisses for you both.

Your Mother,

Berta

From Klara:

I am waiting for good news from Mexico. You travel so much, probably much more than you would wish. I hope that a peaceful future will await you in Mexico. Be careful with other people, not everybody has your character. Once more I am sending you our birth dates. Lots of warm greetings.

Klara

Kisses from Lusia and Genia

From Mania:

I already sent a card with birthday's wishes for both of you but allow me to do it once more. Please accept the most sincere wishes of happiness, good health and the very best for both of you. May all your plans for the future come true.

Kisses,

Mania

From Klara:

My loved ones!

Thanks for the package, we shared it in a fair way since Mania hasn't gotten anything yet. But as I already wrote, don't send us anything. I won't be ashamed to ask you when I have to. Thank God we have everything we need. We live from day to day, waiting for the end of the war.

Greetings,

Klara

From Dawid:

My dear,

I sent the dates, hopefully you have already received them. Hopefully you have heard from Rosner by now. Otherwise nothing new. We are well and send warm greetings.

Dawid

From Genka and Lusia:

Dear relatives in America!

Thanks for remembering my birthday, it's really nice of you! Do people speak English or Spanish in Mexico? I am so proud of you! Everybody envies me that I have relatives in America. And what relatives they are!

I need to end since there is no space left. I kiss both of you.

Genka and Lusia

From Salo:

My dears,

I attach a few lines, but this time I have nothing personal to add, the same old story.

Have you already received the marriage certificates? They should have arrived by now. When do you think you will start your travel to Mexico. Is there no possibility to stay in New York? I wish both of you all the best. Make us happy with good news about yourselves.

Your Salo

From Dola:

Dearest Brother,

I am starting with the news about my "patching up" business which prospers quite well (the shirts' repair clinic). I know that hearing this will make you happy. Everyday I have new "patients." I guess I had an idea that would be good enough even for America. I don't have any time left, and that's good. Staying busy is the best one can do now. Unfortunately I have problems with my health. From having a constant cold I have pus in my head. I attend a clinic and am being taken care of by Klassa himself. I received good treatment, puncture and short wave treatment.

I have to be at the doctor's for a few hours every day. So I must neglect my work for a while.

I have news from Henek. He invites me and then again he asks how I would like it if he came here. He wrote to his brothers. I have to discretely admit it to you, with him here it would be harder for me. It would be best if he stayed where he is. I don't advise him [to do] anything. I don't want to take this responsibility.

Is going to you possible during the war?

How is your health? You complained sometimes about an earache, no wonder after all that you have been through. Please write me honestly how you feel. If you want to whisper something into my ear, please do. Thoughts of you keep our spirits up, and we don't give up.

July 1, 1940

From Berta:

Dear only Son!

We received your last letter from Adele, and I cried when I read it, those were joyful tears. How happy I am when you write me that you are content. You, my everything, have earned it, you were always a provider for your parents and your sisters. The Almighty should reward you a thousand times over, I should only experience knowing that you are happy. You were good to everybody. Whoever talks about you, even though I do not know the people personally, they all say that you are a one hundred percent human being. Why should I not be proud of you, I wish only to have you healthy and well. I am sorry that we are separated from each other, but good news will have to make up for it. I hope to God that we will see each other in good health. Dearest, you write that I should go to Mirisch for help. I did go to see him, he gave me nothing. I do not need anything from him. He only told me when he will have a letter from his wife. He will just report [that]. The last time he had a letter was on June 16. So dear child, I need nothing, I have everything just as before. I had a pair of shoes made and am very pleased. I also got a dress from Dawid, they sewed it for me at home. What else can I write you, [except] that you can be completely at peace on my account and I will close with thousands of kisses.

Your Mother

Dearest Daughter-in-law,

You, my dear, are also the only daughter-in-law I have, so I will tell you that I was visiting your mother and gave her your letter to read. She was touched and filled with joy and told me that she will write you. With affectionate kisses,

Your Mother-in-law

Affectionate greetings to Leo and family and also to Paula and son . . . [illegible] letter I will write her . . .

From Genka:

Dearest Uncle,

You don't even know how much I would like to be with you. You remember me as a teenager, and now I have become a real clerk, but I am not happy. I don't go to the beach, or to the movies, I don't read and in general I do not feel alive.

Thank God, financially we are very well off but I would gladly leave all this for being with you. I hope it will happen sooner or later. Do you think that we will be happy one day? What I see is quite black.

Kisses,

Genka

From Lusia:

Dear Uncle from America!

I see thank God everything in bright colors; I feel good and comfortable in the world, I have enough joy of life for this whole highly respected family of ours.

But now seriously about my profession, I have all the papers ready. I got my exam which I passed very well. When I will have an opportunity I will look for some nice job. In the meantime I send you thousands of kisses and hugs.

Lusia

July 3, 1940

From Mania:

My dearest Brother,

I don't know where to start, should I thank you for a long beautiful letter or for the birthday wishes or for the package you sent? I thank for all of that. As you remember, I will turn half a century on July 19. What did I experience? Nothing and a lot. From my childhood I don't remember much. School years didn't leave nice memories, and I don't have anything to be grateful for (including my orthography).

Youth? Did I have it at all? I married being 20, didn't know anything about life and people, and a year after I already had a child. A child had a child. My parenting responsibilities took over, maybe it was better this way, I didn't have much time to think. Four years after my wedding day the war[24] started which affected me profoundly. After the war the problems with money started. It hasn't broken me though, because I had my hopes and support. Now this, too, disappeared forever. Only ever-lasting emptiness stayed. Sometimes I feel like somebody asked me to sing after my tongue was removed.

This is a summary of 50 years. I know my Dear Brother that you, despite your young age, went through a lot. And many times it hurt me really much that you didn't find a way to me. You thought I am stupid or you preferred to deal with all the difficulties by yourself. But I had for you, my dear boy, not only sisterly feelings but my eyes can also look deeply into your soul. I knew that the office job was not the only and entire reason for your nervous breakdown. We were close but very far from each other.

Okay, that's enough, and now as you say it: straight to the point.

Thank you for the package; it contained coffee, tea, oil which made me very happy but we can get everything here. Milk wasn't there but we can get fresh milk every day. The women bring it like they used to before the war.

Thousand of hugs and kisses.

Mania

From Klara:

My beloved!

We received your letter from June 13. We read this letter many times. Dawid was making fun of us and asking if we already know it by heart. May God give you both health and happiness. That will make us happy as well. You write that you feel so bad that you cannot help us. I assure

---

[24] Mania is referring here to the First World War.

you that we're lacking nothing and may God allow that it will stay like this till the end of the war.

Concerning Dola, I managed to get the idea about going to aunt Rózia out of her head. Last letter from Henek was very tender. It looks like he is not in the best shape. He also wrote that he would give a year of his life in order to know what Dawid is doing (I feel like laughing). When he was leaving he didn't even say goodbye to Mama or to Dawid, although he had enough time and opportunities to do so. The more I get to know people the more I treasure dogs.

Greetings to both of you, as well as to Paula and Leo.

Klara

From Dawid:

Dear Józiu,

I was very happy to get a message from you. You were very lucky and you are doing so well. May God keep us healthy and may we receive only good messages from you.

The address of Leo Kaufmann is 10 Gleason Street, Dorchester, Mass. USA

Greetings,

Dawid

July 7, 1940

From Berta:

Dear beloved Son!

Today I have nothing to write you, just to give you, my love, a sign that I am doing well, which I also want to hear from you both. You write that you have an apartment with a room and kitchen. Did you rent it furnished, or did you have to buy everything?

In the previous letter of July 1, I enclosed a letter from your mother-in-law. Otherwise for today I have nothing more to write you except affectionate kisses for you and also for you, dear Lusia.

Your Mother

From Klara:

Dear Józiu,

I am attaching a letter from Mrs. Raschbaum to the brother of her husband, who is a notary public. She already sent the birth dates. Her husband works on the rail in the Stanislawow area, and his son has a position in Lwow.[25] The other son attends music school and plays on the radio. But she suffers very much that she is separated from them. They are separated because of a sick mother. She comes to cry on my shoulder very often. Now she is more peaceful since she has good news from her relatives.

You write good things to us, too. Here, thank God, everything is well. Greetings to both of you.

Klara

Genka sends kisses via paper. Greetings from Dola.

From Berta (Again):

Dear Son,

A letter, since I have just received your letter of June 24, you surely knew that I would like to know everything you are doing and am very pleased that you are in this place and do not need to travel any farther. I consider myself fortunate to have such a child. I wish for you much success and blessing, that is my prayer to the Almighty. I close with thousands of kisses.

Your Mother,

I will enclose the picture in the next letter.

From Mania:

I have very little space so I just wish you all the luck of this world and also good vacation. I reassure you that I look well. I eat and drink for my future, because whatever I put into my stomach neither fire nor water will take away from me.

Warm greetings for both you and Lusia.

Mania

From Dola:

Dearest Józiu,

I am healthy again, I feel better after the puncture. It was necessary. Unfortunately I am very sensitive to cold. Mrs. Schreiber and Frania

---

[25] These are cities that were in the Soviet zone of occupied Poland between September 1939 and June 1941.

S. declared that they have no patience to write. Your mother-in-law is satisfied with the good news about you, and Frania keeps asking to send you greetings. Nevertheless, I will tell them that they can send every Sunday a letter to Klara and it will be included in our correspondence. We don't want dear Mother to walk to town, and I have no time to do it. At any rate, they know how to keep contact. Writing depends only on their desire.

Kisses.

Dola

Early July 1940

From Salo:

I am joining in with a few lines.[26] I really did not have anything to add this time, it's the same old story. Have your received the copies of the marriage certificate? They should have arrived by now. When do you plan to continue your trip to Mexico? Is there no possibility of remaining in New York?

I wish you both all the best and send warm regards. Cheer us with good news.

From Dola:

Your last letter made all of us weep from happiness. We were in euphoria. We hope you will be able to stay in New York, and won't have to wander any longer.

I needed to undergo some treatment, and feel much better now. I have enough money from my own business. Fashion business is out of the question now, everybody walks without hats.

When we know that you are happy we are happy, too.

Additional Note from Adele:

Best regards to Paula and Kurt from Adele.

---

[26] This letter must have been sent before mid-July, when they learn that Joseph can stay in New York and does not have to go to Mexico.

July 14–16, 1940

From Berta:

Dear beloved Child!

As I already once wrote you that I have nothing important to say, I am just writing you, dear child, to let you have a few lines and to let you know that I am doing well. My dear ones, I hope to hear good things from you.

Dear Daughter-in-law,

Dola was visiting your mother. She said that she had received a letter from you. I let your mother know that every Sunday she can enclose a letter with ours, so I will wait to mail the letter. I close my letter with affectionate kisses.

Always,

Your Mother

The kisses by paper, as I cannot do otherwise. Kindest regards to Leo and family also to Paula and son.

From Dola:

Dearest Brother:

Thank God that you don't have to wander anymore. Maybe in a few years you will become an American millionaire. You are young, everything is ahead of you. I am so touched that you think of me. I always had moral support from you, and I know nothing bad will happen to me as long as I have such a brother. But, My Love, if it happens that Mania stays, I will also stay with her and with Dear Mother. This is why I am here in the first place otherwise I would be far away now. I'll see how it's going to be later on. Up till now I can manage. The last news from Henek was probably from May. I am quite well now but the sea climate would be great for me! Dear Józiu, please do not send anything unless I ask.

I am as fat as I used to be, I am little embarrassed because of that, but who cares? I am so happy to have you over there despite my longings for you. Every time I pass your office my heart starts beating faster.

Your Dola

From Klara:

Your letters are like nectar for us. We get drunk on them. God give you strength for the new project. Here everything is as it was, for which I do thank God. Did you get our letter where I wrote our birth dates? I am curious if this gentleman visited you who was supposed to bring personal greeting from us directly to you? Photographs are unfortunately not accepted at the post office.

Greetings to both of you, also from Dawid and the kids.

Klara

From Mania:

The last letter we received was for Dear Mother, and we patiently wait for the next messages from you. Write if you can stay in New York? Wherever you'll be, I wish you always the best.

Here it is as it used to be and we are very happy because of that. Dear Józiu, don't you suffer because of the heat? Here is very hot, too. But I prefer that to the cold and am very afraid of winter. Maybe God will have mercy on us.

Stay well and happy.

Mania

From Salo:

We received your last letter of March 3 on July 15. Nr. 1 we received yesterday. We are very happy that you with your wife will be able to stay in New York, and we wish you lots of success and first of all lots of happiness.

Dear Mother was twice at Mürisch, Mürisch didn't come to Mother even once. For the Mother's inquiry Mürisch said that he didn't get any directions from his wife concerning mother, and so it is. Please don't let yourself to be fooled by Mrs. Mürisch, because Mother has nothing from him, and she also doesn't need anything. If you do something for Mrs. Mürisch make her pay you well, and do not give her any money, since as far as I know the Mürisch family, you won't see it again.

Warmest greetings my dear Józek, from both me and Mania to you and your Lusia. I wish you lots of fun on your summer vacation. Don't trouble yourself with the packages, good news will bring us more joy.

Greetings for the rest of the family (Leo, Paula).
Salo

Undated, Mid- to Late July 1940

From Salo:

Very dear, beloved Józek,[27]

Yesterday we received your two detailed letters along with a note from Paula of June 13. They came from Vienna. They had a tremendously healing effect on us, added spirit to our hearts, and we all felt filled with new kind of energy. Especially we are happy because of your reassurance that you found yourself in your own professional area, you can take on the same things you did before. Thank God for that! It took away the heaviness from our hearts. May everything go better and better.

I am glad that the documents are already in your hands. Frankly speaking I was already afraid that I am a victim of my own naiveté.

Please try not to worry about us. There is no point in worrying. We will help each other and survive. I have some income as a clerk, not much, but we do not need much. Your mother-in-law said she will write more often. Your sister-in-law is healthy, just a little lazy when it comes to writing. Tomorrow I will visit them both and shake them up a little. Please tell your Lusia that both her mother and sister-in-law are doing well, and are of good spirits. I will tell Franka what you wrote.

The packages came thank you very much. Please do not spend more money on that. Here we can get everything that we need.

Stay in good spirits, and write often.
Salo

P.S. From Mania:

Dear, beloved Brother,

Thank you for the packages but please do not send me anything anymore unless I will ask you for that. At the moment I do not need anything.

---

[27] This letter must be from mid- to late July because they have just learned that Joseph can stay in New York, but they do not yet mention imminent deportation from Cracow.

From Dola:

Dear Józek,

Your last two letters resulted in a fountain of joyful tears. We screamed from happiness! If you really could stay in New York, it would be wonderful, so you won't have to travel anymore. I was lucky, too, taking into consideration the times we live in. My "patching up" business gave me quite an income. I could pay for my treatment, and I still have some money left. Dr. Klassa did puncture, and thanks to short waves I got rid of the rest of the pus. I feel well now. I received a letter from Paula. It crossed with mine, sent a day earlier. Paula started to learn the fashion business, but doesn't have a place to practice. Everybody walks without hats now (I asked Frania but she gently refused). I am staying faithful to my mending business. I still learn English. We are happy with your happiness.

Greetings for Lusia.

Dola

July 21, 1940

From Joseph to the Haifa Lawyer, Samuel Spann:

Dear Dr. Spann,

You notified me in your postcard sent on April 10 that you sent the whole amount of my brother-in-law Dawid Wimisner's money (LP.253.230) to the business branch in London on September 8, 1939. Unfortunately I received a message from this office stating that they didn't receive any money. I asked them to write directly to you concerning this matter (Mr. Rosner is an uncle of my brother-in-law), with a request for explanation. I assume that you did receive their communication and in the meantime succeeded to investigate what happened to this transferred amount of money. I would be very grateful if you would write to me about the results since I am really in a hurry to have this matter explained.

I thank you in advance for your reply and I am attaching an international stamp.

July 21, 1940

From Dola:

Dearest Józiu,

We sent you all the dates. I think that Mania with her husband also will decide for that when they won't have any other choice.

From Berta:

Most dearly beloved only Son

You write that we should mention only facts when we write you, dear child. When I write you, how can I neglect at least to entrust to paper my feelings for you, since I [cannot] talk to you or see you? You will surely know what you mean to me, and it was my joy when you came to see me. I must slowly get used to being content with your letters! I hope that you are content and believe from your letters that it is as you write. I know your good character, that you are not simply chattering to me. May the Almighty grant you happiness and health, together with your dear wife. Do not worry about me, dear child, I am certainly lacking for nothing, without help from Mirisch.

I was at his house, and he told me he had had few letters from his wife, the last letter was from May 24, therefore he cannot help me. I did not ask him to, just gave him the few lines to read, he answered me that he himself had nothing. So, dear child, be careful and do not have anything to do with it, she might take advantage of you. By chance Czarhobrody was at our house, he had connections to him, he said it is difficult to find anything out from him. Again take note that I need nothing at all and I thank you for your good will, as I am convinced that you do it gladly. Doli's date is August 5, 1901. She wrote to Adele about going away, how is she supposed to leave Salo, Malcia, and me behind here, when Dawid travels with the family? But, dear child, do not look at her letter. She is alone and had nothing from the factory. I do not know after all how long her cash will last. Thank God I am healthy. I will now nevertheless mention Mrs. Mirisch's date: born August 16, 1900 Kyakau.[28] Be careful

---

[28] Presumably, Mrs. Mirisch's maiden name.

with your expenses. She wrote to her husband that the relatives had completely moved away from each other. She will have to go work in a factory. Will you be satisfied now with my long letter?

I kiss you both affectionately.

Your Mother

Affectionate kisses for Leo, his wife and son and thank her for the enclosed letter. I was very happy that he is thinking about his old aunt. Kindest regards to Paula, also to Curti, does he already have a position?

Addition from Lusia:

Dearest Uncle,

Now is my turn to be cross with you that you don't write to me at all. But since I am such a graciously forgiving person I am sending to you millions of kisses and hugs despite everything.

Lusia

From Klara:

My loved ones,

We received your letter in which you write that you got our birth dates. But I beg God that we can stay, and won't be separated, since I cannot imagine that. Be careful with Mr. Mürisch. Even if he has the best will, it is out of the question that Mama could get some benefits from him, and any kind of help. By the way she doesn't need any help from the stranger. Be reassured of that, and don't strain yourself too much, as we are trying not to.

Klara

From Dawid:

Dear Józiu,

What concerns your mother, when I will have AP[29] your mom will have it too, please be reassured of that. About packages we don't really need them; but if you feel the need to send something, please send some canned fish. Try to get us legal papers.

Greetings,

Dawid

---

[29] Unclear reference.

From Genka:

I would like to sleep during this time. You cannot plan anything ahead of tomorrow. It is really hot here now but nobody goes away. I don't know what to write you know everything anyway.

Kisses,
Genka

July 23, 1940

From Salo:

My loved ones,
Although I don't have anything important to add, I still want to write a few lines.

Regarding the security deposit, everything is now in order with the landlord Szpitalna.

Friend Mürisch claims to know nothing and said succinctly that he can return no favors. He doesn't seem to value friendship very highly which you stress so much, typical Mürisch, the name speaks for itself, a true son of his father. Don't let yourself be fooled any longer.

Otherwise I don't have anything else to report. Thank God we all are healthy. We greet you warmly and wish all the best, if it is possible please send us a little fresh air from your seaside sojourn just for refreshing.

Salo

From Mania:

My dearest brother,
I can add that for my 50th birthday I received an original gift: 5 people from Poznañ came to share my apartment, including the use of the kitchen.[30] I had to store all my things in one place. The only joy is that you are doing well, may God give you what's best.

Hundreds of good wishes,
Mania

[30] Poznan was located within the western part of Poland annexed directly to the Third Reich. With the intention of making the so-called incorporated territories purely German, the Nazi regime expelled large numbers of Poles and Jews from that region into the General Government. Local authorities were left to find housing for these refugees.

July 24, 1940

From Dola:

My most beloved brother,

I sent a family letter to you yesterday to the address of Leo. When I was coming back from the post office I received a letter from my husband, in which he begs me to try to contact his brothers through you. I wrote to them but they didn't answer, what kind of people are they? He wants them to send emigration papers for him, he doesn't want to stay here.

His telegram to them came back undelivered. I sent them his address; maybe there was a mistake there. I really wish that they wrote to him and consoled him. I wish him happiness which I haven't found with him. He writes very tenderly, calls me "Musienko" like before the wedding but I don't find any trace of sincere concern about me there. He didn't find any work although many others did, which allows them to support their families. I will manage without him. I don't demand anything from him but I also feel that I wouldn't be able to keep giving without receiving anything back anymore. I feel like it is my responsibility to act to his advantage therefore I am asking you to notify his brothers. If the mail doesn't go directly, they can send it to me first. I envy the wives who can count on their husbands' support even if it's long distance support.

Life plays tricks, I found this support outside of the marriage. If I were free, who knows? Maybe I would take a risk. But it's war, can one think about the future now?

Forgive me this egocentric letter, and that I take your attention away from everything else. I don't need to write you about my feelings for you but they are obvious. We never broadcasted them anyway. I agree to make sacrifices for the happiness of the family. It is very hard to live surrounded by hatred. In order to handle this, one needs some support and love. Up till now I have felt betrayed by life but I love it anyway, and maybe with my 39 years I still can think about a joyful future?

I kiss you millions of times. May your life be such as it is in your mother's and sisters' wishes for you.

Dola

Undated, Probably Late July 1940

From Mania:

Dearest Józiu,[31]

You know me well enough so I hope you won't be offended when I specify what you should send for Dola. It will be good timing because her birthday is in August and I know that you would not want to play favorites between us. Please do not send any food. If you can, please send soap, mouthwash, Vaseline, some cotton, and a bottle of glycerin that would be most welcome for both me and Klara for our hands.

About the patching of shirts and linens, Dola has already written to you. My idea was good for something, if only it will be possible to hold on to this place. That is not easy. Henek wrote a nice, tender card this time, asking if she had enough to live. He sensed the situation. He knows that you saw his brothers, that pushed him to write. I personally cannot stand him. He spoiled too much health and blood of Dola.

About Genka and Lusia I am happy to tell you that they are both pretty girls. If only G. would like to be half as good as L. is, then Klara would be a happy mother. Lusia is a gift from God, she loves her mother dearly, is very hardworking, helps around the household and sews really well.

I assure you that our health is fine; we are, if one can use this expression, quite satisfied. We sleep in our own beds on our own sheets.

You wrote that Mr. W. would be happy to help. Unfortunately I will be forced to accept that although I feel very uncomfortable in doing so. But it looks like it is my fate to depend on someone else's good will, and I don't have any choice but to make peace with the situation.

I should conclude this letter with best wishes for your future. Do not work too hard, you understand now what good comes out of it. Take care of your health and your nerves.

---

[31] Probably from late July 1940 because there is a reference to the nice word Dola has heard from Henek, referred to in Dola's letter of July 24, but it is before Dola's August birthday, and there is no mention of the looming threat of expulsion that dominates the correspondence as of July 28.

I kiss you and Lusia warmly. I assure her that her mother is doing well.
I would wish that our Mother looked so healthy and well.

Your Mania

July 28, 1940

From Klara:

Dear Józiu,

If there will be a break in our correspondence please don't worry. Just
wait until we let you know where we are. Maybe God will help us stay.
But it is war, we live like on a volcano and an order is an order.

Anyway, please don't send any packages. We have to get our strength
together and God won't abandon us. We are in good spirits!

I greet you warmly. Also from Dawid and the kids.

Klara

From Berta:

Dearest Children

A few words from me to reassure you that I am healthy, thank God,
that is why I am writing you. Klarcia has written you about the rest.
The children insist that I should give you my date. Whether it will
happen that I should come to see you, that's another question. 1866 –
April 4.

Affectionate kisses for you both as well as for Leo and his family, Paula
and son.

From Dola:

The nightmare of deportation looks into our eyes. There are still some
optimists who think that Jews from Kraków will be able to stay. Dawid
impresses me with his energy. Salo won't be affected by this deportation
law because he is 60 years old. His wife could stay with him. We cannot
be sure though.

Be well, my dear.

Dola

From Mania:

Dearest Brother,
This time only a few words, I don't have patience to write a long letter
and there would be lots to write about. We live in a chaos and uncertainty but maybe all will end well; you have positive thoughts, too. Stay
well.
Warmest greetings.
Mania

From Salo:

If something won't change in the last moment we will be forced to
leave Kraków. Where to? Into Unknown. There may be a break in our
correspondence. I want to alert you that this may happen in connection
to our move. Please don't be alarmed. We all are healthy and send you
best greetings.

Just in case, let me give you Mania's and my birth dates. We don't
know what our destiny is; if we will have chances to survive. When you
will arrange something for other family members, please don't forget us
either. Whether I . . .

[*The rest of this page is cut off.*]

August 1, 1940

From Klara:

Because of lack of space I only send you warm greetings, from both
me and Dawid.[32]

From Mania:

My dear,
We sent a letter for you through Adele. Adele told us we should write
only in German because of the censorship. Greetings and kisses and the
best wishes for the future.
Mania

---

[32] These appear to be short notes added to a letter that has not been found in the collection.

From Dola:

I am trying to stay strong. Unfortunately one gets more and more emotionally exhausted every day. I am happy knowing that you are over there.

Lots of luck.

Dola

August 9, 1940

From Berta:

Dear beloved Children!

I will write the beginning of the letter, then will come the children. Beloved child, we received your July 18 letter on August 8, it is number 2. Dear child, I will not write much. Since the children will write in detail, [I will say] only one thing, that everyone would very much like to be close by you. We are having difficult times. Not with our health, as we are well, thank God.

Beloved child, what do you think about the particulars from Dawid, etc.? Write him a detailed letter, as he is concerned about whether he has the prospect of being in your vicinity, so do not hesitate, write him right away as to how things stand, since we are in this situation, just as Leo or Paula once were, nevertheless be calm. We do not lack for food, just for rest.

I close with affectionate kisses, hoping still to see you. Greetings to Leo and family, Paula and son.

Your Mother Berta

My only joy is when I have a letter from you.

From Salo:

I won't pass this opportunity to write at least a few lines. We are going through pretty rough times now, but we are not the only ones who suffer. May God help us so that everything will turn back for the better, and we will be able to send good news. We received the package long ago. Thank you so much. Please do not send anything more. We cannot provide a future address. Besides, we don't really need anything right now. Just some peace and comfort for our emotions.

Stay well, my beloved ones, and please do not worry when there will be breaks in our correspondence. We will write as often as we possibly can.

For each package, we have paid 1.20 in delivery fees, otherwise nothing. Thus once again wishing you all the best, we remain with greetings,
Salo

From Klara:

Dearest Józiu,

You are writing that you are sending another package, also to Dr. Feliks. You are really impossible. If you haven't done it yet please don't send anything now until we write.

Feliks has an apartment in our house, for free, nothing bad is happening to him. Sending packages is unnecessary.

I already wrote to you that we are dealing with deportation now. In these days decisions will be made who can stay and who must leave. Many of our friends had to go. I pray to God that we won't be separated. If there will be a break in our correspondence that's because of the change of our destination address. Please wait patiently until we send a new address. Now Dawid's sisters are leaving. They used to live in Kraków, now they are going to Szczucin where their aunt lives. Poor Hela has a tough life, in addition to all the losses she also lost her 15 year old daughter who had a head tumor. If we leave, I really would like that we are together with Dola and Mania. Dawid is doing what he possibly can. Our lives are being decided in these days. I ask God to help us to be together. When will God send us the so desired peace? Those who are alive often envy the dead ones now. But a man is stronger than it seems and lives with the hope that it will be better. The only comfort are your letters. You write about heat. Be careful and take care of yourself. Don't drink too much water – I know you like that. How is your throat? Thanks for your wishes that we will be better next year. I am praying for that. It seems that we sinned really much.

Stay well and happy,
Klara

From Mania:

Thank you for your letters. We waited so long for them. Please write, my dear brother, so at least we won't have to worry about you. If your mother-in-law won't be able to stay here, she will go to Busko with her family. She is doing well, and doesn't despair.

I sold the bedroom [furniture] in order to have fewer things that I will take with me. Who leaves voluntarily can take his possessions.

Try not to worry about us. Maybe God won't forget those who faithfully believe in Him.

Stay well.

Mania

August 10, 1940

From Dola:

Thanks for the letter. It was like a healing ointment for me. I am going through awful times connected with the deportations. Salo's and Dawid's cases were reconsidered and they can stay. Because the elderly 70 and up can stay I am trying to be considered with Dear Mother, who is 74 and needs a caretaker. If I don't get the permit, I will be forced to go into the world all by myself, into the unknown. I will manage but everybody here is really worried.

I worried you about my sickness unnecessarily. I am quite well now, I got treatment from Dr. Klassa in Bonifaty. Unfortunately I am very sensitive to cold and only the sea climate can help. But I am not losing hope.

I learned that Henek got citizenship (Russian). I am not going to him. Did you get the letter in which I asked you (following Henek's wish) to notify his brothers. I hope they will write to him. Henek sent telegrams to them which came back undelivered.

As for sending packages, I assure you that up till now we really didn't need anything. If only it could stay that way till the end of the war it would be wonderful. Unfortunately, sooner or later, we will be forced to leave.

I eat dinners at Klara's, now I will start sleeping at Mania's. I will do it for the sake of her peace of mind. Anyway don't write to the old address anymore.

You must suffer because of the heat. Our family hates too much sun from outside; we have enough sun within.

Dear Mother works like an ant, tries to take care of everything, although the current events really affect her which combined with old age and longings for you leave their marks on her. A man is help-less now. Dawid is very good for Dear Mother. He keeps saying: "Don't worry about Mother. As long as I will have enough, Mother won't miss anything either."

My business is asleep now because of the general mood but I do manage and keep the head on my shoulders when all the others tend to lose it. Józiu, are you aware of how happy we are that you are safe over there? I know that you suffer, that you worry about us, but so many people survived wars before and we will survive this one, too.

Mrs. Spitzmann asks you for help since her son didn't honor her with even one letter.

Stay well dear Józiu, take care of your health, don't work too much. Now we can see that this is our only treasure. I thank Lusia for her greetings. Please greet her warmly from us.

Kisses,

Your Dola

August 16, 1940

From Mother:

Dear beloved Children,

On August 15 we received your letter number 3, and it gave us great pleasure to know that you are satisfied with your residence. May the Almighty grant that we are able to send you letters so that you will also be happy. Just now I have no good expectation. Dawid and Klara have gone to look for an apartment, since we do not know when we will move. For this reason, dear child, do not send packages to us or to Malcia. They are moving this week already. I will give you the address later. Dola is also looking for an apartment. We all would like very much to be together, but whether it will work out is a difficult thing. Dear child, be concerned for Dola, as she will be the first one to go. She is the one having the hardest time. Are you taking steps for Dawid and family? He also would really like to leave the house. I am writing you, [but] I do not know if you can do anything for them. I ask you, you are my only joy, so I ask you again to write a detailed letter to Dawid so he will see that you are thinking about them and will do what is in your power. I know that it may be wrong for me to write you such a thing, but a drowning person grabs at a straw to save himself, my heart is full, my eyes fill with tears, we are in front of water. Do not worry about me. Thank God I am healthy, and I am holding on. The Almighty will help in [time of] need, really we have enough to eat and where the need is nearest, there the help is best. Summer here is not pleasant because it rains a lot and is cold, we are also content with these things. I am really sorry to cause you so much pain with this letter. I am forced to express everything to you [in writing] because I am not able to talk to you. I could have still written so much, but my hand is failing me. But, dearest, make light of all this. I hope that it will be different and that I will yet have the chance to embrace you. I close with thousands of kisses for you both and remain your mother who thinks about you day and night.

Dear Leo, affectionate regards to you and your family.

I am going to your mother-in-law about the address.

August 19, 1940

From Dawid:

Dear Brother-in-law,

I read your letter from August 2 and as you requested I signed myself up on the emigration list. I don't understand what is the purpose of that, since also at your request I sent you our birth dates before. I am asking you for a detailed explanation of what you have already done for us. In this letter I expected something more concrete than what you wrote about the emigration registration, and that it may be of use sometime.

I assume that you understand how important it is for me although we are doing well, thank God. This week I was with Klara and the kids in Szczucin to look for an apartment. For now we are staying in Kraków. I am trying to arrange that the whole family stays together as well as I can, and it looks that I will succeed. I have the best chances as a war veteran and because I have always been employed. I expect that you already took care of everything from Uncle Span. Try to find Mr. Kaufmann, because he is a good friend of mine and it's really important for me that you meet with him. He is in his fifties.

I am trying my best for everybody in your family, and I hope that they all are pleased. I just ask you to try to arrange that which you promised us. I can assure you that none of us will be on your back. Lusia finished her exam and got a tailor certificate, Genka learned photography and works pretty well independently. So they both have secured a future, they can earn their bread by themselves. I, as you very well know, will manage myself. I just need a couple of weeks to learn the language. I have a very good friend, a former owner of Wohlworth in Katowice, Mr. Zimberknopf. He has a big business in New York, and we are friends for years.

Otherwise nothing new; I just wait for your explanation of the above. Greetings for you and your wife Lusia.

Dawid

From Klara:

Dearest Józiu,

We got your letter. Up till now we all are together, and may God allow us to stay together and live in peace. Sometimes the nervous system refuses to cooperate. Szczucin is a small town, without any comfort of course, there is not even running water over there. Hard life, but what can we do? Mr. and Ms. Cz. from Katowice live there already. Maybe we will survive this horrible storm. We try not to despair.

Kisses from Genia and Lusia.

Klara

From Dola:

Dear Józiu,

Thank you for the wishes. You made a mistake in the months. Klara was born in September and I on August 5. I am correcting that since the dates may be needed. Here we are having a very unpleasant summer, no warmth outside or inside. Recently I sent a four pages long letter to you. There are fewer and fewer friends here and lots of strange faces.

Dawid exaggerates as always. I sent a letter to the American Consulate today asking for the forms for them and Mania, and he writes that they are already registered.

Greet Paula from me, ask for her forgiveness. I am not in the position to write to her. I'll do it later when I know where I am staying. Stay well and do not worry too much about us. We will get through this.

Kisses,

Dola

From Berta:

Beloved Child!

I have nothing to write you except to send you and also Lusia affectionate kisses.

Your Mother

Your sister-in-law does not know her husband's address. I was at her house . . . [illegible].

Berta

August 22, 1940

From Salo:

My loved ones!

As I wrote to you a couple of weeks ago, we thought that we were among those who would be forced to leave Kraków. In the meantime, we have learned that allegedly my application has been ruled on favorably, and accordingly we will be allowed to remain here a bit longer. Indeed nothing is totally certain, as I don't have anything on paper in my hands yet. We plan to change our apartment, we will take a room with a kitchen, and this way we will get rid of our roommates of whom we have had enough or more than enough. We sold our dining room and the bedroom, and also all the other things we don't need, so we can comfortably fit into one room with the kitchen, and without any roommates. So please send your next letters not to our old address but to the address of the factory.

What concerns packages I would like to let you know that up till now we and Klara each got one package. All the others haven't reached us. Feliks didn't get his either. I am stressing this not to urge you to send them again – on the contrary, please send absolutely nothing more. I promise you that we won't be embarrassed to ask you if it should become necessary. As for now we are not lacking anything.

Many people here register themselves for the emigration overseas. In order not to blame ourselves later we are thinking about doing the same. Norddeutsch Lloyd takes the registrations. You asked for our birth dates in one of your last letters. Here they are.

Gabryel Nachtigall born in Karniowice near Kraków in the Kraków jurisdiction, October 1, 1879.

Amalia Jetti Nachtigall, born in Köty, in the Kraków jurisdiction, July 19, 1890.

As it seems now, sooner or later all the Jews will be forced out of here, thus it is only for such a case.

I heard that you have very hot weather over there, that's also no fun. We cannot complain in this respect; on the contrary here it is cold and rainy. But who pays attention to this? One doesn't even notice such peripheral things like that anymore. What's most important now is that we are healthy. We hope that you feel well, too. Please accept my warm greetings. Big hugs for both of you.

Salo

From Mania:

Most beloved Józiu and Lusia,

I am glad you are doing well. I wish you (and us) that we get only good news from you. Dearest Brother, it seems that you are not getting all the letters; sometimes I write separately to you. Up till now I haven't gotten any response.

Salo wrote already everything. I mean he wrote what he could write. I don't want to lose my last hope and I ask God that he won't let me to be separated from the Dear Mother and the sisters. I can't even accept this thought.

Kisses and hugs,

Mania

August 28, 1940

From Berta:

Dearest beloved Children

How I would like to write you something cheerful. Up until now, everything is as it was, we still live in the old apartment, how long we do not know. I really have nothing to write you, but I do not want to neglect to let you know where we are. But I do not have much to write you about us. I found a letter from my sister from the year 37 that was sent to your address when you lived at Biskuseir 14. The son-in-law's address is S. Sidney Goodman, Radio, 6011 Baltimore Avenue, Philadelphia, PA. Will it be possible for you to find out from him where his mother-in-law is? She is not always with them. I close with thousands of kisses for you both.

Your Mother,

Berta

Affectionate greetings to Leo and family. Is Paula already at home? How is her health? Please ask her to write me when she can. Affectionate greetings to her.

From Klara:

Dear Józek,

Finally I am writing some good news: after appealing our case we got a permit to stay. But I'll let myself to be happy only when I know that Mania and Dola hold their permits in their hands. May God help us to live on dry bread but peacefully I don't wish for anything more. Many of our friends and relatives had to leave Kraków. What cheers us up is that you are happy. I wish you the absolute best. I hope that God will help us and we won't be separated.

Greetings to both of you.

Klara

From Mania:

And I too hurry to let you know that Salo got a permit, and I hope that I will automatically get it as well. We cannot know for how long it is going to be valid. Dear Mother can stay because she is above 70, and everybody above 70 may stay. Now we have only one request: so God will help Dola to stay with us. Otherwise we won't be able to be happy, and even enjoy the fact that we are able to stay.

As always I wish all the best for both of you. Write often, my beloved Józiu.

Greetings.

Mania

From Dola:

Dear Józiu,

I expect to stay here as well. I will let you know as soon as I know. Be well, dear. Don't worry. Somehow we will get through this. What's important, we are healthy. Do you still have such hot weather?

I am as fat as I used to be.
Kisses,
Your Dola

From Lusia:

Me too. Lusia
Greetings from Dawid

From Genka:

We are strong, together, mobilized, and ready for everything.

Undated

From Berta:

Dearest beloved Children,[33]
We received your letter number 4 and I am pleased that you are already rid of the unneeded tonsils. I want to hope that after this, you will feel well and wish for you that from now on, you will have good news. How very much I would like to see you, whether that will happen is another question, I must be content with your letters. Dear child, regarding the packages, Klara and Malcia have each received one, as we confirmed to you. As soon as any arrive, we will let you know right away. My dear beloved child, in a letter I gave you the address of my sister's son-in-law. Please write to him and ask where his mother is, this should not be any trouble for you. Otherwise I have nothing to write to you except affectionate kisses to you both.
I remain your mother who longs for you

From Klara:

Dearest Józiu,
I am very glad you decided to have this surgery. You shouldn't be suffering any illnesses. Do you have to talk so much in your office? This

---

[33] This letter probably dates to very late August or early September because apparently Joseph's letter number 4 mentioned here contains the first news that he had had his tonsils removed, and his number 3 was received on August 15. Moreover, this letter refers to the separate letter that Salo and Mania wrote on August 22, as well as Berta's letter sent on August 28 with the address of her sister's son-in-law.

is the second time I am letting you know that we, also Salo, already have the permits to stay here. We hope that Mania will get it automatically because Salo has his already. We only worry about Dola. Her case was reconsidered and we hope that she will able to stay also. Then we will be really happy.

Greetings and kisses for you both.

Klara

From Salo:

Although I am missing parts for me in your letters for some time now, I will use any opportunity to add at least a few sentences. Recently I wrote you a separate letter together with Mania, hopefully it is already in your possession.

It was a good thing that you freed yourself from the suffering. I hope everything went well. I got confirmation of my temporary permit to stay in Kraków. Mania will receive hers in the next few days. Please accept my regards, all the best for both of you. Mania will write separately.

Salo

From Dola:

Dearest brother,

I hope that America treats you well. Did you get good ice to swallow? Write me the truth. I hope that they did a good job in removing your tonsils. I am well now at least physically. I spent weeks in uncertainty, and I still don't know if I will stay. I have reasons to hope so but still it is nerve wracking. In advance, I thank you for the package, we haven't received it yet. Do you already speak perfect English? I gave it up a few weeks ago since nothing sticks to my mind.

Greetings, kisses.

Dola

[3]

Exit Strategy
September–December 1940

Even while struggling to be granted asylum in the United States, Joseph simultaneously pursued the process of attaining visas for his family to escape from Poland. Having narrowly avoided deportation in the summer of 1940, Joseph's relatives in Cracow did not need convincing that it would be better to leave on their own accord rather than at the whims of the Nazis. "In connection with deportation actions we will urgently need documents stating that we have already taken some steps in order to be allowed entry into America. . . . these documents are very serious and urgent, in any case in order to show the authorities some kind of official or partially official proof that actual steps have been taken to procure entry approval into America," wrote Salo in October 1940. "At this moment nothing really threatens us but people are talking about more severe deportation actions, and then documents like this can really help us."[1]

On December 1, 1940, through Joseph's efforts, the family received Nicaraguan visas. Although the writers had constantly reassured Joseph that they were in no danger, they reacted to the visas as if their lives had been saved. "Today we received the papers from the Cosulario General De Nicaragua," exclaimed Dola exuberantly. "I am at dinner at Klara's. Mania cries from happiness. Dawid got into a state of euphoria . . . and Genka studies the map all day long. . . . In this moment, Dawid reaches his zenith – he produces strange sounds – appropriate for Nicaragua!"[2] Klara was similarly ecstatic. "Many special thanks for the papers you sent us," she wrote. "You cannot imagine with what

[1] Salo to Joseph, October 23, 1940.   [2] Dola to Joseph, December 1, 1940.

great joy we welcomed them. Dawid carries these papers with him all
the time, just like a talisman. . . . having them has lifted our spirits and
gives us courage to carry on. We tried to locate the place on the map.
We have been consulting the dictionary to learn about the language and
people."[3]

So oppressive was the Nazi regime that even Joseph's teenaged nieces
desired to leave their homeland and start anew in an unknown country
across the Atlantic. Genka penned her uncle that "these papers fell like
stars from the sky! Viva Nicaragua! We simply lost our heads out of
joy! . . . Everybody congratulates us and is jealous that we do have such
an Uncle. You deserve a million kisses from the whole family."[4] Genka's
sister Lusia joyfully scribbled: "I am sitting with a pencil in my hand and
cannot find the right words to express what I feel. How to thank you
for such a wonderful present like a trip to Nicaragua? Nicaragua – how
wonderful it sounds!"

But later that December, the family's hopes for leaving Poland vanished. "You gave us a travel route," wrote a dejected Dola. "Well, it
is impossible to leave [the General Government], so don't waste your
energy and money."[5] It was impossible to leave because, in September
1940, the Nazis blocked emigration from the General Government (as
well as from other parts of German-occupied Europe) to reserve the
increasingly scarce emigration opportunities for the Jews in Germany.
For the Nazis, reducing the Jewish population within the Third Reich
through emigration – even by the trickle of people who could still leave
Europe after the outbreak of war – had absolute priority over permitting
the departure of Jews from any other region of occupied Europe.[6]

Not surprisingly, the Nazi ban on Jewish emigration from the General
Government cast an enormous pall over the family. But despite the disappointment about the escape, the family's spirits eventually brightened –
at least on paper. On June 10, 1941, Dola optimistically penned: "It seems
that all your energy and costs connected with Nicaragua were needless
but. . . . there is nothing bad that couldn't turn into something good."[7]
Salo reassured his brother-in-law that "maybe it was supposed to be this

---

[3] Klara to Joseph, December 9, 1940.   [4] Genka to Joseph, December 9, 1940.
[5] Dola to Joseph, February 12, 1941.
[6] Christopher R. Browning, *The Origins of the Final Solution: The Evolution of Nazi Jewish
Policy 1939–1942* (Lincoln: University of Nebraska Press, 2004), pp. 196–7.
[7] Dola to Joseph, June 10, 1941.

way. We cannot know what is in store for us. Sometimes a small failure may spare people from a bigger misfortune."[8]

Sometimes, but not that time.

September 9, 1940

From Mania:

Dearest, beloved Brother,

Because of lack of space I couldn't add anything to the family letter. As always, the rest of the family didn't give me a chance to write about anything new. They already told you everything.

My dearest little brother, you must have suffered a lot since you decided to have surgery. Please accept my congratulations on the successful surgery. May God help you always be healthy. How does Lusia feel? Does the new cuisine serve her well? We miss you and simultaneously we are happy because of your stay in the US. We went through very difficult months, maybe this will finally change.

What Salo wrote to you last time is still not arranged. Many people advise against that. It may happen what happened to Lusia's family.

Many people ask for your address. Should I give it to them? I am afraid they will bother you too much with their asking for favors and questions. Please write me what to do.

As for the coming New Year I wish you all the best, lots of health and happiness.

Mania

P. S. Best greetings for you dear Leo and for your family, as well as for dear Paula.

Mania

September 10, 1940

From Feliks Palaszek:

Highly respected Doctor Holländer,

I thank you for remembering me and for your good heart. I learned from your sister that you sent a package for me. I haven't received it yet. I don't know what could have happened to it.

---

[8] Salo to Joseph, June 12, 1941.

My life didn't change much. Thank God, I, my wife and our child are well. The old travel agency finally went out of business in the beginning of the summer. Another one has been opened "Mittel Europa." Mr. Drachenberg works there. Mr. Bibulski also closed his travel agency. Now he has a grocery store. Countess Borucka is in a horrible state but I think she deserves that for her sadism and harassing us. Doctor Holländer, I hope to receive the package you sent. It takes so long because it's so far, and Red Cross has also much to do.

Once more thank you for your good heart and for remembering me. I wish you lots of health and happiness. I kiss the hand of your wife.

With respect, Feliks Palaszek

Addition from Mania:

Feliks brought this letter and asked me to send it to you. He is doing pretty well taking current times into consideration. He doesn't have to pay for his apartment and has enough to eat. And that's only because he is an Aryan and has special food rates.

We don't need anything from him.

Kisses,

Mania

From Lusia:

Nothing new to report since there is already the second letter sent to your new address.

September 17, 1940

From Berta:

My dear beloved Sweetheart!

So that you do not think about it, I want to write you the truth. I was being treated by Dr. Wasserberg, thank God I am doing very well, you do not need to be concerned about me. Praise God I have good children with me who do not forget their duty to their old mother.

When we received your dear letter, Dr. Wasserberg was at our house for the last time, she was happy that her sister visited you. Dear child, how are you doing after your operation, look at how loyal we are to one another, you were suffering at the same time I was. I hope we will have only good news now. The New Year[9] is coming, so I am wishing you both much luck and prosperity so that I should hear good things from you. Imagine how happy I am to hear good things from you and may the Almighty bless the move with much luck, which you have earned with your good hands and mind, and I hope soon to have a cheerful letter from you, it is my fondest wish to know that you are happy.

In the next letter I will write you more, it is in answer to your letter number 5. I kiss you affectionately and wish soon to hear news from you again. I remain your mother and do not be concerned about me, as I have good children with me, thank God. We got your letter on September 13.

From Dawid:

I greet you warmly. Please try to arrange the papers for us as soon as possible. Forgive me that I don't write, that's because of lack of patience. I hope you feel well after the surgery.

Dawid

From Klara:

Because the dear Mother has already written that she was sick, I won't talk about that. Thank God she walks again. It's already a year since she got inflammation of the gall bladder. She worries about the smallest things, and it's not difficult to find reasons to worry today. And they come not from home but as the result of the general situation. She can consider herself the happiest mother on Earth having a son like you who writes only good letters. Thank God her sickness passed and she is well again. She has to be on a diet.

What concerns Kaufman, he is 50 years old, and I believe you will see him. Please write to us about that. Your mother and sister-in-law stay in Kraków.

Kisses, Klara

Note from Lusia and Genka:

Happy New Year.

---

[9] This refers to the New Year of the Jewish calendar.

September 18, 1940 (Mailed in the Same Envelope as the Previous Letters of September 17)

From Dola:

My dearest beloved Brother,

Thank you so much for a special note for me. I would like to know the truth about how you feel after the surgery? Do you feel relieved? Take care of your health, dear Józiu, because if you don't have it nothing else will make you happy. I am healthy now but I have to be very careful not to catch a cold. I have a tendency to do so. Doctor Bonifratach wanted me to have a surgery of Jama Hajmora[10] but after the puncture I felt much better and I gave up this idea.

I don't understand the behavior of Henek's brothers. Doesn't matter if they want to help him or not, they could write a letter. He is in Drohobycz now, has a passport and he expects to get a job from the Commission of Social Help. He writes so affectionately now: "My Musieńko, you are the only person I have," but what's so characteristic for him he doesn't ask how do I live, how do I handle everything, etc. Just empty phrases. I don't even blame him for that. Many people behaved like he did (Erna is also alone, and with a small child, but she is lucky enough to have the same job as before the war and to get a job is absolutely impossible today). I am happy that I can afford my own place. I still live on Grodzka Street and as you wrote I won't undertake any steps. I will let destiny decide – the war is still here. Do you think that now is a good time to resolve my marriage? I don't even feel bitter towards him, since I imagine that it is not easy for him to send me anything. I just feel strangely cold and cannot imagine our future life together. I have a feeling that life will decide for us.

My "sewing place" completely collapsed. I think that's a result of desperation in our circles. If I only would have the permit to stay the new energy will come and I will come up with something new. I already talked to Mrs. Wurzlow the fashion lady and she said she will take me in. Her condition is to ask you to contact her relatives, and to attempt through your agency to get her son out with his wife (you apparently know him). I think that writing such a letter and contacting her relatives doesn't

---

[10] Presumably a type of sinus surgery.

obligate you to anything. I don't really know how so many people know about you, and keep asking for your address. I don't know if I should give it. Dr. Frischer took your address, he has sisters and brother over there.

I don't know what was unclear in my previous letter. I never had talent for writing and now it's even worse since I started to look for comfort in cigarettes. In fact people don't even think anymore, they became automats pushed by circumstances, quite helpless, so I would lie if I said that I cared anymore.

Dear Mother started to suffer from gall bladder during the war. She has already gotten some treatment, as you suspected, from Dr. Wasserberg. But please do not worry, it has passed, and the good news from you is always the best medicine. Do not send packages. We haven't received any except one, so it's a waste of money.

I am sending a letter from your mother-in-law, who keeps losing your address. She is indomitable. I wish that our Dear Mother had her attitude. I envy only the fact that she has a job, and so does her daughter.

Should I keep writing to Leo's address? Can I write already to Paula? To what address? I won't send letters through Adele any more since I can send letters directly from here via airmail.

Stay well, dearest Józiu, take care of yourself. Do not pay attention to pretentious remarks of Dawid. He is so bonded with his workshop, that I am sure that even if he had everything ready he wouldn't move himself from here. Lusia is our sunshine; incredibly good child, adores Klara. Soon she will go to "Elwira." It's thanks to you again. I mentioned your name, and she accepted Lusia.

Hugs, kisses, lots and lots of happiness.

Your Dola

September 20, 1940

From Berta:

My dearest beloved Children!

Today we received your dear letter number 6 and I will give you my birth certificate. My name is Beila Holländer, maiden name Weiss, born April 4, 1866 in Chrzanow. I am writing little to you today, dear child, since this week we sent you a family letter. You are kissed affectionately by your mother who wants only to see you happy.

My dearest beloved Lusia how happy I am to read your dear letter and thank you and wish still to see you both prosperous, healthy and happy. So for the New Year I wish you both the best.

Your Mother

From Dola:

Mother asks me to say that as soon as a photograph will be taken she will send it to you.

Only this week I sent a letter from your mother-in-law, a family letter, and a separate letter from me directly to Leo. Since a letter from you came during that time, I am immediately writing back. We haven't received any package. We haven't changed the apartment, since Salo and Dawid got permits to stay. I still haven't gotten one for myself.

I am happy that they have it. Yesterday the factory was placed under state ownership. Nothing really changed though. Salo is still employed there. I still have a small share in the factory.

My birth date is August 5, 1901 in Kraków.

I wish you both all the best in the New Year. I send you love; may all your wishes come true.

Dola

From Klara:

Dearest Józiu,

From your wishes for my birthday I see that you made a mistake. I am giving you for the third time the birth dates:

Dawid: November 8, 1890 in Tarnów

Klara: September 27, 1893 in Vienna

Eugenia [Genka]: March 28, 1921 in Kraków

Dola [Lusia]: May 19, 1924 in Kraków

We wrote to the American Consulate in Berlin but we haven't received any answer.

If you want to help us please spare yourself, your health and emotions. How many hours do you have to work? When you will talk to Mr. Kaufman ask him if he has already sent a letter to Mr. Grouper concerning us. I also wish you my dearest Józiu a lot of happiness. Please wish a Happy New Year to Leo and his family, as well as to Paula's son.

From Dawid:

Dear Brother-in-law!
I wish you and Lusia a good New Year, may God bring us all together
again. Greetings.

From Genka:

Beloved Uncle,
It is my turn to write you a few words. Unfortunately, I cannot write
you anything good. Even the strongest person cannot be protected under
such horrible circumstances and can break down. And I particularly with
my 19 years have nothing here that can give me some comfort. When it
comes to studying there is no possibility. I am grateful that I am working
in a store and in this way fill my time up. I hug you, I kiss you, darling
uncle. Genka

From Mania:

My most beloved brother. Forgive me not writing in the former family
letter, there was no space. That is why I just sent you a card. I hope that
you have already received it. As for the new apartment, I wish the two of
you lots of happiness, and all of the best things for the New Year. Dola
and I still don't have permits to stay, and we worry about that.
     We have already sent my and Salo's birth dates but can it really be a
possibility for us? My dear Józiu, I do not know if things will work out
for us but I doubt it. Write a lot and frequently, this is for us the only
comfort in this very difficult period, and particularly for our beloved
mother, it is for her like a good wine which keeps up the strength of
those who are sick. We greet the both of you, and send you kisses.
Mania

From Lusia:

My dear beloved uncle. I am very happy and delighted that you feel
well and are in such good shape now. I wish you a great deal of success
in your work. As I wrote earlier to you, I am learning sewing. As far as
the exam, I need three years of apprenticeship working. So I went to
Elwira Barkanowa on Jagielloñska street. She accepted me only thanks
to you although you are not here. Maybe it will surprise you but it is so.

Apparently she knows you from some trip. So I used this acquaintance and signed up to work there. Other tailors didn't want to accept me at all since they don't have enough work. I work at Barkanowa nine hours a day, with lunch break. I am also working with children but they don't want to pay me. It is very unpleasant, but I feel that this may change. I am finishing this letter because you are probably yawning.

Lusia

From Salo:

My dears! Your letter 6, from which your contentment and future prospects can be inferred, brought us much joy and pleasure. The dear God gives you great good fortune. I have given you the dates for Mania and me already, but I repeat them: Amalia Jetti Nachtigall, born July 17, 1890, in Kety, Gabryel Nachtigall, born in Karniowice by Kraków on October 1, 1878, according to our marriage certificate. Does that have any significance for me, given my age? Accept my best wishes for the turn of the year and please pass on my New Year wishes to Paula as well.

With heartfelt greetings and a hug.

Please also give my greetings to Leo and his wife.

September 25, 1940

From Dola:

Dearest Brother,

I am writing to you to ask you to try to contact the sister of Mr. W. She needs to try to get his son out with his wife since the same thing happened to him as to the father-in-law. Mr. W. wrote already about that to his sister and she promised to help. Mostly it's about asking you for advice, and if possible she wants to arrange that through your agency. They are afraid that she may take some wrong steps, and it may result in a tremendous waste of time and money.

Mrs. W. took me into her salon as a practitioner, so I would like to repay her, especially as she asked me for that.

Sorry I am adding work on your shoulders, you are doing everything for others.

I thank you in the name of Mrs. W.

Hugs,
Dola
Address for Mr. W.'s sister: S. Bilski, 1210 Sherman Ave., Bronx, NY

Another Note from Dola:

I had to write this letter in that way because she wanted to read it. It had to have such content. Please treat it as a business matter, since the sister of W, as they told me, will pay for everything. If you don't want to do this or won't be able to, don't worry.

I couldn't say "no" to her. She hired me but only for two hours daily, not a big deal. And she took me in under the condition that I will contact you about this matter. I took up her offer since I know how to do it and thanks to this my days are filled. In my spare time I read or learn the language. And I listen to the music coming from Miraj. I sigh and long for freedom.

What did Dr. Frischer write to you? I couldn't refuse him when he asked for your address. But I won't do it anymore without your permission. I promise.

I still don't know if I will be able to stay. I am waiting for the verdict every day.

Kisses,
Dola

October 6, 1940

From Berta:

Sweet dear beloved Children

With the beginning of the New Year I will number this letter No. I. We received your dear letter number 7, which for me is salve for my health, as I am still a convalescent and can assure you that I am doing very well and you do not need to be concerned about me. I have very good care since the dear children are around me and take care that I have all the best. I can be proud of my children. One would have to look with a light for children who make use of everything as well as mine. May God grant that I may see all of them have good things. Therefore, my dear child, do not write sparingly. When I have a letter from both of you, it strengthens me like a good wine.

To come back again to the packages, they still have not arrived, who knows if they were even sent off. One package can get lost, but certainly not all of them. So, dear child, can you make inquiries, or must one give proof that they were sent? My dear ones, for the new apartment and the New Year, I wish you all the best – that you be content, healthy, and happy. My sweet child, now I will trouble you, since you are so good to everyone. I am writing you that Adele has complained because she has not had a letter from her son for five months. You have many acquaintances in Palestine. Maybe it would be possible for you to find him with help from some of them. Adele will send you his former address. You can be sure that by doing this you will bless a mother's heart. I can understand what it is like to have an only child abroad and not to know how he is. I will write you more in the next letter, so do not take my words in the wrong way that I trouble you. I kiss you a thousand times,

Your Mother

The children will also write, since I did not leave them any room. Next time I will write to dear Lusia.

Undated, October 1940

From Dola:

Dear Brother,[11]

I am opening this family letter today. Today Mania moved. They rented a room in the same building where Klara lives, on Gertrudy Street 7. I hope they will be happy there. They are glad they got rid of these forced housemates. Lots of "our kind" started already celebrating Yom Kippur. We still are allowed to have hope. We will notify you when we receive the document.

I do too much and have not enough time for my fashion business. I help others: "You know German and have courage" they say. It's true, I do have courage.

I am waiting for your answer for my letters with the copy of the letter to Henek. I will wait until you write. Divorce is possible here. If only he agrees. We all are healthy and pretty much the same as always.

---

[11] This letter dates from shortly before Yom Kippur on October 15, 1940.

Salo's arthritis, Mania's sensitivity, Dawid's optimism, Klara's sobriety, Mother's longings for you, my weak legs and big appetite, Genia's disappointment after making plans about what she will do after high school exam, and Lusia's . . . – I am lacking words of delight. She is such an incredible person in every aspect. May these girls have a bright, good future.

My love, write me soon if I can be an optimist. And take care of yourself. We know it now that this is the only treasure.

Dola

From Mania:

Dear Józiu,

I would love to know more about you, do you still work so hard as you used to. Is it again so emotionally draining? Take care of yourself, respect your health because health is your personal and most important possession.

As Dola already wrote we moved. Although we had our place paid off until December 1, we left in a hurry taking whatever leftovers we did have. We live as tenants at Mrs. Birnbaum in a tiny room. We live on the ground floor, and only Klara from the old tenants lives there also. God help us to be able to stay here till the end of the war. We eat at Klara's. She is a great housewife. There is always space for anybody to join at the dinner table unexpectedly. She often has guests from Szczucin.

Give our greetings to Lusia, and tell her she should thank God day and night for her fortune. You my dear brother, write often and stay well.

Mania

From Berta:

Dearest beloved Children!

The children have written you news. It remains for me only to kiss you both affectionately, unfortunately only on paper. Since letter number 12 we have not received anymore, did you get my letter number 6? I am waiting impatiently for a letter from you. My love, you will certainly know what it means for me to have a letter from you to read. Once again, affectionate kisses.

Your Mother

Greetings to Leo and wife and also to Paula

From Klara:

Dearest Józiu,

Here, thank God, not much changes. We all are healthy and that's the most important thing.

I am pleased with my new tenant; he also has all the comfort he needs. I wash for him, I sew holes in his socks, iron his pants, etc. As you see I am made for everything. I cook every day for many people. Sometimes I start distributing dinner at 1 p.m. and end at 4. I can do it in such a way that it's never too little. Maybe I have a profession for America? Only my hands are not good for the piano anymore. I would like it to be my only worry.

I need to finish because it is already late and everybody is sleeping. I greet you from everybody, kisses and hugs for you and Lusia.

Klara

October 15, 1940

From Klara:

Dear Józiu,

I am writing immediately after "The Judgment Day."[12] It went okay, better than last year, when we all were at the peasant's house in the village, sleeping on the ground barely covered with straw for 14 days.[13] And the worst for me was not knowing about what is happening at home. This year was better, we were all together, and we have good news from you, thank God. That brings us comfort.

Cordial greetings and kisses from

Klara

From Genka:

Dearest Uncle,

I got quite used to current conditions. Like hordes of animals we are also able to adjust to everything if necessary; and that's not such a bad

---

[12] Yom Kippur.
[13] This is the third reference in the letters to the family having fled from Cracow to the countryside during the early days of the war.

thing. We all live with the philosophy wait through and don't give up. Dear uncle, you don't know how much humans must go through, how much do they suffer and don't allow themselves to despair. We all on the outside look like before. We are still pretty well dressed. But what's inside that's a different story! Anyway. One day it will change. What do you think? We have to hang on to the saying: keep smiling. Okay, I am finishing this absurd note, the family doesn't leave me anything interesting to write.

Kisses and greetings for you and the auntie,

Genka

From Lusia:

Dear Uncle,

I feel, thank God, pretty good inside and out. I work 9 hours per day. This work brings me full satisfaction and I am happy to have it. Like every man who works. Greetings for you and the Aunt. Happy New Year. Because our addresses are uncertain please write at the address of the Gertrudy 27 workshop.

Lusia

From Dawid:

Dear Józek,

Thanks for your letter and your attempts to help us. Please tell Uncle Rozner that we are doing fine, and Uncle Heinrich lives in Tarnów as well, but unfortunately he became a widower. What concerns Spann please try to get in touch with him and definitely finish this business with him. I wrote to him already in September 1939 asking him to send everything to the uncle and let him handle this. He wrote me back that he'd do it. Please congratulate Uncle Rozner and Oskar that their kids got married. I greet you and your wife warmly.

Dawid

From Mania:

Dear Brother,

I have to write again. You didn't understand what I wrote before about Marysia and her colleagues being locked up. Dola and I sit like mice on a

box since we still don't have permits to stay in Kraków. We worry about
that. I have to leave some space, so that's all from me. Kisses for you and
Lusia.

Mania

A Line from Dola:

Mania stays automatically because Salo has already his permit, only I
hang between heaven and earth.

From Berta:

My sweet dear beloved Children! This time I am adding a few words,
since I sent a letter to you last week, my dear ones, and no one added to
it. For that reason now they wrote first, otherwise I would not leave them
any space. I am well, thank God, and I look forward always to receiving
good news from you.

Your Mother who kisses you affectionately

October 19, 1940

From Salo:

My Dear Józiu!

We received your dear letter of October 5 the day before yesterday,
very fast for present circumstances. We thank you very much for your
involvement, and insofar as possible I will try to address all your diverse
questions.

First, I would like to console you that the decision to sell the furniture
had nothing to do with our financial situation, thank God for that. For
our limited needs we do have enough and we ask you not to worry about
that. The same concerns Dear Mother, Dola and Klara. The furniture
had to be sold. We are practically furniture free, and we came to the
conclusion that we can live this way just as well, if we won't have other
problems and worries. Today, when one cannot have a maid, it could be
even an advantage. Knowing Mania you will agree.

We have provided our birth dates several times, you surely received
all these letters, but just to be sure I am attaching them again at the end
of this letter.

As you know I have already received the permit to stay, and I was required to provide all the necessary information in order to apply for Mania's permit. Unfortunately, in the meantime some things came up which have postponed approval, and who knows thereby the entire matter and all prior decisions will be reconsidered. Our Jewish hole *[Jüdeloch]* that is another story.[14] It should be known in the next few days. Let's hope for the best. I sent a letter to you via Vienna, which you may have received in the meantime. I am attaching a copy in case the previous one did not reach you. If it is possible, send these documents by airmail.

We were very happy to receive your dear letter, from which we sensed confidence and joy. May God keep giving you all the best, and may you always be in a position to send us joyful letters. We are all convinced about your best will to help us to be able to emigrate to America. We have known each other for years, and I know well what to think of you and your sense of togetherness. So thank you in advance for all your attempts.

I hope this letter is not too long for your patience and close with warm greetings.

Nachtigall Gabriel b. Oct. 1 1878, in Karniowice, district of Kraków

Nachtigall Amalia Jetti b. July 19 1890, in Kety (today German Reich)

Holländer Beila b. April 4, 1866 in Chrzanow (today German Reich)

From Mania:

My Dear Beloved Brother,

You want to talk to us this way via writing; we want it too, but every letter is too small for that. You want to know how we sleep: I on the sofa and Salo in the servant's bed, and we're okay with that if not other things. It is too bad that the summer is past; we are so afraid of winter. Fear of lack of coal, and maybe of change of address. Maybe God won't leave us again this time.

Dearest Józiu, you are our joy, and I thank God every morning and every evening that you succeeded in seeing Paula and Leo. Next time I will write a few words again. Stay well.

Mania

[14] This is possibly a reference to rumors of ghettoization.

October 19, 1940

From Dola:

My dearest brother,
Your every line intended for me makes me so happy. Unfortunately
the letter that you promised to be only for me hasn't come yet. It's hard
to describe how happy your success makes me. I wish you many more
accomplishments. How is your throat? Are you glad you got rid of them
[the tonsils]?

Here we do not live "like in a paradise." I am only worried about the
permit to stay in Kraków. By now I have arranged my life in a way that
I begin to find quite satisfactory. In the morning I work at the factory,
mending business afternoon, evenings with my friends, and around 9 P.M.
back to my little room, where I still live in peace after all the troubles
connected with the forced moves. I could breath and feel free again.
Until the day before yesterday.

Imagine that some horrible creature in a human body wrote an anony-
mous letter about me to the German criminal police[15] where she writes
all kinds of crazy stuff, like for example "She is involved in corpse trading;
has lots of money and treasure," etc.[16] She has charged improbable deeds
that I cannot even write about because they are so disgusting. I had an
hour-long, very unpleasant interrogation and although my conscience is
clean I broke down and finally I started to cry and scream: "how mean!"
They declared that it is a misunderstanding on the spot. I got this piece
of paper so I can find out myself who did it. My suspicions are that it was
a woman (I suspect it 99%) whom I didn't do anything to (a 50-year-old
woman, married with two daughters) but who feels helpless in her anger.
The object of her hopeless love takes care of me, shows me lots of affection and is to me like my own husband never was. He is a friend of the
whole family, especially of Salo. I still don't have proof but with God's

[15] The German "criminal police" was the Kripo, not the more notorious Gestapo. Denun-
ciation for revenge or some other personal motive was not an uncommon occurrence
in Nazi Germany, and thus police authorities, who welcomed denunciations as a key
means of maintaining fear and control, nonetheless had to sort through many spurious
denunciations motivated by personal spite that were not politically useful or relevant.
[16] It was a capital crime at this point for Jews to possess more than 2,000 złoty.

help I will find it. I would take care of that in a small circle of people but definitely. You know how horrible it is in times like these to know that somebody deliberately wants to take your freedom away? They believed me. Sorry I worry you with that but I can hardly think of anything else. Luckily it ended well.

I live a very decent live without personal entertainment. My joys are Lusia and Genia. Especially Lusia is a real joy for the whole family. I have faith in the future. It's strange that despite my age I feel young (although sometimes I feel like 101). I still want a quiet happiness with a good man. I write to Henek, but he seems so far away that even his tender letters don't touch me. We all are healthy but miss you very much. Stay well and may the lucky star never leave you. Greetings for Lusia.

Your Dola

October 22, 1940

From Genka:

Dearest Uncle,

Today it is my honor to start this family letter. Here everything is as it used to be. We all work and earn so we can survive. We are very happy that we have permits to stay in Kraków. You don't even know how important it is for us not to be forced to be into some small provincial town without water and electricity. I personally don't have reasons to complain, but I would like all of us to be together again.

I send kisses to you and to dear aunt.

Genka

From Berta:

Much-loved and dear Children

We received your letters numbers 8 and 10; number 9 has not come yet. What a joy your dear letter was for us cannot be expressed in words. May the Almighty think of you for the good you have done. I wish that you should always write happy letters, that you are content. What can I write you about myself, dear child, other than that I am healthy, thank God, that we all should be happy together. I have also started to number the letters and have already numbered two. Today is number 3, I hope you receive them all.

My sweet child. Old Mirisch came to see me. He said he had received a letter from his daughter-in-law, that she had a good position and now is supposed to get an even better one in her department. She did not mention you, have you spent much for her? Once more I wish you good luck and satisfaction in your enterprise. I would like to spend the whole day writing you. I just do not have the words for what I am feeling. Thousands of kisses to you both, kindest regards to Leo and family, Paula and son. Do you see them often?

Dearest Lusia

How have you organized your housekeeping in your new apartment? I hope you are getting well settled. I would like so much to be able to see everything, what a joy that would be for me. How do you spend the evenings? Do you get together with our family? They are really very nice people. When time allows, write me a few lines. I will be very happy to hear good and cheerful things from my only daughter-in-law. I remain, with thousands of kisses, Your Mother

From Lusia:

My dearest Uncle,

I have the same wish that we all can be together again. I would be so happy if you, my beloved uncle, could write a few lines just to me.

Lusia

From Klara:

I would like to hibernate during this winter like the bears do, to see nothing and to hear nothing. It's only October but it's already cold. Is Lusia aware of her luck? That she is where Janek is? She should thank God on her knees for that. God doesn't abandon us either, of that we had a proof this week. We were nervous wrecks for a few hours but that's all. Dawid's family slept at Micha's on Senacka Street. My deep faith keeps me alive.

I don't know if the world changed or people did, who was your friend yesterday today is your enemy. I've been disappointed by many people. Those are good lessons. Dear Mother is doing well.

Greeting for both of you

Klara

From Dawid:

Thank you for the confirmation from all my heart. I received an emigration card from the consulate.[17] Thank God we are together.
Dawid

From Klara:

I didn't want to tell you this but I was afraid that somebody would inform you anyway, and in some fantastic form. The most important is that it ended well.

From Mania:

Using the left over space, I send you and Lusia warm greetings. I assure you that Dawid is still in a good mood.
Mania

October 23, 1940 Postmark

From Salo:

In connection with deportation actions we will urgently need documents stating that we have already taken some steps in order to be allowed entry into America. I make this request in view of the fact that these documents are very serious and urgent, in any case in order to show the authorities some kind of official or partially official proof that actual steps have been taken to procure entry approval into America, that you provide us with documents that are stamped or certified. At this moment nothing really threatens us but people are talking about more severe deportation actions, and then documents like this can really help us. That would prove that our stay here is not permanent and soon we will be leaving for the US. We need documents for the following people:
Gabriel Nachtigall and his wife Amalia Jetti Nachtigall
Beila Holländer (born April 4, 1866)

---

[17] As becomes clear from subsequent letters, Dawid had received confirmation that they had been placed on the emigration waiting list, not emigration cards.

Dawid Wimisner and his wife Klara and children Eugenia and Dola
Dora Stark

Please send separate documents for each family; and try to do it as
soon as possible by airmail.

October 28, 1940

From Dola:

A few days ago I sent a letter to you. Now I am writing in response
to letter number 11. I am registered with the date of September 27,
1940 under the number 043140. Now I need to wait. The American
Consulate is in Berlin. I don't understand Paula. Following everybody's
advice I wrote to Aniela that we want to add something to the costs of
the trip. How they could have understood that? I am writing to her now
that we had uninvited guests and all the savings are gone.[18] Don't take
it tragically. And please believe finally that we do eat almost like before
the war and I wish that we could live all the time the way we do till now.
The only thing that counts is that we will be able to stay here. The whole
matter went in a different direction but I am sure that Salo and Mania
as well as Dawid with family will stay. Our dear Mother wrote again
(everybody who is 70 and up can stay) asking for me to stay since she
needs me to take care of her. We will see. I won't be in the best situation if
they refuse, but even then I will survive somehow like I always did till now.

I had the best reasons to stay and to receive the pension but I made a
horrible mistake for which not only I am responsible. In January, I was
surprised by a question if I want to stay in the factory as a clerk. Based
on the fact that I am a "quiet" co-owner, I have documentation, I said
I would prefer to be considered as a co-owner. The problem was that
the papers were signed at the law office without a notary public and for
that reason the government didn't validate my co-ownership. I don't get
any pension from the factory and I lost such an important position and
work. It wasn't about pride and honor and the brothers-in-law should
have gotten better information. In addition Salo was not aware of the

---

[18] In all likelihood, the "uninvited guests" were Germans, who, as we know, frequently
searched Jewish homes for valuables.

importance of belonging to the insurance company and took my name off. He kept bothering me about that so much that I eventually agreed. I know that they didn't want to hurt me on purpose but it happened. What hurts is that I encounter attacks now, "see, you didn't want to become a clerk." One thing I know, whatever I'm experiencing and will experience I will take care of it and I will react with a stoic attitude.

Now I am doing really well, I am healthy, I eat enough, I sleep disgustingly often. I go to sleep early, get up at 6:30. The landlady promised to heat the apartment but although the roofs are covered with snow (minus 1 Celsius) she claims that it is warm.

Franka S. and Zosia Sz. declared themselves as commissioned clerks in their own store.

I receive affectionate letters from Henek. I feel that he is hoping for America, maybe for the factory as well. I wrote to him that there are wives here who live from the work of their husbands. He is naively asking if I know how they do it. In general the letters are full of empty phrases expressing sympathy (that I don't need). I am not angry with him that he is over there because many people did the same but I feel like finishing this chapter on 10 years of my life. I don't believe that this man will be able to build something again.

I will wait for the decision about being able to stay and for your opinion. Klara thinks that he won't agree to the divorce.

Dola

From Berta:

My dear Precious

I can write you only a little about myself, since Dola is going to write everything. We received letter number 9, and I am happy that at least you are content, which I sincerely wish for you. We are going through a time that is not always possible to write about. You will also get a letter from Klara, she has written you about many things. Beloved child, be satisfied today with this brief letter. In the next letter I will have more patience. Be happy, as I hope only for good news from you. I kiss you thousands of times, Your Mother Berta

For Lusia, too.

Don't worry about us, we must have hope it will get better.

From Dola (Again):

Write me Józiu why the notary public has not been arranged for me? Was something on the way? I am bitter with Salo who says: "You wanted to be the boss so now you have it." I am happy that he has a good position only because of dear Mania. He himself doesn't deserve it.

Dola

October 30, 1940

From Salo:

My dearest Józiu,

We confirm receiving your letter from October 10 (number 11), and I am in a hurry to let you know that we still can stay in our apartment on Sebastjana 7. In my letter from August 22 I asked you to write to the address of the factory, since the situation was uncertain, and we had to take into consideration that we wouldn't be able to stay. Thank God it didn't come to that, and we all – the whole family – each is in his apartment. I don't know what will come. I wouldn't worry about "betrayal," since every day brings enough stress. So you can still write to our address on Sebastjana.

We received your letter number 10. I am asking you again not to worry unnecessarily, we are not missing anything important. I reassure you that Mania, Klara and Dola have everything that's needed. Understandably everything cannot stay like it used to be, there is a war, and one of the worst in the history.

Don't send any packages. First of all we are not receiving them, so why incur the expense and burden yourself with unnecessary work. Why risk the costs for a "perhaps nevertheless."

We registered ourselves, also Dawid and Dora, with the Consular Division of American Embassy in Berlin; we are on the waiting list, numbers: 43711 and 43712, those are our waiting numbers, not quota numbers.

In order to comfort your wife, yes, according to the most recent regulation, it is possible to send used clothes to Russia. The condition is that they have to be disinfected and certified to that effect. But I am sure your mother-in-law knows that and has already made use of that.

October was very cold this year, we have even had snow.
Salo

From Mania:

Dear beloved brother,
Everybody knows that I don't have a gift for writing letters, and everybody does it for me, so I don't have much to add.
We all sit like on a volcano, our nerves are almost used up. So many months we live in uncertainty and new worries keep coming up.
Please "feed" us with some good news.
Mania

November 5, 1940

From Dola:

Dearest Józiu,
Because my last letter which I sent via airmail was full of bitterness – I wrote it in a moment of despair – I am hurrying to send you this one to cheer you up. As a result of my application, I got accepted by an insurance company again and I got rehired by the factory with the salary of 20 zloty per week. I shouldn't be too happy yet but I allow myself to feel that way because the matter of my staying here seems to be resolved and that's the most important thing for me. I know I don't have to explain this to you.

My dear, we miss you very much. About dear Mother I don't even want to talk, she works like an ant, wants to make everybody happy, but she doesn't always have enough strength and energy. She worries too much about everything (if she only had a nature similar to your mother-in-law. I went to the city with her, and she was walking and humming). Mania looks well. She decided that nobody can take what she eats away from her. Salo always complains a little although many people envy his current position at work. Dawid is still the same, but he is wise and well-informed and seems to understand the situation.

I don't have reasons to complain. Always when the situation seems to be hopeless, something happens and then a solution appears. People are always there when needed, and I can fulfill my plans. I feel lucky.

From Henek as I already wrote to you I get affectionate letters, similar to those from the times we were engaged, but they had the opposite effect on me. I don't believe him anymore. He thinks about times after the war. Maybe he hopes to go to America?

My dear, I hesitated for a long time but now I am determined to finish it. I want to write a letter to him, actually I already did. I am sending you the copy of it and I am waiting for your response. I don't think I should give him any hope. After the war divorce could be more difficult, for financial reasons or because of some blackmailing who knows? Klara thinks he won't agree to a divorce. Please answer me thoroughly if I should send him this letter or rather wait until the end of the war. In the letter I am giving him the chance to say his mind. I wrote it in a provocative manner but I didn't use the word "divorce."

Kraków looks very different now. If you went through the city you would have an impression that you are somewhere else. Many people keep asking for your address.

I don't know if I should give it. Everybody has somebody in America, and they want to send these people to you. Is it in your interest? Advise what to do.

Do you speak well now? I unfortunately don't have time to learn. I feel tired in the evenings. I don't work physically but rather emotionally. I am surprised that I still look pretty good.

Stay well, my Dear Brother. Write only good news to us. How is your throat and other things? We are very proud of you, and all the acquaintances when they hear where you are and what you do shake their heads with admiration, and say "Józek is so clever."

I am ending my "talk" with you. For a real talk, person to person, you never had time, so I am taking revenge on you now.

Hugs and kisses many times. Please always believe what I write in my letters, that's how things are. I don't add anything and don't take things away. Dola

Letter to Henek:

Dear Henek,

I received your letters and I am noticing a sudden change in them, a change for tenderness. Maybe it's just what manifests itself on the surface. This forces me to write to you honestly and openly.

You write that we will be happy when the war ends. Forgive me that I am treating this sentence as an empty phrase, since nobody can predict the end of this war. And I tell myself that your duty is to tell me what I should do and how to live during the war. Should I wait for its end? With whom and how? Our marriage wasn't great (I'll never forget the words you threw in my face: "I married you in order to get out of this little town!"). If we were a loving couple, I would understand that we are waiting for the end of the war in order to be together again. But you have to admit that our relationship called for separation many times before. On what should I base the patience for which you so strongly advise? I will tell you openly I don't have this patience. I am too tired of the times before the war and by what is happening now to be patient. Once more, patience in the name of what? What goals do we have? What memories do we share which would encourage me to suffer and be patient? I'll tell you openly that I don't have this patience and won't force myself to have it.

Before I became your wife I heard similar words, or maybe even more tender ones and what did our marriage look like? Do I have the smallest evidence that this time these words actually mean something? That they are not empty as those before our engagement were? The first time maybe we were mistaken but now we know each other. Think it over honestly. I ask you or maybe even demand for the first time perhaps, that you think thoroughly before you write to me again. There is one more aspect, no less important than others, and namely the material one. Maybe you haven't accepted yet that the factory was completely expropriated by the government. So after the war you would have to spend long years to try to be an owner of empty shelves. In this case, if I had in fact really waited for you, you would have to start to build our lives from the very beginning and give me that which a husband should give his wife. This requires lots of energy, good will and motivation to survive all these difficult times of building a new life, and we would have to do it completely alone since *there is absolutely nobody to count on!* Please keep in mind the practical issues, both for me and yourself, and write back honestly. Not with the phrases but with the whole truth.

Dear Józiu,

I got used to asking you for advice. And now in this important moment for me, although I am sure of my decision, I still cannot make this step without hearing your opinion. So I am waiting for a quick answer. If you don't like something in the letter you may change what you want.

November 7, 1940

From Berta:

Dear beloved Children!

As always I have nothing new to write, thank God I am well. What I hope is that these few lines will satisfy you. Considering all we are going through and staying healthy, it is a wonder that we can stand on our feet. The only thing that supports me is your letter in which you write of your contentment and well-being. You just do not know how happy it makes me to receive such news from you, it gives me fresh courage. Although I am very sorry that I cannot see you, I am happy that you are comfortable in your home. Perhaps the Almighty will give me enough more life that I will be able to embrace you. With my 74 years one cannot hope for a lot, but still I will not lose hope and will trust God.

Dear child, I will write you something more, since you wanted to know the situation with Paula's husband. He married and has gone with his wife to Palestine. That is what Adele wrote us. Something else, Dr. Nalmu Stein is in your vicinity, he will bring his mother over. That is enough news for today, dear child. Remain healthy and happy. Your mother kisses you both a thousand times.

Today I received regards from Frau Eder. Because her son had written to her from your letter number 5.

From Mania:

I want to use this free space and add a few words from me. I live like a true bird now. In the morning I fly out of my nest and come back every evening. We eat dinners at the restaurant, we are forced by circumstances to do so. That is all for today, my beloved Józiu. I have to leave a little space. I send my cordial kisses for you and be well.

From Klara:

Of all the former tenants we are the only ones who still live in this apartment. One of the vacant rooms was reassigned. Within days a German engineer is supposed to move in. We live in two rooms and find it very comfortable. Lusia is very diligent. From 9 to 3 she works at Elwira's and in the afternoon at home, she sews for her customers beautifully. The best proof of this is that her sister is impressed with the quality of her work.

I am sitting and contemplating what else to write, one thought follows another. They could fill a big volume. Nevertheless, I will stick to the saying that talking is silver, silence is gold.

We are all busy and the days pass quickly. I ask God for peaceful times and for good news from you.

With warm kisses

From Lusia:

Mama praised me enough. I only will add that you wouldn't find anywhere in the world another, such a hardworking fatty.

From Genka:

I also work and don't have much time. Now my biggest problem is what to buy for my father for his 50th birthday. As you see I don't have big problems.

November 12, 1940

From Berta:

Dear beloved Son

Your dear letter with the new address made us all very happy. Not everyone has the good fortune to get to such a position so quickly. Only such fine, hardworking men [as you] can accomplish something like that. You deserve it, too, my dear love. How I wish I were a fly so that I could fly to see you, my dear child. My only wishes are to know that you are happy and content. What good fortune it is for a mother to have such a dear son, everyone envies me. I do not tell anyone, but strangers talk about you. May the Almighty grant you that you are well and happy and able to do your work. I go to bed and get up with thoughts of you, my love.

Dear son, were you with the company when Leo and his wife and Paula came to your house? I thought to myself, if only I had been there. Although I was not, it made me happy that you are visiting.

I close my letter with thousands of kisses for you both,

Your Mother

Please give kindest regards to Leo and wife, Paula and son. I am sorry
for Paula that she is suffering so much, enough from her former husband,
now from her son.

Dear Lusia, how have you adapted to circumstances there?

Affectionate kisses, Your Mother-in-law   No. 6

From Klara:

Dear Józiu,

As I already wrote in the previous letter, an engineer lives with us now.
I let him paint the children's room, bathroom, and I gave him all that's
needed including sheets. I am trying to make him happy and I think we
are going to be happy as well. He leaves every morning at 8 A.M. and
comes back after dinner, lies down, and goes out again. He comes back
for the night. I prepare him herbal tea since he coughs a lot. Now I have
two coughing people, since Dawid coughs as well. He shouldn't smoke
and he smokes even more now. When the kids come home the first words
are "He is in" and I benefit from it because they are extra quiet then. I
took a Jewish girl to help, since I didn't have a maid the whole summer
and now in winter I cannot manage by myself. I am glad that the previous
girl left because this kind of people become dangerous.[19]

God bless you, Józiu,

Klara

From Dawid:

We already got a confirmation from the American Consulate that we
are on the list for Emigration Cards.

Warm greetings,

Dawid

From Genka:

Dear Uncle

We write so often that all the subjects are used up. Lusia said that
whatever I will write will be forced and labored, so I'd better not try at
all. I only want to tell you that I am very proud of you.

---

[19] This is one of the few instances in which the family mentions interacting with Catholic
Poles.

Kisses,

Sorry for the smudged ink. The pen, although it is from before the war, is still not too good.

Genka

From Lusia:

Thank you very much for the greetings for Mrs. Barkan, they were nicely surprised. Here the first snow fell already. I can imagine how wonderful it must be over there. You probably will do something wonderful to fully experience the snow. We unfortunately cannot enjoy it. But thanks to my rich imagination I am with you in every one of your escapades. I hope that my presence doesn't disturb you too much. So let me fantasize.

And you enjoy yourselves.

That's what I wish you,

Lusia

November 29, 1940

From Berta:

Dear beloved Child!

Today I am writing just a card. I have already written you several letters and received no answer. Since letter number 12 I have not received any. You have received my previous letter No. 7, therefore this card is No. 8. Dear child, if it is possible for you, please write so that I will at least have good news from you. You will be surprised that no one adds to these several lines. We could write a lot, but patience is lacking. So I close with thousands of kisses for you as well as for dear Lusia. Kindest regards from all, I remain your loving mother who hopes to have a letter from you soon. Berta

From Dola:

My beloved brother,

Your note gave me much joy. Unfortunately, the letter you were going to write me has not as yet arrived. It is hard for me to describe how happy your success makes me. I wish you many more accomplishments.

December 1, 1940

From Dola:

Dearest Brother,

Today we received the papers from the Consulario General De Nicaragua. I am at dinner at Klara's. Mania cries from happiness. Dawid got into a state of euphoria and out of joy he hit me under the rib and Genia studies the map all day long. My dear, you are a genius! Mania and Salo still do not quite believe it, and I am writing this quickly and running to the post office. In this moment Dawid reached the Zenith, he produces strange sounds appropriate for Nicaragua!

December 2, 1940

From Salo:

My dear Józiu,

For some 5 weeks we've had no news from you. We know it's not your fault and we have no doubt that you write regularly, but the fact is that for a long time we have had no news, and that makes us uneasy. The day before yesterday I talked to your mother and sister-in-law Frania, who also have not had any news from you. They both are healthy and in good spirits.

Because of various circumstances we had to leave our apartment. Temporarily we live as extra tenants at Ms. Birnbaum, 7 Gertruda. This is the house were Klarcia lives and where Birnbaum has a pub on the ground floor. So when you write next, please address it: Gabryel Nachtigall Kraków, Gertrudy Street 7, Apartment 13.

The day before yesterday we, Dawid and family, mother and Dora, received the documents for which we asked you before. Thank you very much for your effort and hope to God we won't have to make use of them, but if we do, we hope that they will be really useful. You put so much expense and effort into this and I can't do anything but to thank you from the bottom of my heart.

Please write to us dearest Józiu, maybe via Vienna, hopefully the letters will be faster this way. The whole family is healthy, at least in this aspect we can provide some good news.

Best greetings. Greetings to your wife and to the whole family that lives there.

In the name of Mania I must burden you with something that Mania couldn't refuse. With the Birnbaums, the family with whom we now live, there lives a cousin of the same name and wife who were deported from Berlin three years ago.[20] This couple had two daughters (9 and 12 years old, named Ursula and Ruth), both of whom were given over to a committee (because there was no possibility of taking them along) which sent them along with many others to London.[21] In the beginning everything went well; the parents kept getting good letters and were content. For five months now they've had no news. The parents are beside themselves and do not know what has happened to their children. Mrs. Birnbaum, with whom we live, has a brother in N.Y., Emanuel Birnbaum, living on Eastern Parkway, Jersey City, New York, to whom she has written but without answer. Birnbaum now requests that you try to contact this man either by telephone or in some other way. There is a possibility that after the bombing of London began, the kids were sent away, perhaps to America. Maybe Mr. Birnbaum would know something about the destiny of the children. Maybe there is some organization in N.Y. which would be informed of situations like this one, and they could provide some comfort for the parents?

If you could help in any way it would be really fantastic.

From Dola:

As always I am taking Salo's letter to the post office. Unfortunately I have to go all the way to Podgórze.[22] So I decided to add a few words. Among friends and acquaintances tragic trips into the unknown have already started.[23] Henek made a great gesture. Blood pressure showed

[20] This refers to the mass expulsion of Jews of Polish citizenship from Germany in late October 1938. Among those expelled at this time were the parents of Herschel Grynspan, whose subsequent assassination of a German diplomat in Paris was seized as the pretext for the Kristallnacht pogrom of November 1938.

[21] This refers to the *Kindertransport* or children's transports, whereby a number of Jewish children from Germany and Austria were allowed into England but without their parents.

[22] Podgórze was a dilapidated neighborhood in Cracow. Although Dola didn't know it at that time, Podgórze would soon become the site of the Cracow ghetto.

[23] The expulsion of Jews from Cracow resumed with three police roundups on November 29 and December 3 and 9, 1940.

300 and I cannot be happy because of that, especially as my health doesn't need any help. I couldn't wait to get an answer from you, so I did send a letter to Aunt Rózia. A few days ago I got a proof of her friendliness (I sent to you the content of that letter). Henek asks me to help him to contact his brothers. My moral duty compels me to write a letter to them. I work at the factory until 7 P.M., so I don't go to the fashion lady.

Kisses, Dola

December 8, 1940

From Berta:

Dearly loved children

Do not be surprised that I write only cards. It is not possible to write family letters because it must be written by only one hand. I wanted to write you in my own handwriting so that you won't think about it. Beloved child, we received all the papers, which pleased us greatly. Just one thing was missing, the letter which I await with longing. We have not received any since No. 12, and that made me worry. I hope everything is all right with you two. For us it is Tishab'av.[24] We live with the hope that we may once again be all together. God grant that your efforts will bear fruit. I know you are working for that. Paula wrote us; we did not understand it. Otherwise I have nothing to write except to kiss you affectionately. I would like so much to do it in person.

Your
Mother

December 9, 1940

From Klara:

Dear Józiu,

I type the letter from everybody since it can go out only with one kind of writing. Dear Mother insists on sending you a handwritten version of

---

[24] Jewish holiday commemorating the destruction of the temple.

her letter. She is convinced that a typed version of her letter would lose its charm for you.

Dear Józiu,

Many special thanks for the papers you sent us. You cannot imagine with what great joy we welcomed them. Dawid carries these papers with him all the time, just like a talisman. People envy us, and many of them want you to remember them. Of course the effects of these pages are not immediate or completely sure. And yet, having them has lifted our spirits and gives us courage to carry on.

We tried to locate the place on the map. We have been consulting the dictionary to learn about the language and the people. Now we are awaiting your long letter, which should be here momentarily.

Greetings to Lusia

Klara

From Lusia:

Dearest Uncle,

I am sitting with a pencil in my hand and cannot find the right words to express what I feel. How to thank you for such a wonderful present like a trip to Nicaragua?

Nicaragua – how wonderful it sounds! I got so enthusiastic that I decided to become a journalist over there. What do you think of that? But I didn't betray my profession yet.

I kiss you thousand of times. Grateful Lusia

From Genka:

Dear Uncle,

These papers fell like stars from the sky! Viva Nicaragua! We simply lost our heads out of joy! Aunt Dola makes us call her "senora" and Dad plans the whole future for himself. He even wants to become a newspaper delivery man over there. I would like to know something more specific about the land of our future. Is it a land that flows with milk and honey? What language do they speak there? Everybody congratulates us and is jealous that we have such an Uncle. You deserve a million kisses from the whole family.

Genka

From Dawid:

Józiu, thank you so much for the papers. Since all my family members expressed their joy already there is not much for me to add.

From Mania:

Dearest Brother,

If I thought for 24 hours what words to use to express what I feel I wouldn't find the right ones. I know very well that you haven't forgotten us and will never forget.

We worry so much when we don't have messages from you. Here everything changes very quickly.

From Dola:

I am waiting for news from you. Henek turned out to be very generous. I received a gift from him that I would rather not like to receive. It happened right after I sent him a letter, the copy of which you got as well. I thanked him and asked him not to do it any more. I was carrying this letter for a month waiting for your response, and finally I decided to send it out exactly in the moment he made such a gesture. He asks me to communicate with his brothers since his letters remain unanswered. My moral duty commands me to do so. Our situation changes every day, today we're here, tomorrow somewhere else. Forgive me if my letters are chaotic, it's difficult to control one's thoughts in such a state of excitement. Unfortunately I consider optimists as being fools now.

December 18, 1940

From Dola:

Dear Józiu,

Thank you so much for a long passage addressed to me. I am so happy that you are feeling well but I also very well know how much you do worry about us. If we only could stay in Kraków then somehow we will survive. In the worst case Mania would go to Górki, Klara with family to Szczucin, and I don't have any plans yet where I would go. I was informed that the affidavit is for Russia.[25] I am afraid to send it because somebody

[25] Apparently, Joseph included Henek in Dola's Nicaragua papers. See Dola to Joseph, January 14, 1941.

may steal it. I am not writing directly to Henek. Or somebody may cause me trouble. I wrote to Henek about that. I haven't received the answer to my important letter, and I am very curious how he will react.

My registration number is 043140 with the date of September 27, 1940. The first answer I got had a date April 4, 1940. Then, after I sent a questionnaire, I received a V2. I also learned that it is impossible to leave the General Government. Unfortunately I often feel that this struggle will never end.

How long does a letter via airmail take from Kraków to you? Do you have a furnished apartment? Did you buy furniture?

I kiss you warmly and send greetings for Lusia.

Dola

Now I am writing what Mania dictates to me, since it has to be the same handwriting. We are doing it in order to save ourselves a trip to the post office in Podgórze.

Dear beloved Brother,

The period of writing family letters ended. I don't have much to write although I could say a lot. We are having a very hard winter, and nobody is impressed anymore by either the father-in-law's fate, or Józek's. For example, Mr. Wriszel met the same fate as his son.

In order to comfort you I assure you that we do still have enough to eat, thank God, and I eat as a rule at the restaurant because it is less expensive. Write to us often. We long for your letters very much. I kiss you heartily and send greetings for Lusia.

Mania

From Dola:

I don't go to the fashion lady because she has a minimal amount of work and doesn't have the patience. Life beats her up badly, she stayed absolutely alone. I don't have any obligations towards them. The letter number 13 we did not receive.

December 18, 1940

From Berta:

My dear beloved Son,

How happy I was to take out the enclosed letter from Dola's brother-in-law, that was the best drug for me. Thank God I do not have to take any medicine, I am doing very well, you need to believe me when I write you this. I will not write you about business matters, my heart, as I do not have any. I would like to hear only good things from you two. We received all the papers and photographs you sent, for which we thank you very much, my love. You write that you moved. Did you take a furnished apartment? Write a lot to me so that I can [spend a] long time reading your letter. The longer I read, the more joy I have, dear child.

I am happy that you see Leo and his wife and Paula, I imagine what all of you talk about. Is Lusia now familiar with circumstances there? I asked Lusia but did not receive an answer. I would really like to know how she is getting along. Does she have any diversions? I would like to know so many things, my dear children. I have nothing important to write except [to send] you a thousand affectionate kisses,

Your Mother

Kindest regards to Leo and wife and Paula. Does Curti have a position yet? Since this must be in only one handwriting, all send you affectionate greetings, and if soon you do not have letters often, do not be concerned, as we can send mail only from Podgórze. At present we are still here as we were. Only Malcia has rented a room at the Birnbim [sic] Getrudy. I will tell you one more thing, since you made us aware that we should not write you in Lurnau. I had to give Leo's address to Elwira since Lusia sews at her house and she requested your address. She does not [word illegible] it for herself, only for an acquaintance. If it is not possible for you to accomplish it, then do not give an answer. I was compelled to do it for her because of Lusia. Well, enough scribbling.

From your Mother who kisses you again.

Postcard, December 28, 1940

From Berta:

Most beloved dear Children,

Although I again have nothing important to write, still I cannot neglect to write you a few lines, it seems to me, my dears, that I am talking to you, but there is a difference, since I cannot see you. Dear child, we are staying in the apartment temporarily until January 31. The gods know what will be then. The main thing is that, praise God, we are all well. I hope to hear the same from you. We have not received letter number 13, that is a loss for me, since I am missing my joy in reading. How are you doing in the new apartment? Are you both pleased? I am closing now with affectionate kisses for you both from me as well as kindest regards from all to Leo and wife and Paula.

Your Mother

December 28, 1940

From Dawid:

I received your last letter in which you express your anger that I wrote to you in this way. It really surprises me that you think that I wanted to insult or hurt you. When I wrote that letter I didn't mean anything bad I just wanted things to be sped up. Maybe I didn't express that the way I wanted to but believe me, I didn't mean anything hurtful. I received the papers from Nicaragua for which I thank you once more. Unfortunately I don't have such benefit from them as I hoped to. The most important for me would be to have their citizenship, with their passports confirmed by the German Consulate.

Everybody here says that you are very important over there and have lots of influences on people, so I hope.

From Klara:

Please forgive my husband. He wrote in a big agitation back then; don't be surprised, sometimes such horrible thoughts come upon us that we don't want to stay alive. I know that you moved earth and heaven for us so we could leave. But it's beyond your power. You did a lot and made many sacrifices, including high costs. But I don't know if these papers will save us. May God help us to be able to spend the winter here. Dawid writes about citizenship. Don't trouble yourself with that. In his vivid imagination everything is possible. Thank God we have enough to eat and enough clothes to dress.

From Dola:

I have problems typing these absurd notes from Dawid but he writes under tremendous pressure. Even Klara herself says that he has stupid demands but she asked me to type his letters anyway. I keep waiting for your letters. If only this winter passed, in the summer I won't turn down even a village. Should I send the affidavit to Henek or keep it here for myself?

My dear Brother, I wish you and Lusia a happy New Year and hope that we will spend the next ones together.

Dola

[[4]]

Familial Love, Penned
January–December 1941

In early 1941, rumors began percolating in Cracow about the creation of a ghetto for the Jews. Most Jews believed it would be established in the predominantly Jewish neighborhood of Kazimierz.[1] Instead, on March 3, 1941, the Nazis announced that the ghetto would be created in Podgórze, a secluded working-class neighborhood situated on the right bank of the Vistula River. "Podgórze was a barren area," remembers memoirist Janina Fischler-Martinho. "There were no trees, no greenery, no strip of grass to alleviate its harshness and squalor."[2] In all likelihood, the Nazis chose Podgórze as the ghetto site for more than its unsightly appearance and dilapidated buildings; the neighborhood was located near the Cracow-Plaszów railroad line – a necessary feature for deportations.[3]

While the Germans were erecting the ghetto, Dola informed Joseph that she would soon marry a man named Munio Blaustein. Although Dola and Munio's hasty marriage created turmoil in the family, there was little choice for the newlywed couple; only 17,000 Jews in the Cracow district were allowed to move into the ghetto and Munio had not been included in that group. Whereas Dola had been unwilling to leave Cracow for Henek, she unhesitatingly moved with her new husband to the nearby town of Tarnów. She explained that "Munio had to leave and I ran after him before a Chinese Wall would have separated us forever."[4]

---

[1] Graf, *The Krakow Ghetto and the Plaszow Camp Remembered*, 35.
[2] Fischler-Martinho, *Have You Seen My Little Sister?*, 52.
[3] Fischler-Martinho, *Have You Seen My Little Sister?*, 53.
[4] Dola to Joseph, March 15, 1941.

The rest of the family bid Dola and Munio farewell and prepared to move into the ghetto.

Of course, the family had no idea what lay in store for them in the now-infamous Cracow ghetto. Like most of Cracow's Jews, Joseph's relatives preferred to live there rather than leave the city. "We are very happy that we have permits to stay in Kraków," wrote Genka in late 1940. "You don't even know how important it is for us not to be forced to be into some small provincial town without water and electricity."[5] The "lucky" Jews who received permits to stay in Cracow had only ten days to relocate to the ghetto. As the Jewish families in Kazimierz closed their businesses, restaurants, and synagogues, the character of the historic Jewish neighborhood vanished forever.[6]

On March 20, 1941, the Germans created the Cracow ghetto, which featured 320 one- or two-story buildings, guard posts, and an imposing wall. It was a dreary day, and an icy wind blew harshly as the Jews moved inside. Upon seeing the ghetto for the first time, many were unnerved to find that its wall was crenellated at the top, giving it an eerie resemblance to a row of Jewish tombstones.[7]

In the ghetto, Salo, Mania, Klara, Dawid, Genka, Lusia, and Berta shared a two-room apartment. "Our apartment is not bad and we live together with Aunt Mania and Salo," wrote Genka in April. "Each family has its room and we share the kitchen. We coexist in peace and cooperation."[8] She assured Joseph that the family was "pleased in our apartment. The important thing is that we have full comfort here although it is furnished very poorly, almost funny."[9]

The Jews quickly developed a makeshift community within the ghetto walls, organizing hospitals, orphanages, homeless shelters, synagogues, and a post office.[10] They also started a newspaper and opened stores, restaurants, patisseries, and a venue in which local musicians could perform.[11] "I even take dance classes," remarked Genka about her new life in

[5] Genka to Joseph, October 22, 1940.
[6] Pankiewicz, *The Cracow Ghetto Pharmacy*, 2.
[7] Fischler-Martinho, *Have You Seen My Little Sister?*, 52.
[8] Genka to Joseph, April 23, 1941.   [9] Genka to Joseph, July 16, 1941.
[10] Pankiewicz, *The Cracow Ghetto Pharmacy*, 6.
[11] Pankiewicz, *The Cracow Ghetto Pharmacy*, 10.

the ghetto.[12] Lusia reported that she was also taking courses in sewing, cutting, and modeling, adding: "I am healthy, joyful and full of good hopes as always."[13]

At first, there was an ample supply of food in the ghetto because Jews were still permitted to work in "Aryan" neighborhoods and had the opportunity to purchase food and supplies from Poles. Salo, David, and Genka were among those permitted to work in the Aryan part of Cracow. "I work in the shop," wrote Genka, "but it is uncertain how much longer I will be able to work."[14]

As Genka feared, the Germans soon began to strip Jews of their permits to work in Aryan neighborhoods, causing rampant shortages within the ghetto.[15] After the ghetto was sealed in October, food became increasingly scarce.[16] For the Jews, the hunger pangs merely underscored that they were prisoners whose lives depended on the whims of the Germans. For their part, the Germans strived to remind the Jews of their powerlessness; they murdered more than 2,000 Cracow Jews in 1940 alone.[17]

January 5, 1941

From Salo:

For some time now we haven't received anything from you. We do understand that in times like this one cannot count on regular correspondence but we always worry when your letters don't come for a long time. After all they are the all too seldom bright moments in our daily existence.

For several weeks you sent your letters via Vienna, the last one was supposed to be number 13. Also Adele said that she sent a letter from you to us. It appears that it got lost on the way. Maybe it's the famous "13" which plays its tricks on earth for so long now? If the letter contained something important please repeat it again.

---

[12] Genka to Joseph, July 16, 1941.   [13] Lusia to Joseph, April 23, 1941.
[14] Genka to Joseph, April 23, 1941.   [15] Duda, 66.
[16] Duda, 66.
[17] Roma Ligocka, *The Girl in the Red Coat*, trans. Margot Bettauer Dembo (New York: St. Martin's Press, 2002), 28.

Nothing new here. Concerning pure physical health, Mother and the rest of the family are well, and we must give special thanks to God for that. There is enough to eat as well, of course we have to have very modest requirements. From the packages you sent we received only the first three. Did you try to trace the rest of them? Well, don't try sending us stuff anymore, because it's a waste of food.

How is your life? Are you satisfied with the business and with life over there in general? We hope so and wish you that from the bottom of our hearts. How are Paula and Leo?

May God help us to see each other soon again.

Your loving brother-in-law.

Is the old Mr. Schreiber already in America?

Please use the address of Gertrudy Street 7, Apartment 7.

Mania sends her best to all, but does not write, because different handwriting in one letter is not allowed. Basically she has nothing special to report, in person she would have lots to say but in writing just greets you both warmly. Accept our best greetings once again and write soon and often.

January 8, 1941

From Berta:

Dear treasured Heart,

As always I am writing to you today, dear child, I have nothing important to write, am healthy, thank God. I am sad about one thing, that I have no letter from you. The last letter was number 14, it is already a long enough time since I received it. Letter number 13 has not arrived. Are you at least receiving my letters, I write every week. It is my pleasure to write you both and to read letters from you. My dear child, when you write, write a lot, so that I can read for a long time. We are having a hard winter. The snow is very deep, I do not go out at all.

Affectionate kisses for you both,

Your Mother

Kindest regards from all to Leo, wife, Paula.

January 8, 1941

From Dola:

Dear Brother,

There are such long pauses between the messages! You asked to send you just in case the address of a sister of our good friend. Here it is: Ms. Regine Hütschnecker, St. Gallen, Frongarten strasse 9, Switzerland.[18]

The siblings write to each other regularly, and her brother is every day at our house. What's new with you, my darling? We are guessing that it is not your fault that we have so few messages. We are healthy and have enough food. The winter in normal conditions would be wonderful. There is lots and lots of snow, but it's not freezing cold. Mania works in the kitchen at Klara's. I too go there for dinners.

The nightmare of deportation haunts us, but it's not too long before spring comes. I want to divorce. I wrote to Henek but he didn't answer. He is very sweet and tender in his letters but it's too late.

Stay well, my Dear Brother,

Dola

January 14, 1941

From Klara:

On Jan. 11 we have finally received the letter number 16. It means that number 15 got lost. We miss you so much, and are very happy because of your choice. Here everything is okay. The most important now is to survive the winter here in Kraków. I am glad that you finally received the birth certificate. His wife is of the same age, do the same for her, please.

I think you got the answer for the letter from November 5 where Dawid apologized.

Dear Mother wrote separately last week. Thank God she feels well.

The papers that we received from Nicaragua do not do for us what we expected, although they are validated by the German consulate. What is

---

[18] Little does Joseph know that Dola's "good friend" is Munio Blaustein, his future brother-in-law.

important is to have citizenship papers that are validated by the German consulate.

Greetings from Dawid and the kids, Klara

From Dola:

I have to complain about the Dear Mother who confiscates your letters and nobody except her can keep them for too long. She puts all of them into a little box organized by dates, they are like good omens for her. You would be happy seeing her working in the kitchen. You have to know that Klara has a real diner. No matter at what time of a day anybody can come here and will get food. My dear, don't send anything, at least not now. We don't know how it's going to be later. If we have some needs I will write to you, to whom should I write if not to you?

Henek does whatever he can in order not to lose me. He made a gesture I wouldn't expect. I wrote him to stop since you understand that I don't want to be obliged to anything. Especially that I wrote him a letter and described how things look like from my side. I am not sure what to do with the affidavits in our names. For goodness sake, if I would leave, then not together with him of course. I don't have to explain that to you. If his brothers want to do something for him, fine. If Henek will request an affidavit which is not valid here anyway, what do I do?

I still work at the factory until 3 P.M. every day, I get 20 zloty weekly. Unfortunately my department of "patching up the old underwear" doesn't prosper too well. I should have 5% out of the whole income.

This winter I feel like I haven't felt for a long time, strong and healthy. I prevented my cold in the very beginning of winter. Dr. Klassa gave me very good drops. I also have a warm room and finally I don't have to move every few weeks.

How do you like the American pace of life? How do people live there? Don't pay attention if the addressee will be unknown to you. Does Lusia help you at the office, or stay at home? Klara's Lusia sews really beautifully, she does it for the whole family and she has many paying customers as well. She doesn't do it out of necessity; she really enjoys it. I am writing you honestly that we all are healthy and not hungry and we hold on to the thought to see you soon again.

Greetings for Lusia. Many kisses for you.

Dola

January 22, 1941

From Berta:

Dearest beloved Son,

As an exception I am writing a letter today, because I want to repeat to you, dear child, the letter that Klarcia wrote you in response to your letter to Dawid. Perhaps that letter will not arrive, but mine will. It has to do with the birth certificate you took care of, they are happy and thank you. Now the wife will also send her birth certificate. She is the same age as he, they ask you to take care of it as well.

Dear sweetheart, imagine how your mother-in-law surprised us when she visited us on Sunday. She had found out that we received papers and wanted to know what kind. It is too bad that we cannot write family letters, it has to be written in only one hand. Dear child, I do not always have a lot to write to you, therefore I am writing only cards, I wrote you 4 cards but did not number them. When I write, I think of you, dear child. I forget to number, I am beginning with number 1.

You ask if we need money, thank you at the moment we do not need any. My dear heart, this week we will know if we will be staying or not. I will write you right away, meantime I want to have good news from you. Each letter I have from you is good medicine for me. The letter we just received was number 16, but number 15 is missing. With each loss of a letter from you, I feel how I miss you. I live in the good hope that you and dear Lusia are comfortable. I close my letter to you with thousands of kisses.

Your loving Mother

Many greetings to Leo and wife and Paula.

All the children, since we are together, send fondest greetings.

Address same as before.

February 1, 1941

From Dola:

I received your letter and a post card. I hope that in the spring the mail will travel faster. We also received a long letter from Paula. She is a very dear but a very unhappy woman. What kind of person is her son?

My dear, doing anything in order for me to get my share and to receive some pension is worthless. It's a lost case. I am glad I returned there at all; at least I get 104 zloty every month. Staying there is out of the question however. The relations there are very different now. Mania and Salo received his permit until March, with the possibility to extend it, that's a big deal, worth a lot. The rest of us are still unsure. If I get my permit I will immediately send you a message. There are many people here who are glad that they moved already in summer into some small town. From Paula we know that you are doing well if it were not for your constant worries about all of us. Please don't worry too much. Spare your health for after the war. That is probably the only method to survive.

I couldn't wait any longer for your answer (and I thought that your letter got lost), so I sent a letter to Henek. I could expect anything but that he will use his friend to communicate with me (I rewrote his letter as well as my answer at the end of this letter).

I am 100% decided for divorce. I went to the rabbinate and they told me that both rabbinates would take care of this in the places they are located. I could sign it here and Henek where he is. I have to tell you that according to Henek's wish I always send my correspondence to him at the address of Mr. Marienstraus. I never knew Henek's address except the name of the town. Maybe you will like my response. Do you believe in this illness of Henek?

My dear, I will reveal this secret to you after the war, but you can trust me. I am more reasonable than before the war. Please accept for now that I do manage and I wish that it remained like this till the end of the war. You should also know that I have 5% from fixing old garments. I also sold many things which now became only a burden, and I have some money out of this. I don't have time now to deal with the fashion business. I was able to attend the classes only for a few weeks but I learned fast. Aniela studies fashion.

I wrote to a very trustworthy person in Russia asking for information about Henek, especially about his health. From this source I will know the truth (I didn't write but asked somebody to write for me all very discrete). This person is a brother-in-law of Dr. P. . . , and he is an acquaintance of Henek and is also in Drohobycz.

I thank you warmly for your nice and long letter. I was very happy to receive it. I wish you all the best, my dear. Greetings for Lusia.

Dear Madam,

Your letter and a postcard were brought to me from the post office to be delivered to your husband. Till now I am still in possession of them since I haven't had an opportunity to deliver them to Henek yet. I read both your letters. I am obliged to provide you with an answer concerning these letters. Sending to Henek his belongings is not necessary. These things are not needed. It would be advisable that you sell them and use the money to improve your material situation. You could also do the same with other belongings of your husband.

What concerns your proposal to separate, although you didn't state it clearly but rather camouflaged it between the lines, is certainly possible, from what I know, and you can finalize it according to your will, at any time. My letter is a result of my feelings of responsibility, of the most honest concern, and the faithful friendship towards you, which I have through my relationship with Henek. Please accept the content of this letter in this way, and please don't be upset that I interfere with your private affairs.

Henek is very ill and only God can be a doctor.

So you won't worry too much, I reassure you and stress that I didn't deliver your letters to Henek. May God be my witness: I will *never* do that.

With best regards,
Benjamin Marienstraus

Dola's Answer:

Dear Sir,

I am confirming receiving your letter. I accept the first part but I do not trust the second part of the letter speaking about the illness of my husband. I do not believe in coincidences unless one causes them himself. I would feel very disturbed if my husband lay ill. I am full of positive thoughts about him and wish for his happiness despite the fact that I requested divorce, or maybe all the more because I did.

Since you are authorized to manage divorces, I would like to accept your offer and I request a letter written by my husband that would contain these words: "I agree to a divorce." Please send me information about the health of my husband.

Regards, Dola

To Józiu,

Bye, my dear. Before you will get this letter I really wish that things will go well according to my wishes. Don't pay attention to the sender's address, it's more convenient for me this way.

February 6, 1941

From Mania:

I haven't written for so long because there are things you can experience but cannot describe. In the situation we are in right now the letters from you are the only sunshine. Dear Józiu, please write to us often. Your letters create an illusion that you are close here with me.

Paula wrote to us that she visited you, she wrote how nicely you live and have everything, which makes me really happy. May God give you always everything that you need. Paula is delighted with you; she understands now that I didn't exaggerate when I talked about you. She wishes that Kürli[19] would be more like you. Leo also praised you very much and likes you a lot.

Dola wrote to you that Salo and I have a permit to stay and it will probably be prolonged as long as Salo works here. Dola received notification about her being given a permit to stay, but we don't know for how long. Dawid and his family don't know yet, but the worst situation concerns Dear Mother (things changed), so far she can stay only until February 28, and I don't know what will happen before you get this letter. What can we do? Maybe we will survive.

Dear Józiu, we got two packages with the same content: flour, cream of wheat, corn and bacon. Only bacon we will try to exchange since none of us wants it. I know that Salo asked you for a package, and did it without my knowledge. That was unreasonable, he made you spend this money and now he regrets that.

I assure you that so far we have enough to eat, nobody is hungry, if only we could eat this in peace. Dear Józiu, please do not send packages anymore. When we will need it we will write to you. These times teach us how little we need and that we can be satisfied with very little.

---

[19] Presumably a nickname for Paula's son, Curti.

We both greet you and Lusia warmly. Thanks for the telegram. We were very happy to receive it.

Mania

February 11, 1941

From Klara:

Dear Józiu,

On February 6 Dear Mom has already written back to your letter number 17. Now I'll write a few words. We received your telegram, what a comfort for our hearts! We also got a package which I took to Dear Mother. I was just boiling water for the cream of wheat when your package came. And there was also cream of wheat! But what a difference! Like night and day! We got cream of wheat, flour, corn. That's all very good, we only exchanged the bacon. Mania also received such a package. We are living day after day in anticipation of our identification cards. Our old IDs are not valid anymore. Mania and Dola already have them but they are valid only until March, maybe they will be able to prolong them again.

Thank God that winter is almost over. In summer we can live in the village, we even have rented a room in Grabówka (close to Wieliczka).[20]

Dear Józiu, you surely got my letter where I wrote about the birth certificate for the wife of Kaufman, since she asked us for that. Please send it to us if you were able to take care of that. Kisses and greetings, also from Dawid and the children.

Klara

February 12, 1941

From Dola:

Recently I sent you a long letter but I am going to the post office in Podgórze so I am using the opportunity and am responding to your last letter from Miami (it's apparently so beautiful there). You gave us a travel route. Well, it is impossible to leave the General Government, so don't

---

[20] Wieliczka is on the southeastern outskirts of Cracow.

waste your energy and money. We will write more about that in a letter. I got a permit to stay until March 5. What will happen afterwards? Maybe it will be possible to prolong it.

Mania and Salo received a permit until March 1. We still need to arrange that for Klara with her family; I hope that they will receive identification cards but they all don't seem to be valid for long. I do go to the factory. We are healthy. I don't even know what the movie theater means anymore.

I have to be at home at 9 p.m. I have become so undemanding that I am happy when the day passes without any events. I kiss you warmly.

Dola

February 15, 1941

From Berta:

My dear beloved Children,

Again I have lost a letter from you two, number 18, as I have received number 19. I feel each loss, since reading each of your letters is good for my health. My dears, I was so pleased with your letter of January 4, as I am with all your letters, to know that you are well and content. I regret that you were called away so suddenly from such a beautiful area. Write me good news again.

Dear child, I cannot write much about myself, I would not have enough paper to write everything down. Thank God for everything, that we can walk about. The winter was very hard. We lived in the hope that the sun would shine again, and we could breathe a sigh of relief. Dear sweetheart, do not be concerned about us. You are doing what you can. For the present you cannot do any more to help us. Maybe the time will come when we will see each other again; just now we will have to be patient and satisfied with good letters. I for myself am not satisfied because I cause my dear children worry with my condition. I would very much like to hold out, age counts for a lot.

Under the present conditions as I am writing you, I am again doing very well, the best proof is that I am writing to you. You should not be anxious, it is better to say "one has been sick than one has been rich," thus life has hope.

To you my only Lusia, I say thank you for your letter, which dearly pleased me and I wish to hear only good and happy things from you two. I close with hugs and affectionate kisses which unfortunately are only on paper.

Your loving Mother

From the dear children, affectionate greetings to you, to Leo and wife and son.

Paula and son kindest regards. I am very sorry for Paula that she still must work for her son. Unfortunately not every mother has such children as I do. I need to grow young. I should still (be able) to see something good for all. How hardworking Genka and Lusia are, both are earning. Thank God that Dawid can still take care of himself alone and does not need the children's help.

Dear child, much scribbled today.

I am glad that you will send us your pictures. We cannot send you any, as much as we want to.

February 17, 1941

From Dola:

You are asking how I resolved the situation with my marriage. Something happened that I haven't wished, had not wished either for me or for him. Many people didn't even believe that he was sick. And today on the street an unknown woman came to me and told me that her husband wrote to her that he was at Henek's funeral. Dear Józiu, I just got up from the floor where I lay for two hours as a penance (they told me to do so). He died in December. Although I wanted to get divorced my pain is deep. I wished him happiness which we couldn't find together. I became a fatalist. For 10 years I couldn't get myself to do what I did in his last days or maybe when he wasn't alive any more.

Bye, my dear. When I get myself more together I will write a longer letter. Send your letters to the address of the factory. Mania and Klara have to change their addresses. We have temporary permits to stay but we don't know for how long.

Dola

February 25, 1941

From Dola:

A couple of days ago I sent you a short card in which I informed you about the death of my husband. Although you know very well how it was between us, I do cry because of his death, which was not wished for by anybody. If I had gotten my freedom through divorce I would have a light heart today, and now it is sad and difficult (I write that without pathos). I reacted painfully to his death. This timing that may have something to do with destiny horrifies me!

He died of a heart attack. His heart was weak, and no wonder that he strained it even more. His work in a restaurant added to that. He was a vice director, and stayed up all night long. A state of absolute apathy fell upon me but I am aware that I have to have lots of energy now, and hope that time will do its job.

I was in Nord Deutscher Lloyd and they told me that one can leave the General Government on a foreign passport (but based on the case of this woman in Tarnów it may be only theoretical). By having a foreign passport one is treated according to international rules for foreigners. And foreigners have all kinds of benefits.

If you will be able to arrange these passports, please do it first of all for Klara and her family. They have made the decision and would be ready to leave. Salo and Mania don't seem to show much enthusiasm. They feel too old to start a new life but please ask them directly.

What concerns Dear Mama, please don't have any illusions my dear; the war didn't make her younger, and such a long trip would be too taxing for her fragile health. As for myself, such a move would place me under your protective wings and at the same time offer me a chance to escape. And still, I cannot say clearly what my decision is or would be.

I am commenting on these different possibilities because I want to protect you from incurring unnecessary expenses. Only one thing is sure: Dawid with his family are determined.

We also have to take into consideration that the situation is very uncertain. We would not want to make all the formal arrangements, thanks to your efforts and expenses, and even then these departures might still not take place for other reasons. That would be really awful.

If you decide to undertake any steps (if you think it is a reasonable thing to do) please contact N. D. Lloyd in Kraków, on Adolf Hitler Square 16. They committed themselves to take care of everything and be in touch with you. We, for certain reasons, don't want to make a deposit though it's not about money.

The only bright stream of light for us is the thought that you are well and free over there. Be a lucky child in all you are doing. Stay well, my dear.

Greetings to Lusia.

I kiss you a thousand times.

Please write kindly to:

Mack Liebeskind

620 E 93rd Street

Brooklyn, NY

His sisters are worried. A year ago he showed some good will to bring his sisters over; it's about the brother of Franka, Lusk L. Brata.

I am writing this letter with the knowledge and in the name of the family. They are very busy with moving now. Mania already rented a new apartment. I am simultaneously sending a letter from Salo through the regular post.

Dola

February 26, 1941

From Salo:

Yesterday we received your letter number 22 and your previous letters from Florida. We are very happy that at least one person from our family has a better life, and may God cause that only the best things in life will come your way. You deserve that and we all feel this with our hearts. Not only we but everyone who knew you and had anything to do with you is really happy as well. We and Klara received a package with coffee, butter, sugar and cocoa. We thank you for that. The other packages probably got lost. As I see you wrote to them, and hopefully you will be reimbursed for that loss. It looks like you ordered again all kinds of things for us, through Bulgaria and Denmark. Please don't pay for anything before you know that we received them. It's such a waste of money. Not for a second did we doubt your good will.

About the documents and the next steps I may be able to write in the next few days. That's the thing that interests us the most, and we cannot do anything about this. We had to leave our apartment on Gertrudy 7 within 24 hours. We don't have anything new yet. I wouldn't even start to describe what kind of a problem it is that compels us therefore to neglect all the other problems. Temporarily we stored the few things that we have in the apartment 16 on Gertrudy Street, but we need to wait for the approval. Whether we get it and for how long is a different question. But we don't want to lose our sleep because of that, this too must somehow be overcome.

You asked about my employment; I still work at the factory. How long it is going to be possible only God knows, anyway I try to stay there as long as possible. The salary lasts until the 10th of each month but the most important thing is that one is employed.

At the end one more item of news, a very sad one. Henek: Dola's husband died. You know how his relationship with Dola was. He didn't enjoy any special liking within family for which he was mostly guilty himself but despite all this, the message about his death really touched me deeply. Disregarding his many faults he was a talented man with a good head. May God make him happy where he is now.

We greet you warmly. For a long time now I haven't received a line just for me. Can I ask for that? We will send our new address when we have it. Also Klara had to leave her apartment. So send all the letters for us and Klara to the address of the factory:

Wäschefabrik Port Gertrudy 27

Salo

March 6, 1941

Dola Sends to Joseph the Letter Written to Berta from Munio:

Very Respected Madam,

I regret very much that my departure happened so quickly and I wasn't able to speak to you in person, to present my request as well as to show my love and devotion which I am trying to express in my letter.

It hasn't escaped your attention that Dola became very dear to me during the last 18 months. We both feel such a high level of love and devotion for each other that we can seriously think about spending the rest of our lives together. The only thing that is missing is your blessing Dear Mother, whom I respect so much and love like my own Mother, I ask you from all my heart to be a mother for me, too. I loved my own mother more than anything. I devoted my life to her, but all my giving didn't keep her alive. I would feel blessed by God if I could find her in you. I can assure you that with all my heart (not only in an official way) I always will be a devoted, faithful son, always, like I was for 31 years for my own mother.

I know your heart and your thoughts, Dear Mother, please give me permission to call you this way. I know that you are concerned about your daughter and about the steps she takes. You wonder if she makes the right decision, if this will really make her happy.

It's difficult for me to write about this, I don't want to make an impression of a bragger, and you, Dear Mother, have to see for yourself. You should trust your feelings like Dola trusts hers. I can only assure you that I am an honest man with good character, who will always be faithful to his heart and to his word. And there is no doubt that my heart makes me totally devoted to Dola. I will be an honest, faithful, and devoted husband. By giving us your blessings you will make the connections of our heart sacred. I can assure you, Dear Mother, that you are giving your daughter into hands which are no less loving than your own. I will take care of Dola all her life long.

There is not a right time to wonder about the material side of my life with Dola, there is a war going on. War destroys everything, big possessions, and leaves only ruins. Taking for a husband a rich man without character seems to be a bigger risk than marrying a poor man with pure character and good heart and soul. Please don't think that I praise myself too much. I swear to do everything in order to support Dola in an honest way, and I will take care of Dola's health and well-being. We will try to bring only joy into your life.

In our situation today there is one more thing I need to discuss, it's about the love between you Dear Mother and Dola. I know that Dola won't be able to be really happy without your presence in her life. Therefore I ask you, Dear Mother, to accept my offer of living with us. It will be a pleasure and relief for us, and I promise that we will never treat this situation as a burden.

One more official thing: Because of the sudden death of Dola's first husband we have to wait for one year, as long as the mourning period lasts. Because the situation of the war forces people to do things they wouldn't do otherwise, I am asking you Dear Mother to give us permission for a religious wedding and we will wait for the civil registration for another year.

In any case, I really ask you Dear Mother to let Dola come here to me as soon as possible, in order to make these difficult times easier for both of us. Please understand us both. Dola would feel lonely in Kraków, without friends, only with her family, and with fainting hope that we will see each other again soon as it will be impossible for her to leave the Jewish street. For me to be by myself in a strange place and to work there would be very hard, without the good and faithful life companion.

I ask you for motherly understanding. My letter comes from the bottom of my heart and is written with full seriousness. I will impatiently wait for your permission and your blessings.

I kiss your hand,
Munio Brandsdorfer[21]

March 8, 1941

From Salo:

Dear Józiu,

We received your last letter. You must have gotten my letter in which I am letting you know about Dola's separation from her husband. Today we received three packages from Lisbon, two for the Nachtigalls and one for Klara. What they contain I don't know yet. I haven't gotten to opening them yet. I thank you in Mania's name and my own. Mania will write herself. Recently she wounded her right hand and cannot hold the pen too well.

Today Dola left for Tarnów where she will probably settle down. It is connected with the fact that Mr. Brandsdorfer whom she is very close to lives there and after the official mourning time they may unite. Today

---

[21] On other occasions, Munio uses the last name of Blaustein. It is unclear why he signs this letter Brandsdorfer.

I write only briefly about that. I am sure that Dola is going to relate everything in detail, I myself will come back to this subject later on.

Please forgive me that I am so dry today. My heart is so full as if a belt of steel were tied around it. It is ready to burst.

I am glad that your business is going well. I wish you only successes.

Each of the 3 packages contained 100 grams of tea and 300 grams of coffee.

Your mother-in-law visited us yesterday. What a woman! Full of energy and lust for life, you rarely see this now. She made us all feel energized and joyful. I can only congratulate Lusia on having such a mother.

Salo

From Mania:

Dear Józiu,

Thanks for the packages with tea and coffee. Dear God himself solved Dola's marriage. Dola received our blessings when she left for Tarnów since she will unite with Mr. B. He came here before the war from Katowice, they met here, were friends, he also knew Henek. Now he had to leave Kraków and move to Tarnów. We will send you his letters written to Mother. May God give them happiness. He is not a man of big size but he has a very good, pure character.

Many people received Nicaraguan citizenship. Please try with all your means to get it for us. There is no possibility to leave now but if we had the citizenship it could make everything much easier.

The kids of the Birnbaums wrote already, do not worry about that any more. We still live on Krakowska Street 9 but only temporarily. We will write you about what happens next: we will either leave or move to the Jewish quarter in Podgórze.

March 15, 1941

From Dola:

My Dear Brother,

You will be very surprised at the content of this letter. I was hesitating to write before I knew the details. And today I want to inform you that on Tuesday March 18, I will marry a man I have known for 18 months now. I met him at the beginning of the war, he was always a source of tremendous support for me in the most difficult moments. I am not going to list for you all his good sides (he has bad ones as well) because you may think that I am regressing back to *my* teenage years. I am a mature and experienced woman. I am building upon the goodness of his heart and purity of his character as well as on his intellectual qualities. My farewell to the family was pretty tragic since we don't know when we'll be able to see each other again. But they are comforted by the fact that I am in good hands. The whole family had a chance to meet this man (his name is Munio), and Salo liked him very much. He comes from Poland, he studied philosophy in Vienna where he lived with his family for 25 years. He came to Kraków from Katowice where he ran a big furniture house. Today like everybody else he has lost everything. What's left is the most important, and it is the only thing that counts in a man. We are together in Tarnów. Munio had to leave and I ran after him before a Chinese Wall would have separated us forever.

In Krakow he was a clerk in the local government and he managed wonderfully, he hasn't lacked cookies and wine. Today we do have a problem. But we are not losing our hope. Temporarily we live from our savings. In connection to these material problems I have a favor to ask (before it wasn't necessary): could you please send me a kilogram of coffee, tea and cocoa every month? If you could do this it would mean a lot for me: I would feel like I am living in luxury. All the other things we can get here. Don't send us money. I trust your cleverness that you will manage somehow to send me the mentioned things. Either from the US or through other countries (the first time as an experiment to see if it will arrive). Will the documents you are trying to get for us be of any benefit to us now?

Maybe you will receive a letter from Munio's brother from Paris. They love each other dearly. He also has a sister in Switzerland. His brother's address: Artur Blaustein, Paris IX, Rue Sauluier 13. He had a shoe business in Vienna. He may write to you since he will be equally surprised as you are by what has happened, and he cares about his brother's happiness. I get news from home every day, in this aspect I am in a better situation than you are.

Dearest Józiu, please don't worry about me. I am sure that my decision will lead to a bright future if we survive this terrible war. I will be at the side of a wonderful man who now becomes my whole family. I put hopes in him which he will for certain fulfill.

The civil wedding ceremony is not going to take place, first of all because of a mourning period, second because it's prohibited.

Well, my dearest brother, life surprises us sometimes in a strange way. Maybe I will finally taste some happiness as well? Today I would be a happy woman, if not for my worries about money. But this is like a disease that everybody suffers from, we are not alone.

I am expecting a long letter from you for which I will be impatiently waiting. They send me your letters from home under the condition that I'll send them back as soon as I read them. I cannot know what the future will look like concerning the sending of letters or packages.

I wish you lots of happiness. May God help us to be together again. Greetings for Lusia. Kisses, Dola

From Munio:

Dear Brother-in-law,

I heard so many good things about you from your whole family that I wanted to write to you myself. I want you not to worry about the life of your dear sister. Dola wrote you already a lot; I am being informed about your letters to her, in which you worry if she is not making a mistake. I have to reassure you, my Dear Brother, that both of us decided to unite not only because of the feelings we have for each other. We both are fully aware of the situation, and we are convinced that we can give each other everything we need, and make each other truly happy. From my end, I will do everything in order to be for Dola everything she needs all her life long. I am very sorry that we found each other in these hard times when we don't have an opportunity to give each other as much as we would wish. My heart is full of the best gifts for her. Your family has known me for 18 months now, they gave us their blessings, may it be enough for you dear Józiu to give me some credit I know that I won't disappoint you. I will write a few words about myself to give you an idea who the husband of your sister is: I graduated from the philosophy department in Vienna. I had an export business; and in the last years before the war I had a furniture business in Katowice. After the war I started to work as a social worker in Kraków, and now I am busy looking for a job.

I expect to be able to earn enough in order to support Dola and myself since I have also this quality that I am always ready and eager to do new things. Now we live from our savings and may God help us to survive on that before we'll find something to do. The most important thing is to survive until the end of the war; and I am sure that my optimism for the future will be fruitful, and the sun will shine again for me and Dola.

I would be very grateful to you, my dear Józiu, if you would write me back, and give Dola your blessings. She really cares about that a lot, and she feels that it would be like her father's whom you replace for her now.

Once more I reassure you about Dola: she is in the hands of a man who loves her dearly, and who will try to replace even her brother whom she is so fond of.

I greet you warmly as your new and devoted brother-in-law.
Munio Blaustein

March 21, 1941

From Klara:

Beloved Józiu,

Finally, after several weeks I feel calmer. As I already wrote you, we had to move out of Gertrudy's place, for ten days we lived on Krakowska Street. And now after prolonged deliberation we transferred to Podgórze. This is a Jewish quarter[22] and for the time being we are satisfied. We live in one of the rooms. The second room is occupied by Mania's family. The third one is occupied by uncle and his family. We all share the one kitchen. God willing, we should be able peacefully to spend the rest of the war here. We could have gone to Szczucin, where we have a room. However, one never knows where it would be better. Besides, in addition to not being sure about wandering around, we also did not want to separate from Mother and Mania.

As for Dola, I was not for her getting married right now. But she wanted it this way and we could not interfere. What seemed to attract her most to him was the fact that he offers her what she never had from her first husband (let him rest in peace). Even though, right now he is

[22] "Jewish quarter" was one of the Nazi euphemisms for an official ghetto – that is, a delimited area into which all Jews and out of which all non-Jews had to move.

unemployed, he is very energetic and full of ideas, somehow they will manage.

Thank you very much for the last three packages I received. This makes 5 packages. In each of them there was coffee and tea, only in the first two, as I told you already, there was something else which was particularly appreciated by Mother.

Did you receive the second birth certificate? A week ago Mother mailed you a letter. In a little while Mania will be able to write you. This week she will have the cast removed from her hand. Also Dola is writing you a letter.

Your mother-in-law lives not far from us, she visits us. Indeed, today she is supposed to go to Salo to add photos. I wrote about this matter to Munio and Dola. I am very concerned if, and whether, you can afford all this. Maybe there will come a time when we will be in a position to repay you for all this.

With heartfelt wishes and regards from all of us, including myself.
Klara

March 22, 1941

From Berta:

My dear beloved Children,

I have not written you for a long while, not because of laziness, but my health has been up and down again. I am back on my feet again and doing fine. I wish I could be in your arms and cry my eyes out to your good heart, then I would be calm. My dear child if you receive a letter from Dola, do not be surprised that she has taken such a step. As her mother I encouraged her, since she could not do anything else. She could not get support from anyone and she did not want to be a burden to the brothers-in-law. She was a thorn in the side, not everything she did was right, for this reason we suffered, because we were tired of her. You know that the sisters are fond of each other, so they encouraged her. It was not so easy to say good-bye, but we realized that it would be better for her. The Almighty should help her. She ought to be happy, since she has had a hard time for ten years. God grant that this may be the right thing. I ask you, my dear child, do not be angry with her and think about her. Her address: Herr Ferdinand Birt für M Blaustein, Tarnów.

I close with thousands of kisses for you both.
Your loving Mother
Sincere regards from all also to Leo, wife.
Paula, son kindest regards.

March 23, 1941

From Berta:

My dear beloved Children!

I have a lot to write today, though one cannot confide everything on
paper, we have been through difficult weeks. Salo wrote you, dear child,
that Malcia fell and unfortunately still has her hand in a cast. The work
that we have, we share as we can. We are living together, each has one
room. My dear sweetheart, I already wrote you about Dola. I am happy
that she is not suffering with us. God knows what he is doing so that she
should be free. With us she had no peace, with her all the openings were
concealed, as though she were the stepchild. Her sisters and I suffered
from it. At least she is with her husband among unfamiliar, but good
people. May the Almighty help her. I have enough heartache with two
dear children out of my sight. I comfort myself and hope that at least
you are both content. Dola writes me that she is pleased. She just frets
that you, my dear child, should not be angry with her because of this step
she has taken. For 18 months we saw her husband often. He is a good,
hardworking man and gets along with everyone. Write to them so that
she can be reassured that you will not hold this against her. You know
how she suffered for ten years. Peace to his ashes.

We received the packages you sent. I cannot tell you how many, but
there were a lot. You need not send us anything, only if it is possible for
you to send (something) to Dola in Tarnów. The address is Ferdinand
Birt for Blaustein, Wielke Schody 5/5. Dawid was in an office to send
a telegram, the official said that their office is next to yours, so make
inquiries and take further steps for them, because it is important for
Dawid and family. By mistake Salo did not give you exactly the day of
your good father's Jahrzeit. It is a day later, that is, Sunday, May 4.[23]

---

[23] The anniversary of the death of Joseph's father according to the Jewish calendar
changed with each year's Christian calendar.

Enviable is the person who has not experienced this. Nevertheless, I live in the hope that we will yet experience good things. My love, do not be worried about us. God protects each one, the nearer the pain, the quicker the consolation. Be happy and content.

I kiss you both many thousand times,
Your loving Mother
Greetings to Leo and wife, Paula and son.
Berta

March 26, 1941

From Dola:

Dearest Brother,

A couple days ago I wrote a letter, but we cannot be sure if you receive everything. I am writing again and trying my luck with the help of dear Adele.

I am in Tarnów for three weeks now, where I got married. My husband is a man whom I have known since the beginning of the war, and who always provided support in the most difficult moments. If we would have stayed in Kraków we would have waited with the marriage, but since Munio had to leave we didn't have another choice. Tarnów is a small religious town. Munio wrote a separate letter to you, where he wrote you his curriculum vitae. He lived in Vienna for 25 years, studied philosophy, he is a very intelligent guy. Our family knows him well and gave us their blessings.

Dear Józiu, it's not very easy, of course, but we do hope we will survive. Munio is eager to do any work, and, what's most important, he is an optimist. I am waiting for your reply and your blessing. Thank God that you were spared the harshness of the war.

I would like to ask you again for coffee, tea and cocoa. Many people get these goods from Portugal, maybe it's easier that way?

Wish you luck and happiness in everything.

Please send possible packages to: Blaustein, Tarnów, Wielkie Schody 5/5, otherwise to Klara W., Krakow-Podgórze, Limanowskiego 18/4.

Greetings to Lusia.

Kisses, your Dola

All love and grace – firm handshake – your brother-in-law Munio Blaustein

April 6, 1941

From Berta:

My sweet dear beloved Children,

On April 5, we received your letters of March 3, 7, and 17, together with the telegram, for which I cannot thank you with words. May God repay you for all the good you have done. Everyone was surprised about the telegram, that you think about your old mother like that. How could I not be proud to have such a sweet, good son. May the Almighty yet allow me to experience the joy of embracing you.

Dear child, I wrote to you in a previous letter about my health, thank God I am feeling better, the dear children do what they can, I do not lack for doctors. A doctor comes now every day who prescribes sweating for me. That does me good. Thank God I have everything and do not need help from anyone. Dawid absolutely refused any help from Herr Ritterman. Dear child, be very calm, do not give any direction because Dawid would be very offended, since I lack for nothing except my health, and that is coming very slowly. I hope that I will be restored to health when the warm days come.

Dearest Lusia, how happy I was to read your charming lines, and even though you have only one room, you can be happier than others who have a big apartment. I want to describe our apartment for you, my dear daughter. There are three rooms and three families, and Klara and Malcia each have a room. I sleep in Malcia's room. Uncle Dawid has the third room. We share the kitchen and get along well. The main thing is that we have something to cook. In the same house is a baker named Beigel and there is also a butcher, one should be content, isn't that right, dear child?

Dear children, I know you will be surprised when you receive a letter from Dola. What God makes, human beings should not separate. We were also surprised when we got the news. It is her destiny, such a scheme was prophesied to her when she was a girl, that she would marry the second time. She writes me that she is content. May God grant that it be forever. Thank you, my dear ones, for everything.

My dears, since all the letters do not arrive, I want to send you both congratulations in advance for your birthdays. May you be granted the best and may you be happy and successful in all you undertake, and wherever you turn may you be a light in God's eyes as well as [in the eyes of] other people. How nice it would be if I could show you in person what I feel for you both. So I kiss you affectionately,

Your loving Mother

Your name days – yours, Józiu, June 9, dear Lusia, June 11, am I right? Affectionate greetings from everyone. Dear child, have you received an answer from my sister's son-in-law? The daughter is supposed to be living in New York. Will you take the time to read my letter? I am happy that I could write to you. I kiss you both a thousand times. If only I could, I would like to spend the whole day writing to you. We handed over the pictures in Büro Lloyd. They are sure to come into your possession.

April 12, 1941 Postmark (No Date on Letter)

From Salo:

We received your letters, and as always we are very happy when we receive news from you. A couple of days ago I was at Nord Lloyd and submitted the photos of Mother, myself, and Mania which by mutual agreement by cable message are supposed to be delivered to America by airmail. The same for Dola. Your mother-in-law and Ms. Schreiber are using the same way to send the pictures and documents.

I didn't want to mention Mania's accident in which she suffered a broken hand bone, because on the one hand it served no purpose and I did not want to worry you too much. But I see that somebody has already written to you about it. Thus I want to let you know that the cast was removed several days ago, and the healing thank God is proceeding normally and leaving no external scar. Obviously it will take some time yet until the hand is usable, and therefore you will pardon that it will be some time yet before she will be able to write something personal to you. Don't be disturbed, everything will be okay. Mania sends her warm greetings and best wishes to all. She is always waiting for your messages, and receives them very emotionally. So write often and a lot if you want to make her happy.

Many greetings on my behalf as well, with best regards to Lusia and family.

Salo

Of the announced large packages, none have arrived as yet. Dear Józiu, I think you should send nothing further until we inform you that the package has arrived. It is a waste of money. Concerning the announced greetings through Mr. Rittermann, I must note the following. We knew nothing of the entire matter, because no one informed us, and obviously therefore we could not contact Fleissig. By accident, we were speaking of it in the presence of Dawid, and he told us that about 5–6 weeks ago Ritterman encountered him on the street and told him that he had greetings to pass on to Mrs. Holländer and asked him if mother needed anything. He did not consider the matter particularly important and as he did not think mother was lacking anything at home did not mention it further. Where Mrs. Fleissig is now cannot be ascertained. It would have to be by pure coincidence to run into her. I am telling you this in detail, so that you know that neither R. nor anyone else has done anything for mother. If Dawid had mentioned something of his conversation with R., naturally someone would have followed it up.

April 20, 1941

From Berta:

My dear sweet beloved Children!

I should describe for you the joy I had on April 17 when I received your picture/letter, there are no words with which I could express myself, for me it was a day of double joy. The sweet picture. We could not get enough of seeing it, we passed it from hand to hand. And added to that the fact that my sister is well did not make me just a little bit happy. Imagine getting news from a woman of some eighty years, how glad I will be when all of you get together. Dear child, you write about our pictures, they have already been sent by way of Büro Lloyd and I hope you will receive them. I do not know how Frau Eder sent pictures. I cannot ask her since she is no longer here. I do not know where she moved.

What else can I write to you, my dear ones? My hand trembles. I live in this hope, always to have good [news] from you. As soon as the Almighty grants me life to see you, you can imagine what that will mean to me, to put my arms around such dear darlings.

Dear child, as soon as you have a letter from my sister, please add it to your letter and tell her for me that I long to have a letter from her. I do not find any more words to write except [to send] you, my dear ones, thousands of kisses on paper, because I cannot do it any other way. Goodbye and I wish for more good letters from you.

Affectionate greetings to Leo and wife, Paula and son.

Your loving Mother

Berta

Much-loved Lusia

To give you some news of your mother, I am writing to tell you that she was at our house yesterday, she does not live far from here. She sends you affectionate greetings. Dear Józiu, have you had a letter from Doly? I beg you to write her a letter that should sound like it is from a good brother to his sister. At the same time I am writing you since you asked if Feliks received the package. I do not think so.

April 23, 1941

From Genka:

Dear Uncle,

While I am writing this letter I have your photograph in front of me which made us all very happy. You both look great. I am sorry I write so rarely but I talk about you much more often and think even more often. You are my hope for the future. I didn't change much outside but inside I feel like I am a quarter of a century older. I work in the shop, type very well, take care of the correspondence but it is uncertain how much longer I will be able to work. I spend my free time working on myself. I often regret that I didn't leave with you but maybe it is better this way, I would be only a burden to you. As you certainly know we don't live on Krakowska anymore but in Podgórze (Jewish quarter). Our apartment is not bad and we live together with aunt Mania and Dawid. Each family has its room and we share the kitchen. We coexist in peace and cooperation.

You probably have already our pictures which we sent through Norddeutscher Lloyd with whom my father stays in contact. We all dream about getting these documents. It would bring us real happiness. Our registration numbers in Berlin: 043243–043246

I greet you as warmly as I only can.

Genka

From Lusia:

Dearest Uncle,

I wanted to write to you so many times now but I had to be silent. Too bad. As for now I am healthy, joyful and full of good hopes as always. I am a young teacher now, I discovered my true talent, and I still go to the tailor. I have sewing, cutting and modeling courses.[24] It's going somehow. Dearest Uncle, on April 19 I will turn 17. So I start the 18th spring of my life. In which spring will we see each other again? Will I still be in my teens? I need to finish, there is no more space but I will try to write more often.

Millions of hugs and kisses.

Lusia

April 27, 1941

From Berta:

Most-loved dear Children

On April 25, we received two letters from you, 27 and 28. Number 28 to Dawid came much earlier than 27, therefore we must have patience. All of us sent all the papers and pictures by way of Büro Lloyd, also from your mother-in-law and sister-in-law. Dola also gave her picture and the required paper. Salo took care of it. I think you will already have them, since they were sent a long time ago. Dawid will also write you. Genka was completely disconcerted by the loving words you directed toward her and thanks you very much. She is proud to have such an uncle. Last week she wrote you a letter, also to you, Lusia. She always says she is happy that you also are thinking of her. My dear son, you mention that my birthday is coming closer and I thank you very much for your

---

[24] According to a subsequent letter (Klara to Joseph, October 15, 1941), Lusia taught at Centos in the mornings and at home in the afternoons.

(beautiful fine) telegram. It was quite a surprise to receive something so nice. One can expect that only from such a dear, good son.

Dola writes such good letters and is so content that I am really glad to know that she is happy. You be good to her, too. Write her so that she can be at peace about you and know that you are not angry with her. She received such nice letters from his sisters that it made me happy to read them. She sent them all to me. Imagine, dear child, she got a letter from the sister of the godly, titled Pani. That was the first letter since his ten years at court.[25] It is only now that she has received letters from Munio's siblings that she sees the difference family makes. At least she is not alone and does not need to rely on anyone.

A few words for you, dear Lusia. Your dear mother visits us every Sunday and sends you affectionate greetings. When I go out, I must also visit her. The weather is too bad, it is very cold. I have nothing else to write you. Still I want to mention to you, dear Józiu, that I received a letter from my sister. It was so touching that I cried my eyes out for joy. She was just wishing to see another member of the family when your letter arrived, she said it appeared out of the blue. I wrote her back right away, naturally in Yiddish, she should read it herself. It was not accepted and I had to write it over in German and the sender was Malcia. Mention that as soon as you have a chance, because she will not know who that is. She would have enjoyed it more if it had been written in Yiddish, she could have read it herself.

Adele wrote us that she already received the ticket for the ship.[26] You also had a part in that. Leo takes note that he is again the older brother. He certainly took an example from you, my heart. How lovely it is that all of you will be together. Be happy and many thousands of kisses for you both, which I would much rather give to you in person.

Your loving mother who longs for you, Berta

Greetings to Leo and wife, where is the son? Kindest regards to Paula and son. Does Curt have a position yet?

---

[25] These two sentences are somewhat illegible and their meaning quite unclear.

[26] In contrast to the General Government, where Jewish emigration was blocked in September 1940, Jewish emigration from the Third Reich (including Vienna) was permitted until October 1941. At this point in time, there were still two legal exit routes, overland across the Soviet Union or by ship from Lisbon.

From Dola:

Since I don't know how long it will take for this card to reach you, I am sending the best wishes for your birthday on June 9 now. I cannot express all the details: you know how much I love you. The most important is that Mother feels well again; she lives with Mania and Klara. They all cherish your letters, and cry from joy whenever you write. They send them to me under the condition that I return them back to them. Today I read your letter from March 15 (number 27). If you don't have frequent mail from Dear Mother it is because of the general conditions, and not God forbid the situation at home. My husband got a job in Nowy Sacz[27] so we will move over there. Please send the mail for me to Mother's address. Once more lots of happiness and all the best.

Dola

From Munio:

Dear Brother-in-Law

Because of your birthday please let me wish you for the first time but from the bottom of my heart all the best. They all tell so much good about you, I talk about my brother in a similar way, only the best things.

All the best for you.

Your Munio

April 28, 1941

From Dawid:

We received your letters from 15 and 29 of March and we are very pleased with their content. We see how much work you are putting into helping us, and we are very grateful for that.

I gave everything in the hands of Nord Deutsche Lloyd since they as a German office know best how they should proceed. They told us that they accept these papers only because they are all validated by the German Consulate. They know best what to do and they act without communicating with me. They explained to me that the passports problem has nothing to do with entering this country. The papers we have

---

[27] This is a town 40 miles south of Tarnow, near the border with Slovakia.

right now apparently don't give us any privileges. We would need only passports from over there. They told us that we won't be able to leave for several months since this is how long all the formalities will last. So now it's out of the question, and when the time will come I will follow your advice concerning the route.

Kaufmann has already informed his brother about the birth certificate for his wife.

Thank God here all is well. Do not worry about Mother. She is not lacking anything and is well. We all live together in peace and would like to be with you.

Our registration numbers in Berlin are: 43243-6

In Lloyd they told me that since we are registered over there we won't get a transit visa to USA. Genia thanks you for the wishes. She was very touched that you remembered.

Greetings and kisses for you and Lusia.

Dawid

May 1, 1941

From Munio:

Dear Brother-in-Law,

On the occasion of your birthday, for the first time, from the bottom of my heart, I wish you all that you wish yourself. Here they tell such wonderful things about you. This is great to hear, I feel as if they were talking about my own brother.

Wishing you all the best, your,

Munio

From Dola:

Dear Józiu,

Because I don't know how long it will take for you to receive this, I wish you all the best for your birthday on June 9. It is impossible to express how much we love you.

The main news is that Mania is fully recovered. She lives together with mother and Klara. Mother feels quite well. I am happy with your letters which they sent to me on the condition that I will return them. Today I got your letter of March 15, number 27.

My husband received a job in the *Judenrat* at Nowy Sacz, the place we are moving to. Write to me at Mother's address.

Once more wishing you good health and much happiness.

Your Dola

May 5, 1941

From Mania:

I just want to prove to you that my right hand feels much better; still hurts a little bit when I write so this letter will be written in fragments.

I suspect that I won't remember my accident by the time that you will get this letter. Now I want to wish you and Lusia happy birthday. I don't know if the wishes will come on time. I wish to both of you all the best, many years of wellness and happiness. For you my dear brother I wish lots of success in the business about which they talk here as well.

What concerns Dola . . . the pain in my hand was stronger so I couldn't finish . . . now back to Dola. I agree with Dear Mother and disagree with Klara. Klara thinks that Dola shouldn't get married now. It's easy to say for Klara because she has a husband and children (especially that the relationships between them are better now). It doesn't matter what Dawid is like but he knows that she has obligations towards his family and takes care of them. Dola didn't have anybody. We the three women couldn't give her too much, and the brothers-in-law (I don't want you to dislike them though) didn't behave very nice when she lived with me for a short time. Salo behaved towards her like towards Dear Mother, and it cost me lots of shame and bad emotions. Imagine, in times like this when strangers live in a small apartment together, she wasn't able to live with us. Dawid was also impossible, and Genia contributed to this. Dawid behaved very ugly towards her. She cried too many times because of him, and she felt like an imposer to the degree she wouldn't go upstairs when he was at home. You know her, she doesn't like to subordinate herself and be at anybody's mercy. And for Dawid only those count who are at his service or those who are rich. You dear Józiu are for him like a semi-God because he sees that you are doing something for him. And you should have only heard what he was saying about you a few months before. He said that you forgot the whole family, you cared only about the family of your wife. All four of us worried about that a lot, and Dola told him directly what was on her mind. She pointed out the truth therefore he hates her. Dola didn't want to give up, it is not in our nature, she wanted to stay strong and get something out of life. But she needed to be brave, she needed support from a man. The man who is her husband right now gave her hopes, she found in him all this that she was missing for 10 years. I am sure God helped her; it was her destiny.

Please, Dear Brother, don't think badly about her. She couldn't do otherwise. She didn't want to separate from him. He was deported, and when the last transport to Nowy Sacz was leaving Dola left to be with him.

We got to know him as a decent, hardworking man with very good character, this attracted Dola to him the most. She kept saying that he does what Józiu would do. It's too bad that he is not as handsome as our brother. Yes, my dear Józiu, this was missing in her life: the warmth and devotion of a loving man. May God allow her to have a good life. Dear Józiu, I know you will understand her and will send her some warm, caring words, and you will still be a good brother for both of them. In your next letter please comfort our Dear Mother that you don't think Dola did something inappropriate and that you do understand her.

Dola got a postcard from Adele; she congratulated her heartily and wished her all the best. She said that you contributed to the fact that she received her ship card. Maybe that's because Leo realized that he has sisters, too, and became again an old good brother. So I see that you spread the seeds of peace and may God bless you for that. What concerns the brother of Mr. Ritterman I know how Dawid handled him. Because he didn't have any business for himself in this he didn't even mention that he talked to him. Salo will write to him.

As you know we have a common apartment and I have a passage room. I am never alone and therefore it is difficult for me to finish this letter.

I send you warm greetings.

Mania

P.S. Greetings from the pharmacist Pankiewicz. He regrets that he didn't listen to you last time.[28] Please write to Salo and ask him to tell

[28] The pharmacist was surely Tadeusz Pankiewicz, the so-called Kraków Ghetto Pharmacist, who had the distinction of being the only gentile permitted to live in the ghetto. For four years, Pankiewicz bore witness as the Germans tormented, deported,

his opinion about Dola's husband, in front of me he talks about him very positively; they write to each other, and used to spend lots of time in each other's company. Don't ask Dawid for his opinion, for him Munio is nobody and that's because he hates Dola. He says that they both deserve each other. Please don't be upset that I require so much reading from you.

May 8, 1941

From Berta:

My sweet dear beloved Children,

Since this is my day to write, I do not want to neglect to write you, my dear ones, writing you is my greatest pleasure. Now I have great [*illegible*] to write, I always have to respond, which I am happy to do.

Thank God I receive very good letters from Dola as well as from her husband, both are very content. He writes to me like a son, which I have not heard from the others. I also received a nice letter from his sister in Switzerland, she congratulates me and calls me good Frau Mama. She is unfortunately a widow and has a son who also writes Dola very nice letters. May God grant them happiness, since she has not yet had good experiences. Dear child, have you written them yet? Write, they will be very glad. I sent them your picture, and they both were delighted with it. I have asked them to send it back. I cannot be separated from the picture. Dola said you are already one hundred percent American.

Your mother-in-law was not with us this week, she traveled to see her sister Horowitz on Sunday. Dear children, I have had no letter from you since April, I miss it. How are you? I am very well. Have you made acquaintances there? Dear Józileben, I want to write you something else, how well-known you are, thank God. Dawid went swimming, and there were two men from Bank Holcer there talking about you. When they were finished, Dawid went up to them and said it's good that you did not say anything bad about Holländer. I am a brother-in-law of his. Imagine how surprised they were. Erna's mother, who is in Lemberg near Heneg and who was very sick, wrote Erna a letter in which she also spoke very

murdered, and ultimately liquidated the Jews of Kraków. In 1947, he wrote a critically important account of his experiences, titled *The Cracow Ghetto Pharmacy*.

well of you. My heart, you should be a light in God's eyes and be happy
with your dear wife.

Your mother kisses you thousands of times.

Affectionate kisses and regards from all, kindest regards to Leo, wife,
son, Paula, son.

May 9, 1941

From Salo:

My dearest Józiu,

I just received your letter from March 8 (number 29). Thank you. I still
haven't received the letter that was sent separately to me (number 13).
Of course it is not your fault but we feel deprived, especially Mania who
waits impatiently for every word from you, and reads everything with
fervor. We have already written to you that we all (also Klara, and your
mother-in-law) received the packages you sent to us, with mostly tea and
coffee. I keep repeating that because we are never sure if the letters reach
you. Therefore I am saying it once more that the bigger packages haven't
arrived, maybe they will still come, but you should perhaps make some
inquiries at the company you sent them with, and request your money
back. You are trying to help, spending your money, and by doing this you
always risk that it won't reach us. So before you receive a confirmation
from us that your package arrived, please don't send anything. It is really
a waste of money.

We also wrote you (and I am sure the Dear Mother did, too) that we all
live together, we and the family of Klara Wimisner and Uncle Dawid, in
an apartment in the Jewish quarter Podgórze, on Limanowskiego Street
18/4, each family in a room. Dear Mother lives with us. Every morning
we have the true tribal migration around one bathroom, each of us with
a watch in hand. I also mentioned before that Mania broke her right
wrist when she fell down the stairs. She had to have her hand in a cast for
three weeks. Recently it was removed. The doctors say that the broken
area grew back together and she is almost free of pain, except when the
weather changes, the doctors say that's normal.

Thank God we are all together. Dola followed her husband to Tarnów
like a brave woman should, and like it stands in our Torah: "Don't abandon your closest ones, and follow your husband."

I can answer your question about Mania, taking into consideration our current situation that naturally brings to each and every one of us many small inconveniences, she is not doing badly. The same is true about your mother. But there is a difference: while Dear Mother finds herself in all kinds of kitchen work, and feels there like fish in water, Mania devotes herself to cleaning, and there is not a single speck of dust that would escape her attention, even the smallest one. Mania is going to yell at me for that when she reads this but I don't care; may she yell as much as she wants to.

As you know there cannot be more than one handwriting in one letter so she won't add anything here. She asks me to write something from her. We are waiting for the documents; I know that you are doing everything you can. Hopefully they will come as soon as possible. You will receive the pictures in the meantime.

Warm greetings, for you and your dear Lusia, and all the relatives.

Mr. R. visited Dawid, but Dawid didn't ask for the address of Fleissig, so we can't locate her. If you know the address, please send it in your next letter.

Stay healthy and happy.

Salo

May 11, 1941

From Klara:

From your letter dated March 29 we learned that you received our telegram as well as birth certificate for Ms. Kaufmann. Up till now we don't know if you received our photographs that we sent through the local office. We hope that in the meantime you did get them. It's really important for us, and time is pressing. As I already wrote in two previous letters we live in Podgórze (Jewish quarter) with Mania and Mina.[29] We are waiting for a new address for Dola, since she moved from Tarnów to Nowy Sacz, where her husband got a new position. God help them to be lucky!

[29] Presumably, a nickname for Salo. This is the only occasion in the letters in which this name appears.

Lusia makes progress in her sewing career. She became a teacher of cutting, sewing and modeling. She is very proud of that. The director of the school herself hired her. You can imagine how happy she is when they call her a teacher. She does it with all her heart. We don't know how long Dawid and Genia will be able to work. We hope that till then you will manage to help us out so it may turn out to be OK.

We haven't received a package you mentioned in your letter.

Greetings and kisses from everybody.

Klara

May 16, 1941

From Dola:

A week ago we left Tarnów and moved to Nowy Sacz, where Munio got a job in a small Jewish province. It's a very modest position taking into consideration his abilities but we are very happy that he can work. We will be able to live modestly but without too much stress. We will wait for the end of the war. I really miss the family, but there is no way I can visit them. Only letters make me feel better. Dear Mother is healthy, as well as Mania and Klara. Both brothers-in-law still work, Genia works with her father, and Lusia is a teacher of cutting and sewing. I assume that you get letters from them. If not the fact that we are not together I would be happy. I found a real friend in Munio and I hope everything is well with you. I miss so much seeing you. Stay healthy and happy.

Dola

From Munio:

I great you warmly and wait for good words from you.

May 17, 1941 Postcard

From Dola:

I simply miss your image. Be healthy and happy.

Your loving Dola

From Munio:

I greet you warmly and am awaiting good words from you.
Munio

May 19, 1941

From Mania:

Dear beloved Brother,

Please don't be surprised that I am sending this letter to Paula. The reason for that is that we have a post office in the same building where we live now. It would be a great advantage if not for the fact that D. has new friends there, who tell him about every letter. And as long as I know our gentlemen they can also report the content of the letter since the mail cannot be sealed or glued.

The last letter I sent without a date was mailed on May 5. I wrote it 14 days ago, from time to time and in hiding. I am almost never alone, and Klara would be hurt that I do have secrets from her. But you know that I don't want her to know about everything. Your news that you enjoy getting my mail, despite my style and orthography, made me very happy.

Dear Józiu, I suspect that you are already in possession of the letter from Salo. I am calm since I know that you are able to read between the lines, and you can detect the irony in the sentence about Dola. Believe me, dear Józiu, I miss her very much. She has something that both Klara and I are lacking, a bit of optimism. Now I am at the mercy of the company of my housemates. But I am happy that she is at the side of a man who will respect her and take care of her.

Dear Brother, if you will send any package please send coffee and tea, send it to Dola, directly to her address. I don't want Salo and Dawid to have an opportunity to complain about who deserves what and how much.

Forgive me that I worry you with this message but I prefer that you know what their attitudes towards Dola are. I know you will wonder less that she did leave us although she could have stayed for a while.

Stay well, I kiss you and Lusia warmly.

Dear Mama is better now but still misses you tremendously.

Mania

(note to Paula: Greetings and thanks for taking the trouble to deliver this letter to J.)

May 26, 1941

From Berta:

Much-loved and dear Children

I am now writing only cards since I do not have much to write. I am healthy, thank God, and wish to hear the same from you, my dears. I have not had a letter from you for a long time and wish very much for one. It cannot be as long as it seems to me, since every day lasts a year. I often receive letters from Dola. She is very, very content. He also writes us very nice letters. I am happy that she met such a man. His siblings also write me and call me Mother. Nothing else important except affectionate kisses for you. Also kindest regards from the children. I am waiting for a letter and remain your mother who longs for you.

Berta

May 27, 1941

From Adele:

Dear Józiu,

We also thank you very much for everything you did for us. Hopefully we will be soon lucky enough to thank you in person. I heard from Paula that you and your wife are doing very well, which I wish you from all my heart. I am in letter contact with all your loved ones. They all are healthy and today this is the main thing. Dear Aunt is very happy because of Dola's marriage. Dola lives in Nowy Sacz now, where her husband got a small position. If you believe that your letters go faster through me, please send them to me first. Please, perhaps it is possible for you to do something in Lisbon, there must be no Joint there.[30] In the K.G.[31] we were marked for the next round of tickets. Maybe it will be possible for us to get them for August–September. Hopefully we will manage to do all that, and soon we will be able to go.

[30] Presumably, a reference the American Joint Distribution Committee, which did in fact operate in Lisbon.
[31] Kultus Gemeinde, the official Jewish Community organization in Vienna.

Greetings for you and your wife.
Yours,
Adele

May 29, 1941

From Berta:

Much-loved dear Children!
As I mailed my card to you, Salo brought me a letter from you written
on April 30. We are all surprised that at this time you still did not have our
pictures. Since March, I have sent countless letters to you, dear child, and
also enclosed my picture in one letter. I also thanked you very much for
the telegram and for the letter you sent me. I also sent sincere wishes for
your birthdays, which you have in the same month. In each letter I told
you that Dola is very content. Dear child, the packages from Bulgaria
have not arrived, perhaps you can inquire. It is a pity about the things
and your effort. Do not be angry that I am writing only cards, I really
have nothing particular to write, but every word I write you brings me
pleasure. I kiss you affectionately,
Your Mother

June 3, 1941

From Munio:

Today forwarded from Tarnow we received 5 small packages with 80
decagrams of coffee, 40 decagrams of tea and 80 decagrams of cocoa. It's
touching how fast and precisely you fulfill Dola's requests.

Up till now I thought that only I have a brother who shows so much
love and devotion towards his siblings. You remind me of my Artur like
if you were him. I want to thank you with all my heart for your goodness
and love with which you want to help us and I hope to be in a position
soon to show you my gratitude.

I want to let you know that tea is the most important for us. I am not
sure if you are familiar with my Vienna business (for export and import
under my name) – maybe you heard about that.

I really appreciate your reliability and love. Thank God we live relatively well here. I have a modest but satisfying position. Dola works as
well. It brings very modest income of course but we are pleased with our

work. Of course we were used to different times and situations and we long for them but that doesn't give us an excuse for not being glad right now. Dear Dola is healthy, looks good and happy and I hope that she will never be in a worse situation, as long as she is with me (what concerns "better" doesn't have limits). We receive mail from Dear Mother very regularly, she is healthy and full of energy. Please don't worry about her too much. I have to leave some space for Dola. Warm greeting, your brother-in-law,

Munio

[switching from German to Polish] You can write in Polish to us although I express myself better in German.

From Dola:

Dear Józiu, I thank you very much for the packages. Munio expressed already his gratitude. I am so touched that I still have in you my old good dear brother, it's more important than the content of the packages. I left for myself some cocoa which substitutes for chocolate (I stayed kosher). I really miss you. Now I understand you missing home and Dear Mother. I am healthy, and in normal conditions, I would be happy. Stay well.

Dola

June 3, 1941

From Berta:

Much-loved dear Children!

Although I do not have much to write, still I will find some words to give me pleasure in writing to you, my dears. Were you with Maskor on Pentecost?[32] On Monday, June 2, I was thinking about you, since your naming-day is coming up soon. How lovely it would be, my dear child, if I could also send you such a nice telegram, but we must give up a lot, even though it hurts.

Dear Lusia, your dear mother will visit us as usual on Sunday. At Pentecost she was with us both days, it is a delight for us to talk about the two of you. At the same time, my dear, your birthday is coming soon and I wish you all the best, as only a mother can wish for a child. We

---

[32] Jewish holiday on the fiftieth day after the second day of Passover, celebrating the first fruits of the harvest. In Hebrew, *Shabuoth*.

want to receive happy letters from you two. Dear Józiu, I hope that you will soon be in possession of our pictures. In one letter I enclosed my picture, have you received this letter? Write often, it is too long for me to wait for your letters. Address them directly to us at Limanowska. Write more details about yourselves, not simply about work but just private things, how you are doing. Do you already have a larger apartment and have you bought your own furniture? Oh, how I would like to see how everything looks where you are living.

My dear love, I have very nice and good news from Dola and her husband. They are both very satisfied, thank God. The only thing is that they are far from us and that makes them worry about us. They do not need to be concerned, we are fine. Munio is a good man and comes to terms with every job to earn a good living. Have you had a letter from Dola? She has written to you. Write them, they will be very happy. I have to send them every one of your letters, then I get them back because I collect your letters. Whenever something makes me anxious, I reach for them to read, then it seems to me that I am talking with you, I just unfortunately do not see your dear face. So we are all well here, thank God, and everything is all right.

Affectionate regards from all.

Kindest regards to Leo and wife, Paula and son, does Curt have a position yet?

Does Otto visit his parents often?

Again kindest regards,

Your Mother

Berta

June 9, 1941

From Berta:

My dear sweet Children!

On your birthday, we received a package from Lisbon containing coffee, tea, sugar, soap, three boxes of tinned food, powdered chocolate, which tasted especially good to me. Dear child, thank you very much and be healthy and happy. I want to hear from you. Yesterday your mother-in-law also received a package, came to visit and inquire if we had also received one. We got it the next day. Dola also received the package you sent to Tarnów. She will also write you. We often have news from them. Many thanks from all for the things you sent, but instead, I should send you something for your birthday. Thank you again for the good things we received from you. I remain, with affectionate kisses,

Your Mother

Many greetings from all.

June 10, 1941

From Munio:

Today we received from Dear Mama your letter from May 14. We regret very much that the previous letters got lost, especially those letters in which special notes were addressed to us.

A few weeks ago we sent you a letter and a card and I repeat again (since I don't know if you received this mail) that we did get the package from Lisbon sent by you with 80 decagrams coffee, 80 decagrams tea and 80 decagrams cocoa. We paid tariff and taxes of 23 zloty for everything together.

Hopefully you received our previous letter in which we thanked you very much and shared with you our emotions of gratitude and love. We are touched and happy, and not so much because we received these products but because of the fact that you do care about us so much. Let us thank you again and express our greatest gratitude for your devotion and loyalty for us.

Dola and I are doing quite well, taking into consideration the circumstances we are in. We are healthy and optimistic, almost happy if times were normal. We have regular letters from Dear Mama. She feels well and is healthy. She writes to you very often, and asks us to do the same, so you have messages from us all the time, even if some letters get lost on the way.

I need to leave some space for Dola. Please don't worry about her. She is in good hands.

Love and all the best,

Your brother-in-law Munio

Please give my regards to your wife.

From Dola:

I received your letter from home. It seems that all your energy and costs connected with Nicaragua were needless but, as you write yourself,

there is nothing bad that couldn't turn into something good. I have no
doubts that you would give us a star from heaven if only you could.
You were always doing for us everything you were able to, so of course
you are trying even more today. I have a good secretary in Munio. He
took over and wrote about the packages. I am very grateful for them,
my love. I regret very much that I didn't receive your letter. I value your
opinion so much. I know that from a distance you may have difficulties
to judge the steps I took. It may seem to be unreasonable. But I have no
regrets. I am experiencing true happiness since I found a man of 100%
good character, but I also experience worries and fears. Here we are
doing much better than in Tarnów, and I wish that I would stay here and
survive. I am happy that Mania stayed where she was. Please risk one
more letter directly to us. Stay well my dear and think positively about
us all.

 Kisses,
 Your Dola
 Greetings for Lusia

June 12, 1941

From Salo:

We received your mail from May 14. We see from it that all your
hard work was for nothing. That you did everything that was in your
power we do not doubt. So please don't blame yourself and don't feel
guilty. Maybe it was supposed to be this way. We cannot know what is in
store for us. Sometimes a small failure may spare people from a bigger
misfortune.

 Yesterday we all (Dear Mother, we, Klara, Dola, and your mother-in-
law) received packages. The packages came from Lisbon and contained
coffee, tea, rice, honey, pasta, etc. In the name of Mania and me we do
say thank you very much. I would be very happy if I had an opportunity
to show you our gratitude for all your sacrifices and devotion. Unfortunately, we are always the ones who receive and we have no way to repay
you in any way.

 Health-wise we all are doing pretty well. I still work at the factory. I
have at least some work and not too much time to let dark thoughts take
power over me. How long will I be able to stay is open to question. Every

month they advertise an active position and I do everything in order to get it.

How is your business dear Józiu? Are you satisfied? Do you have some news from your father-in-law and your brother-in-law?

Dola, as you already know, doesn't live in Tarnów anymore since she moved with her husband to Nowy Sacz. He had better contacts there, and the *Gemeinde*[33] held out the prospects of a position there.

Mania just remarked that you and your dear wife are going to celebrate your birthdays. Please forgive me that my sincere wishes will come a little too late. Maybe they can be a down payment already for the birthday next year. I send you both all the best and please be assured that I take an active part in sharing the joy of your successes. I won't try to translate Mania's feelings into words. You know them well.

Please write often and a lot.

Your last letter was number 34; the previous two letters have not yet reached us. Mania asks that if you would like to send another package in the future, please send some rice instead of bacon since we cannot get it here, and maybe some cooking oil – only of course if it will be easy for you to arrange.

Mania cannot add anything since there is only one handwriting allowed in each letter.

Salo

This letter came back to us with the remark that letters to America can go only from Lisbon. So we are resending it and hoping that it will reach you. We all are healthy and greet you warmly. Mother had written in the meantime several cards.

June 17, 1941

From Berta:

My beloved dearest Children,

Today I got news from Adele about what Paula had written her, that you, dear child, have received no mail at all from me and are therefore troubled. That surprises me very much. Not a week goes by that I do not

---

[33] Official, German-approved governing body of the Jewish community, that is, Jewish council or *Judenrat*.

write you, sometimes I even write twice in one week. Dear child, you do not need to be concerned and troubled about me. I am doing very well and I am also enjoying your gift parcels very much. Sweet child, I ask you once again not to be concerned. After all, I am not alone but am with my dear children. They do everything that is good for me. Dola and her husband also write such lovely letters that I am really happy. God grant that we may all be together, and that I may see you all happy, that would be too lovely. Small packages arrive every day now, which we confirm to you. I especially like the powdered chocolate and marmalade, which I eat instead of things from the bakery. Thank you very much, I name you in every prayer.

Dearest Lusia, Paula writes me also that you are worried about your mother. I assure you, dear child, your mother is well, thank God, and is always in a good mood. We see each other only on Sundays, when she visits us. During the week she is busy. The business is not going badly, and people like to go to her store. She wrote you last week.

Write her diligently so she will be happy.

And write me a few lines, too.

With thousands of kisses, I remain

Your Mother

Affectionate greetings to the relatives.

Dear Józiu, have you still not found an opportunity to speak to my sister?

Dawid wanted me to ask you, have you had news from Uncle Rosner?

Affectionate greetings from all.

June 17, 1941

From Klara:

Dear Józiu,

This is already the second week during which we enjoy the packages sent by you. Thank you very much for everything. We got 3 big packages all good things (Dola received her package as well). Then we got 7 small packages, all from Portugal, and paid for in Lisbon as it is stamped on the ticket. We also received a notification from Warsaw from the trading company Jutrzykowski that there is condensed milk waiting for us. A separate thank you from the children for the powdered chocolate.

When will I be able to pay you back? For now you have to accept "thank you" but for a hundred times. I know you will be relieved to know that we received all this. Please send the packages to Mother's and Mania's name since Dawid is being asked too many questions at the post office. The packages arrive whole on the outside but inside the papers are torn. The last package of coffee for me weighed 22 decagrams and for Mania 35 decagrams. Is that how much you intended to send? We received a letter from Adele that you worry because you don't have news from dear Mother. It is strange since she writes every week. You have to be patient as we are waiting for the mail from you. We know that not all correspondence reaches us. Thank God we all are healthy. My nervous system improved and the old Klara doesn't exist anymore which makes me very happy. We have one household with Mania and we are happy this way. Dola writes too that she is happy. She finally feels that somebody takes care of her. May God give her as much as possible since up till now she didn't experience any love in her marriage. If it is nice we will all go to Krzemionki Park on Saturday, we'll take a blanket and will be breathing fresh air. It's difficult though to find a quiet spot since this is a paradise for children and besides there are masses of goats. The ladies bring them to pastures. Before they had dogs on leashes but now they can benefit from having a goat and having a dog is a luxury. Dear Mother also writes to you and asks you to send some rice, that is her favorite meal.

I great you warmly and send you kisses. Klara

Greeting for Lusia and all the relatives from all of us. We haven't received the letters that you wrote to Dawid. In this moment we got from the post office 5 packages of raisins for which we all thank you.

June 23, 1941

From Berta:

Much-loved dear Children!

This week we received some packages, which we acknowledged to you. Today Malcia received two packages of coffee, Klarcia got coffee, sugar, and rice, which is the best food for me, and so, my dear child, I thank you very much, especially for it. It was just what I wished for, as I was about to ask you for rice, but you, my love, always know my thoughts. Everything would be very nice if only I had a letter from you and an answer to my letter. Since March I have written countless letters and cards, and you write that since February you have received no letters from me, that concerns me very much.

I ask you once again to write me often, in the meantime I kiss you affectionately.

Your Mother

June 24, 1941

From Mania:

I can't find words to thank you for all the packages you sent. We enjoyed coffee and even more tea. We have good coffee substitutes here and therefore many people cannot appreciate real coffee.

Since May I have written four times, I assume that some of my letters have found you. I repeat that Dola writes often and is happy. If only her husband could get this promised job. Dear Mother writes separately every week. She would love to write everyday. She wants to feel like she had you next to her. She misses you very much and tears of joy run on her face when she reads your letters.

We sent to Dola some things from the package you sent like honey, raisins, sardines, chocolate, etc. Dear Józiu, I know it doesn't make any difference for you, so please send packages directly to their address, in the previous letter I gave you the reason. Dola wrote that she received 80 decagrams of coffee, 80 decagrams of tea, 80 decagrams of coco, and two small packages. She is very sad that she hasn't received a letter from you. She really wants to know what you think about her second marriage. Nothing bad, right?

I assure you that she got a decent man and if times were normal she could be happy. Please write to them again. Dear Mother will be happy too if you will.

What's new with you? You wrote a couple months ago about Cuba? It didn't succeed?

Dear Józiu, don't work too much. Take care of your health. Maybe God will be merciful and we all will see each other alive again. (Umaju Selu)[34]

---

[34] The meaning of this phrase remains undecipherable to the editors.

I personally don't worry too much that you didn't succeed to arrange the matter. Maybe it's better this way. There is nothing bad that couldn't turn into good.

Don't worry about Genia and Lusia, they don't overwork. Lusia is still the same sweet good daughter. Unfortunately Genia didn't change; in many ways she is like Dawid.

I am repeating what Dear Mother has already written: we received 14 small packages all together. In addition I got two packages of coffee and Klara got a big package with coffee, rice and sugar today. Dear Mother is very happy.

My dear, I think this is all for today. I send you lots of kisses. Please kiss Lusia from me and assure her that her mother is doing well.

Mania

June 24, 1941

From Munio:

Just to let you know that everybody, dear Mother and the siblings, are doing well. Please do not worry. If you are missing some letters it's because they get lost. We are OK.

Love,
Munio

From Dola:

Dearest Józiu,

Please do not worry about us as Munio wrote. Every few days I receive mail from home where everything's all right, thank God. Your mother-in-law visited them a couple days ago.

Kisses,
Your Dola

June 26, 1941

From Munio:

Everyday we receive mail from Dear Mother, and we too write to them every day. Dear Mother and the rest of the family are doing well. We are healthy and content. Yesterday we got a package from Kraków, in which they added things from you: bacon, honey and chocolate – incredibly tasty. Lots of thanks!

Don't worry about us. Warm greetings to your wife.

Your Munio

From Dola:

Dear Józiu,

So you don't worry too much we write to you three times every week, and they write separately from home. Please don't worry. Thanks for the packages.

Dola

June 27, 1941

From Munio:

Dear Józiu,

I just wanted to reassure you that Dear Mother and the siblings are doing well – in case you are not getting mail from them directly. Please do not worry about them.

Your brother-in-law Munio

From Dola:

Dear Józiu,

As Munio already said please be worry free. I receive mail from home every few days. Praise God – everything is OK there. Your mother-in-law visited them a couple days ago.

Your Dola

June 30, 1941

From Berta:

My much-loved dear Children,

As always, I joyfully take pen in hand to give you a sign from us and also at least to speak my mind in writing, since I cannot do so in person. Above all, you have our best thanks for the canned milk you sent, which benefits us greatly. There were six cans that came from Warsaw. We divided them among ourselves and also sent one can to Dola. Dear child, you know in advance what you should send, you always know my thoughts exactly.

And if you want to send something, please address it to me in care of Wimisner, Limanowskiego 18/4.

My dear love, last week I received from Adele and Paula a letter for Dola. I answered right away and believe that you will get a letter from me from Adele. Thank God I get good news from Dola, both are very satisfied. Munio, Dola's husband, wrote me that he had written you three cards. Have you received any of them? Write to them. His siblings call me Mama and are glad that their brother has come into such a family, and I can appreciate the word Mama, since they have been without parents for a long time. He is really a very good person. God is rewarding her now after what she suffered for so long, and I am satisfied that she decided to take this step. No one can think badly of her for it. She had no home, and now she keeps house and cooks. She writes that it is worth going to the trouble for such a husband. Dear child, should that not make me happy? Now for me, my health is good, thank God, I just miss your letters, for which I have to wait a long time. I hope you have received mine, which I send weekly, I would most like to write every day, if I knew that you would get all my letters. I miss your letters. I kiss you affectionately.

Your Mother

Many greetings from everyone, also for Leo, wife, son, Paula, son. Does he have a position yet? Dear child, I just wanted to mail the letter when the children each received some packages from you. Malcia got soap, cocoa, and chocolate, and Klarcia got cocoa and chocolate, from Lisbon, which I acknowledge to you on behalf of the children with best thanks.

July 3, 1941

From Dola:

Dear Józiu,

I send postcards to you because they reach you faster and I really want you not to worry too much. We all are healthy. Dear Mother is writing separately.

I received two chocolates from my sister-in-law in Switzerland. I sent them to Mania for her birthday. I got the package from you; thank you very much. Don't worry about us.

Lots of kisses,

Your Dola

July 8, 1941

From Dola:

My dearest beloved Józiu,

There is not a single letter from you. Why? Are you mad at me? I could call myself a happy woman today. My husband got a position as a secretary in the region. He is doing very well. Now I can understand your longings for the family. Yesterday I got a letter from Dear Mother and the sisters. They all are healthy, thank God. Today I received four cans of sardines from the Carlos Company from Lisbon, sent by you a long time ago to Tarnów. I thank you with all my heart. I will recall how they tasted. But for practical reasons I prefer tea. I lead a modest life, I heat with wood in an iron oven (Nowy Sacz doesn't have gas). But I am very glad, almost happy if not for the permanent longings for the family that you know as well as I. I always think what Dear Mother is doing, how are the sisters and the children. Please write to me directly. I really would like to have a message from you.

I am very happy that you are doing well, and that all of our family stayed in Kraków. All the best,

Your Dola

The following letters from Dola on July 9 and 11, 1941, were sent together to Munio's sister, Regine Hütschnecker, in St. Gallen, Switzerland, who added her own letter of July 21 when she forwarded them to Joseph.

July 9, 1941

From Dola:

Dearest brother,

Do not be surprised that you are getting this letter from my sister-in-law. It is easier for me this way and I want you to get this letter. Dear Mother worries very much that for a month now we haven't received any news from you. She also fears that maybe you don't get her mail either. Please send all the letters to Regine (Munio's sister) who will immediately answer you after contacting Dear Mama. Here everything is all right.

I always repeat the same things in every letter since I don't know which ones you do get. So today, too, I repeat that Munio got a position as a secretary of this region. It's connected with many great advantages for us. I live in modest conditions but I am really happy. Only my longing for family and you are always with me. Only now I understand your longing. About all our people from Kraków, I am happy to let you know that they all are healthy. Dear Mama writes to you 2–3 times a week, she feels well but she misses you really much. Dear Józiu, I am so hungry for some letters from you directly to me. Since my wedding I only got news written by you to Dear Mama. I am afraid that you may be angry with me. But you do send all these packages to me. I received up till now all together 80 decagrams of coffee, 80 decagrams of tea and 80 decagrams of cacao, and yesterday (at the old address) four boxes of sardines. All these packages are sent by Carlos Company in Lisbon. I also got from home many good things from you.

How are you doing, my dear? Are you healthy? Are you happy?

Kisses for you and Lusia.

Greetings from Munio.

Your Dola

July 11, 1941

From Dola:

Dear beloved Józiu,

Today again we received two packages with 40 decagrams of tea in each. Sender is Carlos Campos from Lisbon. To keep track of this: we received everything at the old address in Tarnów, and it was sent to us here. I also received many good things from home from your packages. I always express in my letters feelings of true gratitude, I don't need to use too many words, you do know how I feel. Here everything is all right, especially that my husband as I already wrote got a position as a secretary. We couldn't wish anything better for him today. I have news from home 3 times a week with handwritten notes from Dear Mama, who is healthy, thank God. I am writing this letter to my sister-in-law because I think it will be faster this way. Send your replies also to Regine who will immediately send it to Dear Mother or to me.

My Dear, I didn't hear anything from you directly to me for a long time, and you do have something to say to me for sure. What are you doing, are you healthy, do you have lots of work? Take care of yourself since we want to see you happy again some time soon.

Kisses,
Dola

From Munio:

Thank you very much. Greetings from your brother-in-law Munio

From Dola:

Dear Regine,
Please be so kind and send this letter to Józiu. I will be very grateful for that. Once more I thank you for the great chocolate, it tasted really good. Please don't spend any more money for such luxury. How are you doing? Please write to us soon.

Greetings and kisses,
Dola

From Munio:

My Regine,
I don't have much space left. We both, Dola and I, are well and glad. If we didn't miss our families we would be quite happy. I often get news from Artur and much more rarely from Hanka. How is everything with you? Did you get the permission for a clothing package? It would be very needed. Please send my and Dola's letters to Józiu.

Kisses, Your Munio

July 21, 1941

From Regine:

Dear Brother-In-Law of my Brother,
Please allow me to introduce myself this way. I am a sister-in-law of Dola (a sister of Munio). I have the honor to help you to stay in touch with your family. Please write back to me fast so I can send it to your dear mother and to Dola.

In case you are interested to learn something about me:

I live here as an emigrant from Vienna. A year ago I suddenly lost my beloved and unforgettable husband. We will celebrate the first anniversary of his death soon. I am here with my 15-year-old son who goes to high school and is an excellent student. We possess affidavits and hope that we will be able to go to America soon. Then we will have a pleasure to get acquainted personally.

We live in great pain after losing our dear husband and father, and therefore we also miss the rest of family which is so spread out in the world. May God send help for us all.

Greetings from me and my son Kurt.

Yours,

Regine Hütschnecker

July 14, 1941

From Berta:

My dear sweet Children!

How I was revived today by your dear letter, which I had awaited with longing. Every day was so long for me after the mail came. I wanted it to be the next day, but then again and again I waited in vain. So you can imagine, my dear child, that Dawid brought me the letter early. He knew very well the joy I would have, and he read it to me so that everyone would know what you had written. Do not be surprised that I had such a longing for your letter. The last one, No. 39, was from May. No. 37 came today, so again I am missing one of your dear letters. I have not let a week go by without writing you. When I write, I imagine your dear face. Since March, I have sent 19 letters, along with cards, many of them registered, and I am waiting for answers to what I have asked. (Dear son)*, how happy your letters make me, they always bring news. So you have already visited my sister, your aunt. I imagine her pleasure and will write her. It is just a pity that I cannot write her a letter in Yiddish. She would enjoy reading it, because she knows my handwriting very well, since our handwriting is similar.

(My dear love)*, you will get a letter from Switzerland, which will surprise you. At my request, Dola wrote her sister-in-law and asked her to write you, I thought surely you will get it sooner from there. Meanwhile, I received your letter on July 14 and answered right away. Concerning the packages, we confirm that we received some from you, but whether all you mailed, I do not know. The most important thing is that I have letters from you. For your peace of mind, I will tell you that I am doing very well as far as my health is concerned. Do not be concerned, just take care of yourself. In my old days, I should have joy from you as well as from all my dear children. Malcia wrote you four letters. Have you received them? Your mother-in-law was here yesterday. She visits us every Sunday when she does not go to visit her sister Schanzer. She is in Lagewnik and sends warm greetings to you both. Thousands of affectionate kisses from me to you. Each one would like to add a few words, but that is not possible, so they all send affectionate greetings. Dola and her husband always ask me to give you warmest regards from them. (She received the package, which came from Tarnów to Neu Sandez.[35])*

*These parentheses are contained in the text.

From Berta to Her Sister Whom Joseph Will Visit:

My beloved Sister and your dear Children!

Today I received a letter from my son in which he informs me that he received a letter from your son-in-law, and he writes that he and his wife will travel to see you. How happy I am that after such a long time you, my dear sister, will see my child. I can imagine the joy and would like to be fortunate enough to be there and also to meet your loved ones. Who would have believed the families would come together like this. Do you not have a daughter in New York? I can remember that, years ago, a woman came from there to Kraków and visited us. She brought greetings from you as well as from your daughter and said she was your neighbor. She also said your daughter was a milliner. Where is this daughter? Maybe she is not far from my son. Will you please let me know right away if my children visited you? How glad I am that in our old days we can know of each other at least through writing. I would very much like to write you about each sister, but each one is somewhere else, and I do not even know where they are. I am enclosing for you a small photograph. You should remember me well if we resemble each other. Please also send me a picture of you.

To be sure that you know my exact address, I will repeat it

Krakau Podgórze

Limanowskiego 18/4

in care of Klara Wimisner

[35] Neu Sandez is the German name for Nowy Sacz.

That is my daughter, with whom I am staying.

With affectionate kisses for you and your loved ones and with kindest regards from my children, I remain your sister

Berta

July 14, 1941

From Salo:

Dear Józiu,

For more than 4 weeks we have not received any letter from you. Hopefully it has nothing to do with your health, and you all are in the best shape. Now this is the most important. Dear Mother writes one card regularly every week. Do you receive them? We all are healthy. If we only knew that you are feeling well too, it would be a great relief for us. Your mother-in-law was here yesterday. She is doing well; as a single woman she is very strong. She sends her greetings. When the letters from you come we always share them with each other. Please write to us soon. Wishing you all the best, I also send a warm hug.

I wrote this letter in the office. On the way home I found a letter from you from June 21 (number 38) which made all of us very happy. Mother is glad that her sister sent a message and the pictures. The last letter from you was number #34 so three letters sent in the meantime are missing.

Once more – all the best,

Salo (G. Nachtigall)

July 16, 1941

From Genia:

Dear Uncle,

Every time I eat tasty chocolate from you, and this happens pretty often, I feel guilty that you Dear Uncle always remember us and I don't even write one word. First of all, I want to make something clear. You, Dear Uncle, write that we all work so hard, that's not true. We don't work hard at all, and our work is not unpleasant. We are busy only in the mornings, and the afternoons we have free. In the mornings before going to work, Lusia cleans and I go shopping. In the mornings I work in our office, and afternoons I have for myself. I even take dance classes. But please don't think that I am "lightheaded." I also read a lot and study. Entertainment and "fun" is out of the question but I really cannot complain. Mrs. Schreiber [Joseph's mother-in-law] visits us a lot and always is elegantly dressed.

I am afraid of winter because my fingers and toes are frostbitten and I don't have mittens or snow shoes. But somehow I have to survive. The most important thing is not to give up, right? We are pleased in our apartment. The important thing is that we have full comfort here although it is furnished very poorly, almost funny. Some old junk that keeps shaking in all directions. Almost everything is leased anyway. But we have a beautiful light room with two windows.

The letters from you Dear Uncle are always the best gift and a big attraction. Dear Grandma always cries with joy and the whole family snatches them from each other's hands. We all are really touched that you remember us. We try to go from one day to the next. I am curious what are you doing in this moment when I am typing this letter to you on our old Erica. I would give so much to know. I believe that everything is possible, things are just more and less probable.

I also would like to let you know that Grandma is totally sweet and everybody adores her. All our family and even others call her "Grandma" and all respect her very much. Thank God she is healthy and happy. She helps Mom in the kitchen, and in the afternoons she goes to this little park and gossips with other grandmas.

What's new in your life? Is Aunt Lusia still so beautiful? Probably yes. I kiss you both.

Genia

July 17, 1941

From Klara:

Dear Józiu,

This letter returned to us a month after we sent it. So I am sending it once more through Lisbon. In the meantime we received from Warsaw 6 packages of condensed milk, 9 pieces of soap, coffee and tea, so everything that you described in your letter.

Stay well.
Klara

July 27, 1941

From Berta:

My dear, much-loved Children

How happy I am when the day comes for me to write to you. Since I have a certain day for writing, I feel then as though I would like to speak to you, my dear child. I am just curious whether you are getting all my letters and cards. After a few weeks, Salo and Klarcia got back the letters they had written you. We have acknowledged the packages received from Lisbon, only the ones from Bulgaria and Danu[36] have not arrived. I thank you especially for the rice and the canned milk, which I enjoyed very much. Dola also received the packages which you sent to Tarnów. They were forwarded to her in Neu Sandez, and she wrote you at once. You should get all the letters we write to you.

Dear children, I asked in my letter if you are settled now, did not get an answer, so when you write, please tell me in detail how everything looks in your apartment. As usual, everything is fine here and we are in the best of health. Each of us has our own pursuits.

Dearest Lusia, for you a few words from your dear mother. She visits us very often and sends you and Józiu warm greetings. She has the same longing as I do to see you both.

Next time I will write more. Your last letter was number 28, not as I told you number 27.[37] Again we are missing some, and I have been waiting for them for a long while.

Affectionate kisses, unfortunately only on paper, kindest regards from all

Your Mother

---

[36] Presumably, an abbreviation for Denmark, which was referred to in this context earlier.

[37] Because Berta and Salo earlier refer to letters 37, 38, and 39, apparently Berta has confused the letter numbers here.

August 5, 1941

From Berta:

It is my "writing day" so I won't pass the opportunity to write to both of you and send you my love. I always receive good letters from Dola thank God. They both are very happy.

August 10, 1941

From Berta:

My dear sweet Children,

It is not possible to write how happy your dear letter made me. You write that my sister cried with joy. My joy was doubled, to have such a good letter from you, my dear child, and added to that to have such good news from an older sister after so many years (and be reminded) of the old days. I wish I could have been a fly so that I could have been with you and seen all that. Along with your dear letter, I got a letter from Dola and her husband. They are very content and happy with each other. He said he wishes that Dola will be as happy with him as he is with her. God grant that we may all be happy with one another.

With my letter I also sent a letter to you from Salo. I am curious if you receive all our letters and cards. In each letter we acknowledge the packages we have received, the last ones arrived in June. Dola also confirmed to you the packages she got. Have you received any mail from her? How glad they would be if you would write to them. They are living in Neu Sandez. He is secretary in the *Gemeinde*, and they are very content. For the first time she knows something about life. I am very happy that I experienced knowing that she is pleased. Since I do not have anything special to write, I will also write a few words to my sister, which I hope you will give to her when you see each other.

Dear Sister,

How happy I was when I received a letter from my son, telling me that you, dear sister, are happy and doing well. It was not a small surprise to learn when reading the letter that you were all together, which I had not counted on at all. How lovely it would be if the Almighty allowed us to be together in our old days, He gave hope to the living, and I look forward to that very much. I just do not know if it will happen. In any event, I am pleased that you have met my only son, and the other children from their picture. I would like to look forward at least to having pictures of your loved ones. Please try to give me this pleasure and send me pictures of all your family. That will be the loveliest present for me. I close with affectionate kisses for all.

Your sister Berta

Many affectionate greetings from my children.

August 11, 1941

From Salo:

We haven't received anything from you for such a long time, and we are not sure if you get our letters. We got our mail back with the remark that the mail to US can go only through Lisbon, so we tried again this way. We can only hope that the letters will reach you. We are convinced that you also write regularly, only the current situation causes us not to receive our mail. We hope that everything is well with you and that you are happy. What amazes us is that many people do receive mail from America. Do you have any news from Mr. Schreiber and Józek? Yesterday I spoke to your mother-in-law and her daughter. Both are well. They worry, too, since there is no news from their relatives. Here everything is all right. Dear Mother is well and takes care of our physical existence; on Sundays we cannot miss cholent,[38] we also have sausage. What else can you ask for? Mostly it is Mother who takes care of us. Klara and Mania help. Dawid also plays a big role. He seems to be really devoted to preparation of culinary delicacies. If he weren't a great salesman, he could easily support himself as a cook. Now and then the change of weather reminds Mania of her hand, but by and large that is also overcome.

You ask if we feel at home in our apartment. By all means, simply splendid and diversified and nonsleeping is provided for.

---

[38] A long-simmering stew that was a traditional dish of East European Jews.

Stay healthy, my dears, and write even if there is no certainty of arrival, and be well. From the entire family I add warm greetings, even if no one else can write more, because more than one handwriting is not allowed.

Yours, Salo

Just before mailing this letter, you letter number 41 arrived. Mother was extremely happy about the news from her sister there, also Mania and Klara wept from emotion. No wonder, as they have not seen the aunt from America for 57 years. I showed your letter to your mother-in-law, who has also had no news from you for a long time. I would note once again, that 3 letters are missing, as the last one was number 37. Once again greeting you. Salo

August 13, 1941

From Mania:

It seems that I have especially bad luck since you haven't received any of the four letters that I have written to you since May. Otherwise you would definitely write back, or at least you'd confirm receiving the letters. Your second to last letter was number 37 and the last one was number 41 in which you wrote that you had visited the new found aunt.

So we needed the war in order to connect – after 57 years – with the family members we didn't know? We are doing well, thank God, and we enjoy living in the new apartment. Up till now we haven't had any visitors. What makes us really happy is that Dola is content. I have only one request: I just ask dear God to give health and strength to the dear Mother, so that we all survive this war and will meet together again.

Dear Józiu this letter will probably find you after your vacation already. I wish that the strength you will gain during your vacation will serve you for a long time. That everybody likes Lusia is not news for me, I am used to this. Did she change at all? From the photographs it doesn't look so. Klara changed in the sense that she has a body like Genia now. Lusia and I stayed true to our fat bodies. I don't know about Dola.

I thank you once more for the packages you sent, and that you sent separate ones straight to Dola. I send warm greetings to both of you.

Please give my regards to Dr. Tertelbaum and his wife.

Mania

August 18, 1941

From Berta:

My dear beloved Children!

Although I am not sure that the card will arrive in time, still I wish you much happiness and good health in the New Year, that we may be able to see each other soon, this is the only wish I have. How sorry I am that I have not yet received the letter from my sister, I wonder if it will arrive at all. Have they visited you? Write and tell me who all was there. Here everything is fine and we are healthy, thank God, just very anxious. I have very good news from Dola, thank God, she also is longing for us, maybe she will be able to come here for a few days, if only I had the same prospect for you, my dear ones. I pull myself together and tell myself that everything comes with patience. Affectionate kisses for both of you as well as for Leo and family. Where does Paula's son have good work? Once more, affectionate greetings from all.

Your Mother

August 25, 1941

From Berta:

My dear, much-loved Children!

Today I received your letter, which is dear to me. And I am very happy that you were pleased with your stay. I am also very glad that you have received at least some of my letters. I write every week, and it is my pleasure, it is my opinion that I am talking to you, sweet child. If only I knew that you are receiving all the letters. The children have also written you but as yet have received no answer from you. Gizia[39] also wrote you a letter and is waiting for a reply. In all my letters I have acknowledged the arrival of packages we have received. In one letter I even asked when it would be possible for you to send me rice, since there are many things I am not allowed to eat. I am following a diet, mostly light foods. Thank God I am doing pretty well, I pay good attention to myself, as do the children. They would like to give me everything I need so that I look good.

---

[39] Affectionate nickname for Genka.

As far as your mother-in-law is concerned, she also received packages the same time as we did, which I acknowledged in a letter, as she was here when I was writing. She visits us often, looks good, is in good spirits, was also here this Sunday. I always give her the letters to read. I must also send the letters to Dola so that she can read them, then I get them back. In her letters, she sounds very content.

I also got a letter from Adele, saying that Paula does not see you so often, does the poor thing have so many demands, it is too bad that she has no joy from her son and still must work for him. Not everyone has successful children, so I thank God for your well-being and good health.

In a card, I have already sent good wishes for the New Year, but perhaps the card will not arrive, so once again I wish you both all the best I could possibly wish. It was not very hot this summer, only a few days were very warm. Otherwise there is nothing new with us, everything is just fine. I close with thousands of affectionate kisses,

Your Mother

Kindest regards to you from the children as well as to Leo and family, Paula and son.

I have still not received the letter from my sister. Has anyone in her family visited you? It will be a pity if the letter she wrote in Yiddish should not arrive. Dear child, you will be surprised that I am making you aware of this, but you know that Salo is very sensitive and you are not answering the letters he has written you, which bothers him. You may not mention when you write him that I have written this to you, he is the same Salo he has always been. Dawid is completely different.

August 29, 1941

From Klara:

As much as I ask God to get lots of good news from you, I also ask God that you get all our letters. Dear Mother is healthy, thank God. Sometimes she goes out and sits on the bench with her old friends. She likes sitting on the balcony where it is quiet and she enjoys fresh air. I wonder if you received my letter from August 17 which I sent via Lisbon.

I confirmed receiving all the packages, thank you for all of them. Dawid didn't get any letters from you.

I am glad that you used the summer to rest, and that you went for a vacation. Without any problems, right, like always? Dawid and Genia still work like before but I doubt that it will last long. Lusia works here as a teacher. She continues learning sewing and cutting. Kisses,

Klara

September 17, 1941

From Berta:

Dola went home yesterday. We enjoyed having her here for a short time. Soon after she got home, I received a telegram from her letting me know that she arrived safely. Everything is fine with us. I am healthy, thank God. I do not have anything particular to write except to send you affectionate kisses,

Your Mother

Kindest regards from all, also from your dear mother-in-law. We all wish you all the best for the New Year. Kindest regards from Dola and Munio. Greetings to Leo, wife, Paula, son.

September 30, 1941

From Munio:

Dearest Józiu,

Our mail to you reminds me of our prayers to God. One never knows if they really reach Him.

Dola received as an exception a permit to be with Mania for 8 days that she was happy to use. We support ourselves as best we can. We have enough wood and potatoes for the whole winter. Everything is OK here, and we are content. Please keep writing to my old address. All the best. Your Munio

From Dola:

Dearest Brother, as Munio already wrote, I was at home and found everybody healthy. We cried for joy. Today we are all together in our thoughts. May God give you health and happiness. Also please give best greetings to your Lusia. I talked to her mother. She is perfectly healthy and happy.

Kisses from the heart,
Dola

October 9, 1941

From Berta:

Dear much-loved Children,

Since the holidays are ending today, I can tell you that we spent them well, but not as we always did before, of course. But for the present time, what we can endure is good for us all. How are you doing? I do not have anything special to write, praise God all are well. I received the letter from my sister. She still cannot believe that she has really seen my son. Are you still receiving letters from them? Did they visit you? How lovely it would have been if I could have been there. . . . if it will be possible to see you both. I live in this hope of yet having that good fortune and all of us will be together. I close with thousands of kisses. Your Mother

October 15, 1941

From Klara:

We haven't received anything from you since your last letter in August. We are impatiently waiting for news. Especially since you said that you had to look for a different income source. May God help you in every assignment and protect what you do. I wish you happiness and success from the bottom of my heart. As Dear Mother has already written, Dola was here for a few days. She praised her husband very much. Only now does she feel that she is being taken care of. Genka still works with her father, Salo works as well, and Lusia teaches in Centos in the mornings and at home in the afternoons. Being a teacher was her dream. She takes sewing lessons.

It's already the third year that we spend every holiday in a different place. Thank God all went well. May God allow us to spend the next holidays together. Your mother-in-law comes here often. Franka[40] moved in there, and the Horowitz family too. I kiss you warmly, please greet Lusia as well.

Klara

October 20, 1941

From Berta:

Dear much-loved Children!

I really do not know, my dear ones, what I should write you. There is nothing new, everything is as it has been. There is just one thing I would like to know, whether you are receiving our letters. We write diligently every week. Six weeks have now gone by since we got your last letter. Frau Fleißig had a letter from her husband every two weeks. Yesterday your mother-in-law was here and wondered how just your letters are getting lost. Every day I wait for the mail, unfortunately in vain. I do not know what to think. I miss your letters as a hungry person misses bread, so please write often. If one letter happened to get lost, not all of them would. Thank God, I am doing well, as are the others. Stay healthy. I kiss you affectionately,

Your Mother

Greetings from all, also from your mother-in-law. She is displeased that Lusia is not writing.

November 2, 1941

From Berta:

Much-loved, sweet Children!

I unexpectedly received your dear letter today along with the picture of my sister. I was so happy to have them and read with tears because at least one of us is holding out well. And especially happy that you, my dear darling, have gotten to know an aunt and her family on your mother's side, since I will not have the good fortune to see them all. Stay in contact with them, that way I will sooner have news of her. How should I not be

---

[40] A sister of Joseph's wife, Lusia Hollander.

happy with you? You write that you are proud of your old mother, but how could I not first be proud to possess such a treasure that is greater than a fortune?

Dear child, at the same time, I received two packages of coffee, each weighing seven pounds, from the firm Jose Joaquim Pires, Catte Rus Auguster 89, 4th floor, Lisbon. Malcia received one package 42 from the same firm. Salo has acknowledged them to you.

What else can I write you? I would like to sit here the whole day since it seems to me I am talking to you, my child. I sent word to your mother-in-law right away that you had had a letter from her grandson. She came with Franka to read the letter, too. Is it possible for you to copy what he wrote?

I close my letter and would like so much to embrace you and to kiss you both. Stay well and happy. Do not be concerned, everything will be all right.

I thank Leo and Paula for the good wishes. Adele is surprised that Paula writes so seldom. I wrote her to say that you wrote me that she is content. Again affectionate kisses and from all, kindest regards,

Your Mother

Klara and Gizia wrote to you. Have you not yet received their letter?

December 15, 1941

Postcard to Regine Hütschnecker, Switzerland, from Dola:

As you know Hanka left Vienna[41] and we wait every day for news whether she is coming here. We have regular news from Arthur. How are you doing? What do you do now? Here everything is in the best order thank God. Please be so nice and send all the letters to Józiu from Mother and from us. We don't write to him separately in order to save writing space. Please let us know how you are doing.

Kisses and hugs,

Your Dola

---

[41] Numerous deportations of Jews from Vienna to Lodz, Minsk, and Riga started on October 15, 1941.

December 22, 1941

Postcard to Ms. Regine Hütschnecker in Switzerland from Dola:

We received your letter of the 7th, for which we thank you very much, as well as for the announced package, but it is always sufficient to have a few lines about how you are doing. Here everything is OK. Munio works hard in his old position, which he can keep unsalaried, although in January we receive the concession to collect the "small lotto." Good news from Arthur; we still don't have Hanka's address. Please show ours and mama's correspondence to Józiu. Kisses, Dola

December 23, 1941 (Mailed through Regine Hütschnecker in Switzerland)

From Berta:

Dear beloved Children

I am writing you just to reassure you that I am perfectly healthy and that, praise God, we are all doing fine, so that you can be without worry for us. I am happy that I will have good news of you from Regine and also that you can read my handwriting and can have no anxiety about my health. Many, many affectionate kisses for you and Lusia. I am expecting a letter soon.

Your loving Mother

Very dear Frau Regine, sincere thanks and kindest regards to you and also to your son.

Hollander

December 5, 1942

From Regine Hütschnecker:

Dear Mr. Holländer,

Yesterday I received a check for $50 that you sent from the bank. In this moment I cannot send it to Dola. But I will hold it for her. Thank God they are healthy. I received a message from them.

Unfortunately I have to inform you that your Dear Mother died peacefully and without pain on August 28, 1942. It is unfortunately God's will, and we humans cannot help it.

I am always happy to hear about Dola and the others. I asked you before to write a letter to Edith Loew in Buenos Aires. She can immediately send you $300. Did you receive this letter? Please keep the money for my older brother. I ask you for a quick answer.

Dola writes in every letter "Greetings to Józiu."

Lots of warm greetings from my son and me.

Yours,

Regine Hütschnecker

Index

Made in the USA
Middletown, DE
04 April 2018